Accidental Apostle

Finding your calling by doing what is needed

Accidental Apostle

Finding your calling by
doing what is needed

Ben Taylor

2019

Dedicated to Catherine, Isaac, Hudson, Grace
and Elijah…

…and to all those who because of their faith are too
good for this world
(Hebrews 11:38)

Contents

Foreword

At this point in a christian book you'll usually find a nice comment from a well known christian celebrity endorsing the author and the work he or she is doing.

It's not business as usual though.

Instead, here are some comments from people who have become disciples of Jesus and much loved co-workers through the work God has entrusted to us. These people are the reason we do what we do and why I have written this book. They have quietly entered the kingdom of God and begun to help their friends and family enter it too.

Their changed lives can speak for themselves...

"We pray about where to go and then go there to tell people about Jesus and find people of peace. We read about things in the Bible and then it actually happens when we go and obey Jesus. Finding people who want to know about Jesus is the main reason why we are doing this. Finding 'gentiles' who are uncomfortable going to a church because it's a cliquey thing and it's not for everyone. It is hard to go out – but you just need to pray and get the Holy Spirit behind you because we're walking in Jesus' shoes. Get involved with this work because Jesus is with us"

Trevor, Brother and Co-worker

"I was at a bus stop with my friend when the team approached me and asked if I wanted prayer. We then arranged to meet up at a pub every Tuesday to read the bible and pray. Since finding Jesus and being baptised I have stopped using drugs and my life is much better now. I've been gathering people in my house who want to be saved and know more about Jesus. I have now baptised more people and it's really good."

Rachelle, Co-worker

"It's about helping people find the right path and helping people with anxiety and depression. I got baptized to see my life changed. I wanted to stop getting into trouble and find the right path. Jesus has helped me to stop carrying knives and this mission is needed to help others escape the life of crime and those who are struggling. It's good bringing people together and when we gather we share our highs and lows and pray for each other."

Jake, Co-worker

"This is the Lord's work and we want to make our heavenly Father happy. We want to spread His name and message, and help people love and understand one another. So many people are apprehensive about the system of religion, and the wickedness of the church has driven people away. The church is full of Pharisees but the more we think about Jesus the more we do His work and His light shines into the darkness around us. When we gather together it's real church where we join as one and care for each other."

Khalin and Andy, Co-workers
"This work is bringing hope to people who are lost and bringing light to communities. It teaches people to be selfless and to put others before yourself. We're learning what it really means to have faith in Jesus and to build our own community instead of just going to church. It's a refreshing and new approach to these ancient beliefs and we are bringing the truth to those forgotten or marginalized by society and the church. Just like Jesus did"

Danielle, Grace and Ian, Co-workers

"Are we beginning to praise ourselves again? Are we like others, who need to bring you letters of recommendation, or who ask you to write such letters on their behalf? Surely not! The only letter of recommendation we need is you yourselves. Your lives are a letter written in our hearts; everyone can read it and recognize our good work among you. Clearly, you are a letter from Christ showing the result of our ministry among you. This "letter" is written not with pen and ink, but with the Spirit of the living God. It is carved not on tablets of stone, but on human hearts."
(2 Corinthians 3:1-4)

Introduction

The last thing I ever thought I'd do is write a book.

To put it bluntly, millions of people around us are slipping to an eternity without Christ and are pretty much living a hellish existence here on earth.

I feel we have enough information in the Bible alone to be getting on with things without the plethora of christian books available.

Providing yet more information about what we are supposed to be doing as disciples of Jesus isn't really going to help the situation. Believers in parts of the world where they only have the Bible and not all the other 'add ons' of western christianity seem to be doing a much better job than we are anyway.

So I'm writing this rather reluctantly. I am not an author but feel something needed to be done, so I got on with it.

If you take away nothing else from this book then I hope that you will get on with it too. You don't need to wait for a fanfare, a pat on the back, a voice from heaven or a public commissioning service. Stop expecting someone else to do it and get on with it yourself.

You don't need money, possessions, degrees and theological training to follow Jesus and fish for more people. To do it, you just need to do it. The honour of Jesus, the salvation of the nations and the credibility of our faith is at stake!

Me and my wife Catherine recently felt God was leading us to stop and reflect on our last 10 years of ministry. It's been a rollercoaster with Jesus. We've made lots of mistakes, acted with a lack of wisdom on many occasions and the intensity of mission on the front line has been costly on our marriage and family life.

But we had to get on with it.

I felt I needed to write this book because I believe there's a whole army of people just like us! People who God is calling and who will learn what they need to know through the foolishness of simple courageous obedience. They don't need to *know* any more. They need to get on and do what they already know.

People who can't sit still in church meetings while everyone around them is slipping to hell.

People who feel compelled to "go" even though they don't know any of the answers or what they're going to do when they get there.

People who just can't keep on talking about what Jesus is saying but have to get on with it.

People who see the great spiritual need around them and want to do whatever is needed.

I believe you discover your calling in life as you get on and do whatever is needed, not through spiritual faffing, reading books and theorizing about things. Our churches have become breeding grounds for professionals not pioneers. We look to certificates and qualifications instead of humility and intimacy with Jesus and we prize head knowledge instead of heart obedience.

I discovered my calling by accident. I never set out to be anything, I just wanted to obey Jesus and do whatever was needed. There's been many times where I've had to stop and be reminded of this along the way.

I've taken some of the things I have learned from the life of Paul as a basis for this book. He was an "Accidental Apostle", someone who wasn't concerned with titles and positions but poured himself out for Jesus and others. His calling was forged through serving and giving everything to 'get the job done'. His focus was never on a title, calling or job description. His focus was Jesus. In this book I will attempt to unpack what the calling and work of an apostle might look like as most people have no idea about the importance and necessity of these gifts to the church or are put off by the showy, empire building apostles who surface on TV and at conferences.

If you're looking for something polished and clever that gives you all the answers then put this book down and look for something else! There are also other great books available about important themes such as vision, strategy, making disciples and church planting,some of them written by friends and people I love and respect. Many of these books have impacted us greatly and we're very thankful for them. But as I sat down to write this book my overwhelming feeling was that there is something missing. I meet lots of people with a vision but years down the line nothing has happened. I meet lots of people looking for practical tools and training but they lack the heart and passion to push through hardships that come up.

There's a great work that needs to be done in the world today. Most of us have talked about it. Some of us have prayed about it.

Are you one of those who will do something about it?

I hope that this book will provoke and inspire an army of accidental apostles to action. If you have that spark in your heart from God I pray that with every page you read it will grow until you are totally consumed.

(If you don't have that spark within then I suggest you stop, lock yourself in a room and get on your knees because without that we have nothing and reading this book will be a waste of time!)

Many believers may find some of the things written in this book hard to understand and receive, just as some of Jesus' disciples did in John 6:60-70,

"Many of his disciples said, "This is very hard to understand. How can anyone accept it?" Jesus was aware that his disciples were complaining, so he said to them, "Does this offend you? Then what will you think if you see the Son of Man ascend to heaven again? The Spirit alone gives eternal life. Human effort accomplishes nothing. And the very words I have spoken to you are spirit and life. But some of you do not believe me." (For Jesus knew from the beginning which ones didn't believe, and he knew who would betray him.) Then he said, "That is why I said that people can't come to me unless the Father gives them to me." At this point many of his disciples turned away and deserted him. Then Jesus turned to the Twelve and asked, "Are you also going to leave?" Simon Peter replied, "Lord, to whom would we go? You have the words that give eternal life. We believe, and we know you are the Holy One of God."

This book is an attempt to speak the truth in love so that Jesus receives more glory! The content of this book is what I continue to wrestle with and what we seek to 'live out' on a daily basis with those we are discipling and training,

"I solemnly urge you in the presence of God and Christ Jesus, who will someday judge the living and the dead when he comes to set up his Kingdom. Preach the word of God. Be prepared, whether the time is favorable or not. Patiently correct, rebuke, and encourage your people with good teaching. For a time is coming when people will no longer listen to sound and wholesome teaching. They will follow their own desires and will look for teachers who will tell them whatever their itching ears want to hear. They will reject the truth and chase after myths. But you should keep a clear mind in every situation. Don't be afraid of suffering for the Lord. Work at telling others the Good News, and fully carry out the ministry God has given you. As for me, my life has already been poured out as an offering to God. The time of my death is near. I have fought the good fight, I have finished the race, and I have remained faithful. And now the prize awaits me—the crown of righteousness, which the Lord, the righteous Judge, will give me on the day of his return. And the prize is not just for me but for all who eagerly look forward to his appearing."
2 Timothy 4:1-9

Chapter 1

Chosen to take God's message

Acts 9:15

When I look at a lot of people around me who are part of churches, in positions of influence and who call themselves pioneers or leaders I feel concerned.

For many, serving Jesus has become just a lifestyle choice or the next step on their career ladder.

I remember being in one situation where a church was planning to pay one of their leaders a part time wage so he could give more time to this 'calling' This would involve him reducing his hours in his other paid job. I really liked this guy but he had become a product of "churchianity" (churchianity is a strange make believe world where so-called followers of Jesus gather together and do things in His name but never stop to question if what they are doing is actually what Jesus wants) He stood up and told us all about this great step of faith that he was making. I sat there trying to understand what he was talking about. Yes it would involve some changes but really it was just a career choice for him and his family. Instead of doing his other work for 3 days a week he'd now be doing church leader work (whatever that is!) instead, and getting paid for it.

Things like this annoy me.

If this is what stepping out in faith has become then no wonder our nations are in the state they are! If this is what the church has boiled faith down to, then God help us!

My experience of being 'called' by God had nothing to do with working hours, pay, or anything like that! When I signed up to give my life to Jesus and the work of the gospel I didn't even consider what the terms and conditions were. I felt like I was going to die if I didn't give my whole life unreservedly to my Lord and saviour. It was everything or nothing! 24 hours a day, 7 days a week, 365 days a year. It would be the determining factor in my relationships and family life. I think Paul echoed this sentiment in 1 Corinthians 9:16 when he said,

"Yet preaching the good news is not something I can boast about. I am compelled by God to do it. How terrible for me if I didn't preach the Good News!"

I often feel very foolish when I look at, and listen to, a lot of other believers. I'm actually quite clever academically and can think up great ideas and plans myself. But life in God's Kingdom has nothing to with any of that. In fact, like Paul said in Philippians 3:5-12, we're realising more and more that all the stuff which the world (and increasingly the church) thinks is important is actually rubbish! What matters is Jesus and working with him to grow His flame in other people until the ends of the earth are reached with the gospel.

This book is not for people considering how much they might get paid to do ministry work or who are worried about if they can afford to serve God. If you're asking those kind of questions I personally think you've misunderstood the whole point!

My hope is that I can in some way follow the examples of people like the Apostle Paul, William Booth, Jim Elliot and Hudson Taylor. People who laid it all on the line for Jesus and were used by Him to build His kingdom amongst the darkness in their generation. (You can google their names to find out more!)

After everything is said and done (and we all say and do a lot!) lasting fruit comes only from doing the will of our Father. As I shared at the start of this chapter, it concerns me that you rarely hear people talking about doing God's will despite the cost to them. I long to see people responding to God's call on their lives, but I fear that many of us are so consumed with ourselves that we are not even listening to Him.

When I look back on our last 10 years, there was one thing that kept me going. It wasn't the quality of the training that I have received. It wasn't the support of others (often we had no support anyway!) And it certainly wasn't the financial reward, because there isn't any! What kept me going was Jesus Christ and His call on my life.

And that is where our journey begins...

First Flames

It was August 1998 and I remember the night well.

I was at a youth camp and it was the summer before I went to university. I had just turned 18 and was fresh home from an alcohol-fuelled coming of age holiday in Majorca. For that week I was drunk most days and made a lot of decisions that I deeply regret.

Having 'lived the life' (or so I thought!) for a week, I now found myself at a christian youth camp going through the motions again. Reading the same old things from the Bible, praying the same old prayers and seeing the same old friends. I had been baptised a year or so earlier but found it easy to play at churchianity. Do the right things, say the right things. Say sorry to God when you do something wrong. But nothing really changes much in your life! It really is a joke and God cannot stomach it, that's why he said He would vomit people like this out of His mouth,

"But since you are like lukewarm water, neither hot nor cold, I will spit you out of my mouth!"
Revelation 3:16

But that summer night something happened.

I don't really remember what the sermon was about that evening or what anyone else said. All through the meeting I was gripped by a prophecy that I had written down in my youth Bible a year or so ago. I can't even remember where I heard it, but it's message was that God was calling 11th hour workers into His harvest fields, that these workers would be fearless, committed and bold and that they would take the Gospel to the ends of the earth. It was loosely based on Jesus' parable from Matthew 20.

When God is moving, you often do things which seem foolish in the world's eyes and as the meeting that night was drawing to a close I did something before I thought about it.

At this stage I must confess something very important. I know it's really bad, un-British and goes against most of what I have learned from western christianity, but I often do things I feel Jesus is asking me to do before thinking about it. Lots of people have tried to help me grow out of this and to see that sometimes Jesus just wants us to settle down and not to ask too much of ourselves and others. But it's no good, I just can't do it, when Jesus asks me to do something I have to do it no matter what.

Back to that August evening, I got up, went to the front and said I had something to share. I read out the prophecy and challenged myself and the whole camp to lay their lives down for the gospel in a way that would radically transform all our lives and relationships. I thanked people in the marquee that night for their friendship, but preached that I could no longer drift through life having fun, getting an education and settling down to some kind of middle class mediocrity where we practiced a form of godliness but denied it's power (2 Timothy 3:5) God was calling us all to radically re-orientate our whole lives around Him and His work. I publicly invited some of my closer friends to join me in laying my life down for Jesus and His work and then sat down.

God had called everything into question and I mean everything. Was I prepared to lay down everything for the sake of the gospel? Career? Social standing? Reputation?

I was a mess. So were others. And I got the sense that a few people were questioning who this spotty 18 year old was and who had given him permission or authority to call the whole camp to lay it all on the line for Jesus?!

I was crying all night and I felt terrible. I was a 'high achiever' (whatever that means!) at school and on the sports field. I had a good group of friends and had a loving family. But that night I had a taste of the true spiritual reality of life and that I was one day going to give an account of my life to the living God. And that scared me. Achievements in this life mean nothing when compared to obedience to Jesus Christ.

Faced with the reality that my life was actually not my own to enjoy away, I felt changed overnight. I've always been someone who's been focused and gives 110% to anything I do. But overnight God had changed the whole trajectory of my life. I was now living for Jesus and the spread of the gospel. I went to university a couple of months after that with the strong conviction that the main reason for me being there was to spread the gospel amongst anyone I came into contact with.

I don't know if you have ever had that feeling or conviction where you are literally compelled and consumed by the Holy Spirit to such a degree that you find yourself doing crazy things on a regular basis? Well my 2 years at University were like that. I often look back at that time when I felt God's calling on my life so strongly. At the time I felt alive and was conquering fears on a daily basis as I shared Jesus with friends, prayed for the sick and gathered people in my room to learn more about Jesus.

We're told in our churches that we shouldn't be too 'full on' with our faith or we will put people off. Well I've found the opposite to be true. Living a humble and loving life where you are completely honest and up front about Jesus Christ and His power to heal and set free is like a breath of fresh air to most people. More and more I find myself in situations where people say things to me like, "Why haven't any christians laid hands on me before and prayed for me?" and "Why has no-one shared with me about being saved from sin before?" When I train people to share the gospel and plant churches I always tell them that there are people out there literally waiting for an encounter with God.

We, as the church, have watered down everything about Jesus and His work! Let's get back to how it is meant to be and root out the fear of man from amongst our ranks for sake of the lost world around us!

The reality is (and the Bible shows this as well) that the more you follow Jesus the more you offend religious people who favour fear and control over obedience to God! At university it was my fellow believers who were offended not those around me who were drinking and sexing their way to Hell.

So be warned, if you follow God's call on your life you can't follow what others want and meet the endless demands that worldly thinking will try and put onto you.

As Jesus' half-brother tells us in James 4:4,

"Don't you realise that friendship with the world makes you an enemy of God? I say it again: If you want to be a friend of the world, you make yourself an enemy of God."

Being a friend of God sets you at complete odds with the world and everything that it tries to tangle up in its demonic tentacles! I used to be part of churches where people described as apostles used to fly in from around the world. Dressed in expensive suits and paraded at the front of churches they were like celebrities and everyone in the church seemed to be playing along. I looked at these so called apostles and although they appeared well meaning, it all seemed so different from the apostles that I had read about in the Bible and in history. It all felt like a bit of a game. Their goal was to serve their own interests, build up their own empire and to promote the status quo. Harsh words maybe, but sometimes they're needed. They didn't appear to be people who'd laid it all on the line for Jesus, were not afraid to speak the truth in love to their flocks and who'd taken the position of a servant.

Forget the romantic ministry lifestyle dream! Being truly called by God will mean that you have regular run-ins with the managers of the status quo. Unfortunately nowadays these mangers of the status quo are more often than not also known as 'church leaders'!

So as I'm sure you will already know, following Jesus is not easy and one of the major tests is whether we are willing to lay our reputations on the line and whether obeying Jesus is more important to us than being liked by those around us!

Give yourself

One of the great joys that comes from following Jesus is that life is never boring.

After my time at university I spent two years working at a church in the north of England helping to build a ministry there. I then met Catherine who was living in Australia at that point. Through a series of miraculous (and at times very hard!) events we married on June 1st 2002 and then lived in Australia for 4 years. During most of this time in Australia neither of us could work due to health problems and it was a time of great soul searching and I suppose you could call it a wilderness experience. We then felt the Lord leading us back to the UK in the spring of 2006 and that is where we will pick up the story.

When we returned to the UK my health was recovering and I got some part time work as a carer. During my time in the spiritual wilderness I had come to the conclusion that I would never do 'full time christian work' again. I remember announcing this to Catherine (goodness knows what she thought of it!) and giving her a long explanation about how my experience of christian ministry had really been completely inward focused, not impacted any of the people in the area around us and was solely focused on building up our own little world.

Being part of a church was fine, but being paid to be glorified spiritual babysitters who just drank coffee all day, wrote newsletters and spent all week preparing boring sermons was, in my not so humble opinion, pointless, hypocritical and completely self serving. I would never be having anything to do with this world that in my view was cliquey and I would get a job where I could have an impact in the 'real world'

But God has a sense of humour!

I think God likes us to have strong opinions, but to be open to developing these opinions in the light of fresh revelations and humility. I have to admit that I am not very good at consensual decision making or being in situations where people are not clear on what they think. I get impatient when people take a long time (or longer than I would take) to process their thoughts and come to a place of knowing their opinion. I process quickly and see the world in a very black and white way. Thank God that He is helping me to realise my pride as I thought everyone was like that or should be like that. Praise God that we are a body made up different parts who work things out in different ways!

Anyway my strong conviction had led me to become a carer and I loved it. I felt like I was making a practical difference to the people I looked after and their families. I had opportunities to speak about my faith and pray for people when appropriate to do so. We became very involved with the local church fellowship I had grown up in and it felt right for us to start leading a home group in our house and to begin encouraging prayer where we could.

I started to have some strange feelings though. It was like the more we prayed, the more I had this feeling that I had to literally give more to God. I tried to push it down and ignore it but it got stronger and stronger. I can't even explain the feeling to you, but it was like I sensed God was asking me to give Him more of myself and my time. It got to the point one night where I could not sleep and I felt that I would not ever have any peace again unless I yielded my will to God. I woke Catherine and explained that I felt God was inviting me to quit my job and to pray. We talked and prayed and the next morning I went into work and quit.

Looking back on that time, it was another episode where God changed the trajectory of our lives. It wasn't some magical out of the blue moment, but a number of prayerful steps that we made together in response to how we felt the Holy Spirit was leading us. God has been reminding me lately about that time of our lives when we felt such a strong conviction that we must simply "give ourselves to prayer and honour the Holy Spirit" It was foundational to our calling and something that we so easily forget! When you find yourself surrounded by new disciples and churches, have a growing family and are getting invites to go and help people in other areas, it's easy to forget where you came from and how God led you into this work in the first place. Looking back this was another time of responding to God's call on our lives.

We were not receiving a wage or money from any church or organisation and because of my strong dislike for christian personalities who seem to constantly be asking for money we decided we would not make any of our needs known to anyone. We would trust God that He would provide for us as we obeyed Him.

During that time God drew out many insecurities in me. I would often be asked, "so what do you do?" It felt like everywhere I went people would ask me that question and I began to feel like God was trying to make a point to me. I'm someone who struggles to separate who I am from what I do. My identity can easily become tangled up with my achievements or work. During that time I felt I was doing nothing, so it was hard to answer anyone who asked me what I was doing! In my worldly mind I wasn't working and I didn't know what to say. I sensed that this season of intense prayer was birthing something but I didn't know what.

I'd go for long walks in the countryside around us, praying and interceding for our town and country. Then I'd go home and worry about whether God would provide for us as a family because I wasn't "doing" anything. I'd ask God to help me to give myself to Him deeply but then I'd get my diary out and look to see what meetings I'd arranged to make me feel like I was doing something and having an impact.

I still struggle with many of these things. I find it hard to do nothing with Jesus! I wrestle with the idea that my gracious Father is content with me when I just obey Him instead of working hard day and night for Him. And I find myself easily looking for purpose and peace in activity and plans rather than simply resting in Christ.

If God is calling you, He will lead you into situations where He can put His finger on the real issues in your heart! Speaking from experience - if these foundational heart issues are not worked on then it won't end well for you! You can be busy 'serving God' but without inward change, everything will come crashing down around you! Life with Jesus is like an iceberg. The main part of the iceberg is unseen below the water line and just the top is visible. In the same way, the hidden work of God in your heart is the most important aspect of life. What you 'do' in His name is just the tip of the iceberg!

If you're like me, you can make things happen, push doors open and generally try and do Jesus' job for Him. There's often been times where I've had to stop and think about whether I'm actually doing the will of Jesus or just doing what I think is best. Or worse still – am I doing things to build up my own insecurities or need to appear successful! Often it's my wife or those around me who 'encourage' me (sometimes it doesn't feel encouraging!) to stop and think for a bit.

So let's constantly be mindful that being called by God is firstly and most importantly about being called to be WITH him and not just to do things FOR him.

Jesus called His disciples so they could be with him first and then be sent out second (Mark 3:14) I must confess that recently I have re-looked at my goals and measure of success. As someone who feels called by God and focused on a clear vision from Him, I find it easy to slip into a work based measure of success. In that scenario my life becomes more or less peaceful and joyful based on how much nearer I feel I am to the number of churches we want to see planted etc. Although this is not necessarily bad – these goals must come out of the most important thing which is being with Jesus. Don't get me wrong, I have no problem with healthy church planting goals. But I'm realising more and more that joy and identity comes first through Jesus. Recently I've been challenged with these two points:

1) Jesus wants to plant more churches than we can hope for and imagine anyway so maybe we can let go of it all a little bit

2) I need to re-orientate my measure of success around the more important work of being with Jesus

I won't go into how I have done this, but if you feel God is calling you to be with Him more and to serve Him, then I'd urge you to prioritise personal prayer and meditation on scripture as the most important work you have. Anything else that has any lasting fruit for God's Kingdom will come out of that.

Back in those early days I remember struggling with how God would provide for us. Not only was there no guaranteed income coming from anywhere, but I was basically spending my whole time praying and reading the Bible. It was a double whammy. We had to learn to trust God completely for everything we needed. But I also had to learn that God's grace and goodness isn't dependent on whether I think I have worked hard enough to deserve it. Do you ever have those days where you feel you need to stop and ask God to show you if you're still walking in His will or whether you've gone completely mad? I have a lot of those days! I remember one day where I just felt like my life was so different to even my fellow believers in the church. In many people's eyes (including my own!) I wasn't working, but I had this great burden and sense of calling that was consuming me!

A lot of my friends were questioning what I was doing at that time and I found it hard to communicate anything in response. Giving yourself to prayer seemed to be a very foolish thing to do in the eyes of many brothers and sisters around me. And believing that it's possible to live by faith and not to be concerned about money, food and posessions seemed almost offensive to other believers.

Having had the blessing of meeting brothers and sisters in Christ in other parts of the world, it is always hard to see the lack of passion and devotion to Christ in us western christians. May God raise up fools from within our ranks and people who value nothing but Jesus,

"Our dedication to Christ makes us look like fools...."
1 Corinthians 4:10

I was having one of those days where I was battling with things.

Was I really following the will of Jesus and was giving myself to prayer a legitimate way of life? Was it ok for me to give myself completely to Jesus in prayer and to believe that He will meet all our family needs? I learnt pretty early on to go to the scriptures for everything. If you haven't learned to do that yet then learn it quickly! When faced with any question or challenge, there is always wisdom and direction in the scriptures, if we're willing to read it and meditate on it.

I also learnt pretty early on that soldiers of Jesus need to fast. As far as I can see, the Bible clearly sets out that fasting from food is an important spiritual practice. It's great if God leads you to fast from TV, Social Media and other things that we waste hours of our life on. But for me fasting means not eating food, and that hurts! But guess what - it's meant to. If we cannot deny our bodies what it craves for then how can we expect to obey Jesus when we're used to giving our bodies and worldly desires everything they scream for?

So as I always do (and urge others to do as well!) I went to the scriptures in prayer and fasting. I asked God to show me whether I was on the right track or whether I'd lost the plot. Around lunchtime I felt the Lord leading me to read Acts 6. As I read the start of the chapter God began to speak to me.

It's not hard to picture the scene in Jerusalem. There was lots of need. Lots of people. Lots of things needed doing. And right in the middle of it all were some ordinary people who were trying to follow Jesus. Pretty similar to how life is always like right?! Some people were starting to grumble because needs weren't being met (Acts 6:1) It's often interesting to see how the pressure of meeting needs reveals what is in people's hearts. Often we think that situations are an attack from the devil or that everything is going wrong or it's all too much. Sometimes it's neither of those things and it's just an opportunity for us to grow! If we are never faced with situations that feel too much then we may never learn to rely on Jesus and draw on His wisdom! Jesus deliberately asked His disciples to meet the needs of the multitudes to test where their faith really was (Mark 6:37-44) What's interesting in the feeding of the 5000 is that Jesus doesn't tell them to pray about it or to ask Him to do a miracle. He tells His disciples to feed them. Sounds like an invitation to faithfully 'get on with it' doesn't it? What's the point I am trying to make here? Well it's often easy to hide behind a fake spirituality that allows us to sidestep actually doing anything Jesus has commanded us to do. Let's look at some other examples.

Jesus has commanded all His disciples to heal the sick. Not to pray for the sick. Not to ask Jesus to heal them, but to do it. I probably can count on two hands the number of people I know who are regularly actually doing what Jesus said here. I know hundreds of other so called believers who are praying for people and asking God to heal people. But God has asked us to do it (Please hear what I'm saying, I'm not suggesting we have any power to heal people. Of course it is Jesus' power. But he has entrusted His power and authority to us so we can get on with it here on earth! So why are we faffing around in prayer meetings rather than laying hands on sick people in our communities and commanding their sicknesses to go in Jesus' name?)

What about another example?

Jesus has commanded all His disciples to go into the whole world, to make disciples of all nations, to baptize people and to teach them to obey all of Jesus' teaching. And not only that, Jesus has promised to be with us as we do it! (Matthew 28:18-20)

What else do we need in order to 'get on with it'? But how many of us are actually doing what Jesus asked us to do? And how many of us are doing lots of other things at and for our churches, but they're things Jesus has never asked any of his disciples to do. I challenge you to reflect on how much of your life and the life of the church you are part of is focused on helping people obey Jesus and doing what He has already told you to do. Jesus commanded us to,

"Go and make disciples of all the nations, baptizing them in the name of the Father and the Son and the Holy Spirit. Teach these new disciples to obey all the commands I have given you. And be sure of this: I am with you always, even to the end of the age" Matthew 28:19-20

A disciple of Jesus is someone who hears and obeys Jesus and helps other people to do the same. Simple, but not easy! Let's be really honest with ourselves, how much of our time and energy is spent on actually praying, thinking and acting on the main thing that Jesus has asked us to do? We need a reality check. When we meet the Lord who we claim to worship, He is going to ask us if we have done what He has instructed us to do.

It's really simple, He's going to ask you and me if we made disciples of all the nations by baptizing people and teaching them to obey Him. All the other christian stuff we fill our lives with is nothing.

What else needs to happen so that so called believers in the western world actually start doing the will of Jesus? We surely don't need more books, seminaries or sermons. Maybe an army of accidental apostles who change the entire spiritual landscape through foolish obedience and loving service will shake the church out of her slumber?

Our loving heavenly Father often tests us to see if we will grow through situations rather than resort to fear-based responses and worldly wisdom. In the story from Acts 6 we see that 'The 12' are faced with an opportunity to grow. Maybe you're reading this book and you are facing a crossroad in your life and ministry? Maybe something is stirring in your heart but you can't quite explain it? We would do well to heed the wisdom of 'The 12':

"We apostles should spend our time teaching the word of God, not running a food programme"
Acts 6:2

I'm talking to accidental apostles here - have you been called by God? Don't get drawn into feeding programmes and physical need-meeting exercises! I know everyone is called by God and everyone is called to ministry but don't neglect the more significant spiritual work that God has entrusted to you. We will look in later chapters what this work might look like, but I urge you to stay true to your calling and not to be pulled away by human needs or opinions. Don't get drawn into activity that carries no gospel seed!

Question everything you are doing and ask whether it is going to help spread the gospel and make disciples to the end of the earth.

God spoke to me through these verses. Here I was praying and fasting about my current situation and here you have some ordinary men in Acts 6 who realized that there was something even more important than feeding people:

"Then we apostles can spend our time in prayer and teaching the word"
Acts 6:4

I'd quit my job caring for people because I felt God calling me to give myself to prayer. But I was struggling to see this as a valid, significant and legitimate use of my time. Wouldn't it be better to use my time to work hard helping people practically or to earn a good wage for my family?

No. Obeying Jesus is the most important thing. If we do that, then everything else is added to us (Matthew 6:33) God was calling me to the significant and important work of prayer and teaching the word, and if we are concerned with the building of God's Kingdom then this is of critical importance.

Back to Acts 6 and we see 'The 12' appointed spirit-filled men to continue with the feeding programme because meeting physical needs such as this is important, but not at the expense of meeting people's spiritual needs. So I felt encouraged that I'd left my important work of caring for people's physical needs but God was wanting me to understand that there is something more needed than that. And that was to explore the call to be an accidental apostle and to give myself to prayer and the ministry of the word. I have now come to understand that this calling is foundational and sacrificial in nature and provides a platform for others to build on which is why Paul wrote that apostles are 'first' in the church (1 Corinthians 12:28) as we all, of course, build on the one true foundation that is Jesus Christ.

What's your food?

Jesus had some things to say to His Disciples in John 4 about food and nourishment.

Jesus was weary from his journey and sat next to a well. He ends up meeting the Samaritan woman and this encounter opens up a whole town to the Gospel. It's the kind of scenario accidental apostles long for! However you also have the good old disciples who, in this story, have gone to another place to buy some food. We don't know whether Jesus had asked them to do this or whether it's something they had decided to do themselves.

Either way it meant they missed out on Jesus' encounter with this woman of questionable character and an opportunity to see God's kingdom breaking into a whole village through this person of peace (For more about people of peace read on!)

I cannot help but think that this is a picture of the church. Do we often miss out on what Jesus is doing because we're off doing good things that we think are needed? Like the disciples, are we on a mission to meet needs and complete tasks that we think need completing? Or are we following the mission of our heavenly Father. Jesus uses the opportunity to teach his disciples about what real food and nourishment is,

"My nourishment (food) comes from doing the will of God, who sent me, and from finishing his work."
John 4:34

We should heed this warning from the Lord we claim to serve.
Is doing and finishing the will of God more vital to you than having your own needs met?

What is God's calling on your life?

What are you passionate about?

What needs to change so that your life reflects your calling and passion more?

Chapter 2

Called to the gentiles and to Kings
(and to the people of Israel)

Acts 9:15

More and more I realize that everything is about people.

It may seem a strange thing for someone like me to say. I mean, I'm what many people call a *"full time Christian worker"* so my job is people!

Or rather it *should* be!

As I look back on my life so far, I see that there have been times when, actually, other people were not my main priority. Often ministry or projects that I was involved with and even leading, were really about me! Serving God can often, become, about building a platform for yourself, instead of building a platform for Jesus and others. We pray and think about how we can become more effective, how we can feel more fulfilled, and if you're anything like me, how you can do a better job. Whilst these are all good things to consider, they don't deal with the most important issue that actually it is not about you, it is about others. To put it another way, spiritually immature people think about how God can lift them up, spiritually mature people think about how they can work with God to lift others up. This book is for people who are ready and willing to lay their lives down for Jesus and others.

Without that nothing makes sense!

Paul writes this in Romans 12:1-3:

"And so, dear brothers and sisters, I plead with you to give your bodies to God because of all he has done for you. Let them be a living and holy sacrifice – the kind he will find acceptable. This is truly the way to worship him. Don't copy the behavior and customs of this world, but let God transform you into a new person by changing the way you think. Then you will learn to know God's will for you, which is good and pleasing and perfect."

You cannot even understand God's will without sacrificially laying your life down for Him. So this is where everything starts, with Jesus and why He issues this challenge to anyone who desires to follow Him:

"If any of you wants to be my follower, you must give up your own way, take up your cross daily and follow me"
Luke 9:23

Following Jesus starts with sacrifice and surrender, not signs, wonders and strategy. You can have the most wonderful church planting strategy and vision but without a sacrificial and humble spirit you might as well screw it all up and throw it in the bin. And we know what Jesus said in Matthew 7:21-24 about people who relied on signs and wonders instead of sacrificial obedience. (If you don't then take a read of it!)

I recently read a book about humility and I was deeply challenged. Like many others, I have been guilty of looking at the outward appearance rather than the heart. I've met a lot of people with amazing gifts and charismatic vision. But their work has amounted to very little because they have failed to recognize what the most important thing is,

"The Lord doesn't see things the way you see them. People judge by outward appearance, but the Lord looks at the heart"
1 Samuel 16:7

There's been many times where God has had to humble me when I haven't wanted to humble myself! I am trying to change the way I 'work' and to look for humility in potential co-workers and team members instead of just vision, calling and enthusiasm. As I value this more in myself I'm sure it will become a greater value in our teams! Only then will we see abundant and lasting fruit in our lives.

Unless a seed falls to the ground and dies

I remember a few years ago when God was leading me to travel around the UK. We would go to visit other believers who had also begun to meet, more simply, in homes or public venues. Often these meetings were ''us 4 and no more'' type scenarios where the people were meeting in a home because it was more convenient for them. Or they were people who had been hurt by more traditional forms of church. Others have written at length about "Simple Church", "House Church" and "Organic Church" and how believers can meet in more informal and relational ways. If you google those phrases you'll find lots of great books on these topics. Whilst it's great that existing believers are discovering more informal and relational ways to be church together, that is not my interest or the point of this book. This book is about the need to plant churches amongst the gentiles. My strong conviction is that the Lord of the harvest wants to build His kingdom amongst a new people, as well as preserving the old wineskins that exist for those who are already believers in Jesus.

What grieved my spirit about that time of travelling was the lack of what you could call 'missional DNA' in most of these so called churches. There was no sense of sacrificial mission for lost people or any fervent prayer for those held captive by satan and his demonic armies.

As I hope you are beginning to understand, the whole reason and motivation (apart from glorifying Jesus of course!) for doing what we do is to see churches planted amongst people in the harvest. And that is, I believe, the heartbeat of an accidental apostle. Without the foundational apostolic DNA of mission (what this book is all about!) what's the point? All you're doing is re-arranging the chairs on a sinking ship. And by mission I don't mean a once a year attempt at inviting people to a café style church meeting. I mean a fall on your face and give yourself to Jesus for lost people unreservedly type of mission! God hates our token gestures and is asking for our whole lives. Are we prepared to pray with blank diaries, open chequebooks and willing hearts? If not, then we've missed the point and our worship has become a farce.

I remember some friends who stopped their church meetings in a hired hall to meet in a home. They felt God had given them the words from John 12:24 where Jesus says,

"I tell you the truth, unless a kernel of wheat is planted in the soil and dies, it remains alone. But it's death will produce many new kernels – a plentiful harvest of new lives."

They'd been given a book about more informal ways of being church so they felt God was leading them away from hiring a building and sitting in rows, to meeting in a house. Early on into their journey away from the church building we begun to build a relationship with them and the church that was meeting in their home. It became obvious that even though their 'way' of doing church had died, the people hadn't! The leader still delivered a sermon for the church in their house, everyone else all listened and did nothing and no new people were added. The only difference was that it happened in a home instead of a hired building and everyone sat in a circle instead of rows. So as our relationship grew we were able to help them die not only to the way of "doing church" but also to their way of "being disciples", which is really the main issue facing all of us.

You see, being part of Jesus' church really has nothing to do with what we like, what we're comfortable with and what makes us feel good. It's not really about where you meet either. If that's what you're about then you'll never understand God's will, like it says in Romans 12. People all around the world are putting their hope in fashionable church models and strategies when really the answer lies in people's hearts. Are people prepared to lay their lives down completely for Jesus and others? If you are not, then you'll never see abundant lasting fruit. You can forget about the latest teaching series on finding your God given purpose. You can shelve your plans for the exciting new café church. And you might as well stop standing up and preaching each week. Because Jesus has already told us the truth in John 12:24. A harvest of new lives will only come through the death of seeds! As Dietrich Bonhoeffer once said,

"When Christ calls a man, he bids him to come and die."

So for our friends, everything had to change, where they met, what time they met, what they did when they met and ultimately who they were as disciples of Jesus. Over the space of a few years God led them on a journey to give themselves to a certain people group in their local town and they were able to form a simple church with some of these people who wanted to learn more about Jesus. Everything changed because they were prepared to live sacrifically for the sake of the Gospel and others. Their lives became less about what suited them and more about what God was doing in the other people.

Most denominations here in the UK have now come to the realization that everything must change and they are exploring new forms of being church. However I fear that for many they are still missing the point. The nations are not going to be discipled by merely a re-branding exercise, it's going to take wholesale death and sacrifice from the people of God. It's going to take men and women of courage who forsake all for the sake of the Gospel and are prepared to leave the culture of churchianity to infect the cultures around us with the seed of the Kingdom.

I believe that we are now in a time here in the UK and Europe where our starting point is no longer the church. Shock horror!

We need a new harvest field based understanding of mission rather than a church based understanding. Our lives must start to revolve around what God is doing in the world, rather than what He is doing in our church meetings. I've been involved with trying to train churches and believers for over 10 years now and I've come to the realization that if we believe that God's work will be finished solely through mobilizing, 'firing-up'and training christians then at best we will be sadly disappointed and at worst we are wildly deluded! There are simply not enough existing believers to go around, so somebody somewhere needs to start raising up disciples, churches and leaders directly in the harvest like Jesus' disciples did in the Bible.

My hope is that God will raise up many accidental apostles who lie awake at night thinking about what it would look like to plant churches in the harvest and to mobilize teams to see movements multiplying across whole unreached people groups and places.

You might disagree, but that's the real question I think needs answering today. How are we going to see many thousands of churches planted, strengthened and multiplied in the harvest with new people? Where leaders are appointed from amongst these new disciples and where the workers become 'them' not 'us'

That's what keeps me awake at night.

What about the 99%?

If God is calling you to be an accidental apostle then you're going to have to get used to upsetting a few people and going against the grain!

At the time of Paul's calling, the religious landscape was not that different to the state of affairs here in the UK now. You had a bunch of legalistic leaders who were trying to maintain and preserve a dying form of religion and who were preventing the nations from entering the Kingdom of God. Jesus had spoken out against these religious leaders in Matthew 23:13,

"What sorrow awaits you teachers of religious law and you Pharisees. Hypocrites! For you shut the door of the Kingdom of heaven in people's faces. You won't go in yourselves, and you don't let others enter either"

I've had the joy and despair of travelling to many places in the UK and have seen churches of all shapes and sizes. And I have to say that worryingly it appears that a lot of believers in Jesus are really good at shutting the door to the Kingdom of heaven in people's faces! I'm convinced that a lot of people just don't want to see other people coming to faith in Jesus because it will disrupt their life. I hear a lot of believers saying that people don't want to know about Jesus. But here in the area of the UK where we live the harvest is literally too plentiful! There are too many people wanting to follow Jesus! I used to think Jesus' words in Matthew 9:37 were a joke. But they are not, and if we are prepared to let go of our convenient christian meetings and what we like, then we too will stop shutting the door to the Kingdom of heaven in people's faces and start to see many people entering it! The harvest is plentiful.

Paul was called to the gentiles and to kings first and to the jews after. We've found it helpful (although not entirely correct from a theological point of view!) to classify people as jews or gentiles. So if you have grown up in churchianity as I call it, then you're a jew and if you are not familiar with churchianity then we'd class you as a gentile. So the fact that you're reading this would suggest to me that (according to our crude and untheological method) you are a jew. By the way I class myself as a jew as I have grown up in and around churches.

Now the problem for people like us is that we have become very used to a certain way of doing things, have a very set way of thinking about church and quite frankly we find it very hard to build relationships with sinners because we've become experts at living morally acceptable lives and meeting with other people like us. The idea that God could be at work amongst notorious sinners, prostitutes and tax collectors is hard for us to get our heads around, or even worse is actually offensive to us. For many jews, myself included, they are often led by the spirit of religion and not the spirit of Christ who was the friend of sinners. This attitude is offensive to God and contrary to Christ. After all, Jesus is with us in our church meetings right? Not with the sinners in their homes, pubs and workplaces.

For people who have not grown up in churchianity I would class them as gentiles. Many of these gentiles either don't know anything about Jesus or believe that they are not good enough to join the jews. You might think this is funny, but it isn't. After over 10 years of mission to the gentiles I've seen that actually there are many people searching desperately for a saviour but feel excluded from churches (or should I call them religious meetings!) Jesus is deeply upset about this and it leaves us with a problem!

One short sighted answer to this problem is to make our jewish churches more appealing to gentiles. However it doesn't really work because from experience the jews don't really want to change everything they know and love, and if we pluck a few gentiles out of the harvest and christianise them we sever any future missional opportunities amongst all their friends and families.

Accidental apostles see another option though, and we will come to that later!

If we're being really honest, for most christians and churches, the gentiles are an afterthought. Yes they might have great vision statements about making disciples of all nations but in reality their idea of success is maintaining the status quo and keeping the peace.

How far we have fallen!

Jesus called His first disciples to follow him and learn to fish for more people (Matthew 4:19) Jesus' community was formed on the cutting edge of mission to the gentiles, not miles from the front line where they could do whatever they wanted in safety.

I remember back to the time when we were beginning to sense the discomfort that comes from God's calling on your life. We were involved with a church and attended the weekly meeting on

sunday morning. But for months I'd sit through the meeting trying
not to cry. I looked around at all the people we loved and had a
heart to encourage and help. It all seemed be working fine for
everyone else, but not us. The only way I can describe it is that God
had taken our hearts out of that church and the people around us
and had put it with the 99% of people in our town who were not
following Jesus or part of any church. It was a very hard time and
we had to let go of a lot of people we loved to embrace what God
was calling us to do.

So many people are quick to jump on the latest christian
bandwagon. Yet they miss the point that it is all about people. All
we've ever wanted to do is to help people find Jesus and become
everything that He wants them to be. No church model or
programme will ever do that, it's people serving other people in
love! In the early days of our work, many of my friends would
joking refer to me as the "anti –church". Although it was quite
funny, inwardly I felt sad that they didn't have any idea about how
hard it had been for us to leave the church we were part of to
pioneer this new work. For us it's always been about people and if
God hadn't sent us out we would still be joyfully serving amongst
that church trying to help and equip people around us to be all that
Jesus wants them to be. What we're doing now is in some ways no
different, we're just doing it amongst the gentiles and amongst
people who were previously not God's people. So am I anti-church,
well yes and no! And I'll let you work out what I mean by that.

Each week at the end of the Sunday morning meeting I'd hear
people saying things like, "Wasn't that a great time of worship?" or
"Wasn't that a great service?" I became increasingly uncomfortable
with this mindset and begun to wonder what God thought of our
'services' and what he would say about our times of worship? I had
an increasing conviction that God isn't really that happy or pleased
with our times of worship if 99% of people in the villages and

towns around us don't know about Jesus or if there is no vision and practical plan for how they could meet together as church in their own homes, at the pub or in a café. I believe the best way Jesus is worshipped and glorified is when people call on His name for salvation and then obey Him ongoingly as His disciples. So that's the worship I have committed my life to. Of course we still sing songs sometime, but everything has been reframed around the calling and conviction that God has given us. Here in the UK and Europe it has to be about the 99% of people who are walking in darkness and not about us!

So I'm passionate about seeing people called and sent to the gentiles and to kings and also to the jews. Most people I know feel called to do the opposite. They feel sent to the jews (existing churches and believers) and then also the gentiles and kings. But I've committed myself to work with teams who are focused on going directly to the gentiles to plant churches with them. Just like Peter wrote in 1 Peter 2:10 we can now say to new disciples and churches we have planted,

"Once you had no identity as a people; now you are God's people."

And we long to see many more people becoming God's people when before they were not. There is potential for this everywhere. But we need an army of accidental apostles to make it happen! And we need teams who act as spiritual scaffolding to encourage the growth of these disciples, churches and leaders who are growing and multiplying in the harvest.

Some friends who are church Planting here in the UK and abroad talk about the *"brutal facts"* when they are casting vision for church multiplication. Confronting the brutal facts means accepting the current reality and seeing it as what it is objectively.

When we first sensed God calling us here in Somerset (a county in the South West of the UK) I remember God showing us how there are approximately 1 million people in the county. As we prayed and wrestled with this, I discovered that the motto of Somerset is an old anglo-saxon phrase, *"Sumorsaete Ealle"*, which means *"All the people of Somerset"*

The *'brutal facts'* help us to see how many people there are in the places we feel called to and to see the sheer scale of the missionary task before us. We cannot be precious about anything, our lives, our churches or our ministries. This spiritual battle isn't personal. We, as soldiers of Jesus, have a huge and urgent mission ahead of us and countless millions of souls are waiting for us to liberate them and train them to be disciples of Jesus. May God help us to honestly reflect on our efforts in light of the brutal facts and the will of God revealed in scripture!

Through prayer, our conviction is that God has called us to help catalyse a movement of disciples, churches and leaders that multiplies until the gospel reaches all the people of Somerset. (visit www.benandcatherine.org for more info) For that to happen we need thousands of churches that meet simply in homes, cafes, pubs and workplaces and which can grow and multiply in the hands of what many would call ordinary untrained disciples who are devoted to Jesus Christ,

"The members of the council were amazed when they saw the boldness of Peter and John, for they could see that they were ordinary men with no special training in the scriptures. They also recognized them as men who had been with Jesus."
Acts 4:13

So everything is about the people! What will it take to see entire people groups transformed with the gospel and what would the

churches look like as these new disciples begin to gather to follow
Jesus together? And what would it look like to appoint
indigenous leaders from within these churches?

This is what accidental apostles think about, pray about and weep
about. They are pioneering fathers, looking to see how they can
labor with God to see Christ formed in people who were
previously not God's people. They see their spiritual children in
faith and are prepared to leave the safety of buildings,
denominations and tradition to see the living Christ at work in new
churches and spiritual communities and to recognize and develope
leaders from amongst them. They are prepared to find common
ground with the people they are called to and through prayer and
fasting find the grace to become all things to all people in order to
win them. (1 Corinthians 9:19-23)

We live near Glastonbury (The new age centre of the Universe!!)
and the apostolic task of becoming all things to all people is never
more obvious than when we as a team work there! I must confess
that I use it as an opportunity to model and practically show to
those on the team how our churchianity can act as a stumbling
block to those God is calling there. If we cannot look beyond
outward things to see the heart, then we will be unable to perceive
and see the grace of God at work in people who look, sound, dress
and live differently to us. When Jesus sent his disciples out to go to
towns and villages in Matthew 10 and Luke 10 we see that he gave
some simple instructions to them. One of these instructions was to
take nothing with them. (We'll look at this in the next chapter!) The
Lord of the harvest knows better than we do about harvesting but
we still love to lean on our understanding. If only we would take
nothing but the gospel when we go to plant churches. Instead we
take everything! Remember, Jesus wants to multiply disciples and
churches until the nations are discipled, not just recycle the

dwindling pool of existing believers! When Jesus sent out church planters in the gospels and throughout the new testament they went in 2's or a small team and had to rely on the power of the gospel to grow a new people from scratch. They were sent out like sheep among wolves!

Most church planters today take everything except the kitchen sink with them. They take centuries worth of churchianity, great plans for buildings and often they take with them (or attract) a ready made congregation of other well meaning christians or people who are disgruntled with the last church they were part of. You know who suffers from all this - the lost people who we say we're doing it all for! In reality everything we take with us totally disempowers any new believers who come to faith through our work because we're imposing our 'jewish' churchianity onto them, rather than going in humility and seeding their families and culture with the gospel and nurturing what grows amongst them as they begin to obey all of Jesus' commands. I've met many people who have shared a vision to plant churches amongst the harvest but after a year or two they give up. Often it's because they lack the patience and perseverance to develope and nurture the small signs of fruit they see. They're looking for instant and exciting results that justify their ministry instead of giving themselves unreservedly to the long haul of planting the gospel into new people groups and places and tending to the new disciples, communities and leaders that will grow. For many who've studied these kinds of kingdom movements around the world, they observe that movements are the overnight success stories that were 10 years in the making. Are you ready for a lifetime of hard work?

We were very blessed when we begun our ministry because 99% of the believers around us (including those in the church we were part of) didn't understand what we were doing and didn't want to get involved. Although it was hard at the time, with hindsight we're thankful that God led us in this way so we learned how to do the real work of ministry in the harvest rather than the pseudo-ministry of babysitting unhappy christians! We've always been about seeing new disciples, churches and leaders growing up out of the harvest and to be quite frank, the majority of believers I know say they don't feel called to do that, don't want to do it or give up when they hit the inevitable spiritual trials and suffering that Jesus promises to everyone who does His work.

For accidental apostles they understand what it means to go *"far away"* to the Gentiles just as Paul was commissioned to do,

"Go, for I will send you far away to the Gentiles"
Acts 22:21

For us it felt like we were being sent far away even though we never left the town we were living in! In some ways it would have been easier to be sent to a foreign tribe somewhere amongst an unreached people group. We would have had less awkward conversations with church goers and over protective church leaders in our region. But the reality is that the UK is unreached and needs missionary pioneers who are prepared to deal with the huge shifts in mindsets and practices that are needed to plant churches amongst the foreign cultures that are right on our doorstep. So we need accidental apostles that are sent to young people and gangs, to immigrants, to different music scenes and to all the different types of people and places around us. The possibilities for the Gospel are endless if only we would see with faith and act with courage. Most situations we now find ourselves in seem a million miles away from what life used to be like for us in the church we were part of. God has helped us to go far away to the gentiles and I believe He is calling many others to do the same.

As we've tried to respond to the Holy Spirit, looked to make disciples and planted churches here in the UK I started to notice that we were seeing fruit amongst a certain type of people. Now God loves everyone, don't get me wrong. But I think he has a special place in his heart for notorious sinners. You know the kind of people that the world would look down their nose at? The kind of people most christians would never dream of associating with. The kind of people that if we're honest, we've written off in our minds and hearts before we've even spoken to them.

Wherever I go I keep getting into situations where I meet people like this. They might be the biggest drug dealers or gangsters in town or the people with the most notorious reputation. I've learned how to act with people like this and to be honest I feel more at home now with people like this rather than with a lot of fellow believers. Why? Because they have become *my* people. We've seen lots of these kind of people baptized and start gathering together as churches. This work is full of challenges and heartbreak, but woe to me if I do not pray my heart out for these people and plant churches amongst them!

I remember during a time of prayer a while ago I suddenly had a vision of an army of people. I immediately felt like they were the people I was called to. They looked a pretty rough and ready mob, I have to say. But one thing stood out, they all had razor sharp teeth. To be honest they looked pretty fierce and I think they would be the last kind of people most believers would ever dream of approaching. They certainly didn't look like christians! God has called me to them though so I must go! Lord may you continue to raise up churches and leaders amongst the sharp toothed army who will bring freedom through Jesus to notorious sinners, tax collectors and prostitutes. May all these people around us who are not God's people become His people!

Is God planting your heart amongst the gentiles? Is he calling you to the 99%?

"Then I heard the Lord asking, "Whom should I send as a messenger to this people? Who will go for us?
I said, "Here I am, send me..."
Isaiah 6:8

What's the message?

In Acts 9:15 God declared to Ananias that He had called Paul to take His message to the gentiles. So what was the message that Paul was sent to proclaim?

At this point I want to look at some examples of what the message wasn't.

The message was not "Ask Jesus into your heart"

After Jesus had led me to quit my job, I had the privilege of travelling to a number of other countries to see what God was doing there. I saw how underground house churches were multiplying in China. I experienced open air gospel events in Kenya. And I witnessed pioneer evangelism in the villages of India. In these places it seemed like the gospel was spreading rapidly and the disciples and churches I met were carrying out the Lord's work selflessly. Returning back to the UK, I was met with the same old arguments like, "God is at work overseas but it's hard ground here in the UK" I used to go along with this faulty and unbiblical way of thinking which crushes faith and takes away any sense of responsibility in us to pray, preach, make disciples and plant churches. The things that our brothers and sisters were doing in these countries were completely different to the things we do in our churches here in the UK, so it's no wonder that they were experiencing a different result. Throughout scripture we are told that the Kingdom is about sowing and reaping and that if we sow the right seed with the right attitude then God will reward us because he will not be mocked,

"Don't be misled – you cannot mock the justice of God. You will always harvest what you plant"
Galatians 6:7

So I came to the conclusion from scripture that God's will is for the gospel to bear fruit in every culture, in every place and amongst every people. And if there is fruitlessness, then it's not due to the hardness of the ground or God's heart, it's due to us, our methods or the seed we're planting. I reflected on the messages that I had received in churches growing up and the continual stream of sermons, messages and words that are available to us online and I realized that the Bible is true, we do harvest what we sow!

We're planting a message that says God wants to build up our lives, make us feel good, make us successful and solve all our problems. So we get a harvest of people who think Jesus is their own personal genie who will appear when we need help and do whatever we ask Him to do for us. Churches consult their members in the same way that a business measures consumer satisfaction and believers remain like babies tossed to and fro because no-one dares to speak the truth in love (Ephesians 4:14-16)

Jesus' message was not *"believe in me and I will come and live in your heart and make everything good for you."* He isn't another option for you to put on your mantelpiece next to the statue of Buddha and your medication! He says that new life is available to you if are willing to die to your old life and obey Him. Maybe if we started planting the true seed of the gospel then we'd see a harvest of people who are selfless in their devotion to Jesus and His gospel?

Jesus did talk about dwelling and living in us – but only if we obey Him and trust Him,

"All who love me will do what I say. My Father will love them, and we will come and make our home with each of them."
John 14:23

So let's spread the message of the Kingdom and urge people to submit to Jesus' rule in their lives so that Jesus comes and lives with them!

The message was not "Come to our church"

Churchianity has turned discipleship into a spectator sport where our hope is that lost people will turn up at a church service. I have forgotten how many depressing conversations I have had with people who seem unable to see the opportunities for discipling people around them because their whole focus is trying to get their friends and neighbors to come along on a Sunday and hear the anointed leader. When will the body of Christ *wake up?*

I was talking with one friend who'd helped to organize an event at her church. The event was an opportunity to connect with local ladies from their town. As a result of that event my friend invited one lady to come to their church on Sunday morning. Apparently it had been a 'good' meeting and the visiting lady had enjoyed it. My friend was really excited as she talked about this story, but then her passion seemed to drain away as she shared her hope that this lady will come to another Sunday service one week. I listened to my friend as she shared how she was praying that the lady would come again and that there would be a good preacher that week.

Am I missing something here?! If the discipling of the nations depends on inviting people to good Sunday morning services then we might as well all pack up and go home.

I must confess I felt like shaking my friend!

God has called all of His children to invite those around them to follow Jesus Christ. You and I are the answer, not meetings or leaders. My friend is an amazing follower of Jesus and has the spirit of God in her, but her message to those she knows is "Come to the church" rather than going into their world and sharing how Jesus has come to people! My friend has an open door with this lady but instead of seeing the opportunity to bring God's kingdom amongst a whole new group of people, she's waiting for this lady to come to her church on a Sunday. And in my experience the vast majority of people are not at all interested in church, however they're interested in Jesus! But we'll come to that later.

The message was not "Say the sinners prayer"

If you're an evangelist then you won't like this, but Jesus has called us to make disciples and not just converts! Jesus called His followers into a life long commitment to obey Him and commands us to do the same. Yes we enter the Kingdom through repentance and baptism but according to the scriptures it's not 'job done' when that's happened. As with all the giftings in the body of Christ we must all be careful and realise that often we only see in part. To an evangelist the most important thing is always getting people saved and baptized and this is crucially important. But it's only the start of the process. Just as a pastor will always see that the development of a new disciple is always important. We need all the parts working together and looking to God who brings the increase,

"Each of us did the work the Lord gave us. I planted the seed in your hearts, and Apollos watered it, but it was God who made it grow. It's not important who does the planting or who does the watering. What's important is that God makes the seed grow. The one who plants and the one who waters work together for the same purpose. And both will be rewarded for their own hard work."
1 Corinthians 3:5-9

So no-where in scripture do we see any emphasis that praying the sinners prayer or reciting a doctrinal statement has any bearing on someone's eternal destiny. Paul says in Romans 10:9 that,

"If you declare openly that Jesus is Lord and believe in your heart that God raised him from the dead, you will be saved."

We know that salvation isn't obtainable through works and comes only through grace. We know that only God knows the desires of someone's heart. But I think we can conclude from scripture that public repentance and baptism is the first step of discipleship that Jesus and His disciples commanded people to make. Baptism is the public declaration that you believe Jesus is Lord and you are turning away from you old life through faith in His saving work.

Being a disciple of Jesus isn't just saying a prayer or putting your hand up at the end of a meeting. It's a decision to take up your cross, deny yourself and follow Jesus in community with others every day for the rest of your life (Luke 9:23) So when you're doing the work of an evangelist remember that the mission is to make disciples and not just converts!

Interestingly in Acts 2:37-41 we read Peter's response to the question, *"What must we do to be saved?"* Peter doesn't lead them in saying the sinners prayer, he instructs them in the way of discipleship. Peter says the following,

"Each of you must repent of your sins and turn to God, and be baptized in the name of Jesus Christ for the forgiveness of your sins. Then you will receive the gift of the Holy Spirit. This promise is to, to your children and to those far away – all who have been called by the Lord our God"
Acts 2:37

Peter calls them to be disciples who repent, get baptized and filled with the Holy Spirit and then spread this message to their families and friends and others who are far away. That message was for everyone from day one and it's the message we train our teams to share with anyone and everyone who responds to the gospel.

The message was not "It's all about loving people"

Whilst none of us would doubt or question the importance of loving people, it's not the primary thing Jesus has commanded us to do. Jesus has commanded us to make disciples, which involves helping people to understand their sinfulness towards God and to obey Him despite the resistance they will encounter from within and without! Making disciples is both the most loving and unloving thing we can do! It is the most loving thing we can do because it is the only thing of eternal worth that we can offer to people. But often it can also appear or feel like the most unloving thing because you are confronting people about their lifestyle and rebellion to God.

What you or I think is not so important though because I hope we've become obedient disciples of Jesus. What He thinks is the most important thing,

"Obviously I'm not trying to win the approval of people, but of God. If pleasing people were my goal, I would not be Christ's servant."
Galatians 1:10

Contrary to popular belief, preaching the gospel is not tidying someone's garden, giving out flip-flops at nightclubs or even prayer walking your town. All these things are good things to do if God leads you to do them, but without planting the seed of the gospel, nothing of eternal value will grow in anyone's life. There are a million and one ways to share the gospel and to clothe it in humble and loving works of service if required. But woe to us if we don't preach the gospel and make the way of salvation and life clear to people. At the end of the age Jesus is going to ask every one of His followers whether they made more disciples and we won't be able to hide behind religious good works, charitable deeds and kind things we did for our neighbors. He's going to ask us all if we baptized people and if we taught them to obey all His commands. And if you're a leader in the church of God then this is a serious and weighty responsibility as you're called to equip those in your care to be disciple makers and church planters!

Charles Spurgeon once said, _"It is the whole business of the whole church to preach the whole gospel to the whole world."_ Imagine the whole body of Christ being engaged with the missionary task of discipling the nations! That's God's will for His body and He's given gifts to the church so that everyone can be equipped (Ephesians 4:12)

In the book of Acts, the believers were scattered due to persecution. Unlike most believers nowadays, they did not take time out because life had been quite tough for them, they did not keep their heads down and begin to slowly build relationships with people and they didn't keep travelling back to Jerusalem every Sunday because there was great preaching and kids work there. The Bible records what they did in Acts 8:4,

"But the believers who were scattered preached the Good news about Jesus wherever they want"

Gospel and others first. Our comfort second. There is no other way for a disciple of Jesus. Whilst there may be times and seasons in our lives where God leads us through times of healing and rest, this is in the context of walking with Him towards His vision of seeing the Kingdom coming on earth as it it is heaven.

Jesus' message

If you've been a jew (church-goer) for any length of time then you will already have a lot of information and ideas about what Jesus' message was when he walked the earth. However often this is all second hand information. It might not necessarily be wrong or bad information, but it's not revelation. It's not what Jesus is saying to you and expecting you to obey. It's quite fun when training believers in how to make disciples as most have never actually read the Bible themselves and thought about how they are going to obey what God just said to them through it.

I want to encourage you to open the Bible and see for yourself what Jesus' message was. We have this amazing living book full of truth and revelation but most of us never open it ourselves and feed on it.

When we begun our journey of being disciples of Jesus and making more disciples we realized that the best thing to do in any situation is go to the Bible yourself and not to rely on the ideas and thoughts of other people. God speaks through the Bible in amazing ways and if you would just allow it to speak to your hearts and those you are seeking to disciple then, like us, you'll be amazed,

"For the word of God is alive and powerful. It is sharper than the sharpest two edged sword, cutting between soul and Spirit, between joint and marrow. It exposes our inner most thoughts and desires"
Hebrews 4:12

So here are some words from the scriptures that will help us to understand Jesus' message.

"From then on Jesus began to preach - repent of your sins and turn to God for the Kingdom of heaven is near"
(Matthew 4:17)

When we started on our journey of working in the harvest with gentiles we had no idea what to say! Any mention of the word 'church' or 'christianity' just killed every conversation we were trying to have with people. So I turned to the gospels and read them through. I wrote down in my journal the question, "What was

Jesus' message?" and put down on paper everything that stood out to me. Quite quickly I saw what Jesus' message was. You cannot really argue with scripture! Because I didn't know what to do and we were seeing no fruit at that time in our work, I decided to just say exactly what Jesus said! So in my conversations I would literally invite people to repent of their sins and turn to God because God had a whole new life for them. It was a very simple thing to do, almost foolishly simple. Guess what happened? We started to find people on a regular basis who wanted to repent of their sin, turn to God and enter His Kingdom.

There is great value in admitting we don't know what we are doing and searching the scriptures for guidance on everything, from what to say to how to overcome obstacles you're facing. At the school gate, in homes and at the park, lots of people in our town were now being invited to enter God's Kingdom through repentance and faith.

"Heal the sick, and tell them the Kingdom of God is near you now"
Luke 10:9

After seeing these initial breakthroughs with people, we then started to get into a lot of houses and social circles and this created a new set of challenges. What do we say and do now that we were with people who are spiritually open?

Can you guess what our clever strategy was? Yes that's it, we turned to the scriptures and did what it says.

So we saw that Jesus instructed His disciples to do some things when they enterered a household or 'oikos' of people (We'll go into this more in the next chapter) In Luke 10 and Matthew 10

Jesus told His disciples to eat food with the people, to heal the sick and to declare that the kingdom of God had come or was now near to them.

So that's what we did.

I put on some weight because I ate food with a lot of people. Sick people got healed because we laid hands on them and commanded them to be healed in Jesus' name. And many gentiles understood that the kingdom of heaven had come to their homes and that God wanted them to worship and obey Him there instead of thinking they needed to go to a holy building or sit in a row for 2 hours on a sunday morning. It was an amazing time, and all we did was what Bible said. If we could do it then anyone can do it!

So it's clear that Jesus' message was that when people repent of their sin and turn to God then His kingdom invades their world. This is what I live for! To see God's kingdom increasing on the earth as it is heaven, to see people living together under His rule and living His way! If your experience of God's kingdom coming is limited to what happens between 10am-12pm on a Sunday morning then you need to get out more.

I often explain Jesus' message to people using the following illustration. I explain to them how I am a British citizen and because of that I have a British passport. Because I am citizen of this kingdom I am subject to the laws, regulations and authorities of that kingdom. In everything I do I am accountable to this kingdom and the king or ruling authority.

Jesus invites us to become a citizen of His kingdom and to live according to his rules and regulations and to live under his rule as king. We enter His kingdom through repentance and turning to God. This involves baptism and a turning away from the old kingdom that we were living in. Joining Jesus' kingdom is a total commitment to subject every area of your life to Jesus as your king and to live according to His standard.

Let your kingdom come on earth Lord as it is in heaven!

"The Spirit of the Sovereign Lord is upon me, for the Lord has anointed me to bring good news to the poor. He has sent me to comfort the brokenhearted and to proclaim that captives will be released and prisoners will be freed. He has sent me to tell those who mourn that the time of the Lord's favor has come, and with it, the day of God's anger against their enemies. To all who mourn in Israel, he will give a crown of beauty for ashes, a joyous blessing instead of mourning, festive praise instead of despair. In their righteousness, they will be like great oaks that the Lord has planted for his own glory. They will rebuild the ancient ruins, repairing cities destroyed long ago. They will revive them, though they have been deserted for many generations."
(Isaiah 61:1-5)

Jesus quotes these prophetic words from Isaiah when he stood up and read the scriptures in Luke 4:18-20. What's interesting from these words is that we see two parts of Jesus' work. We see the liberation of prisoners and then the rebuilding of ruins and cities. From an apostolic perspective both are equally important and needed. You cannot rebuild people and places if the workers are still imprisoned by satan. And there is not much point in setting people free if they do not join the rebuilding work needed in their own lives and in those around them.

So we need an army of liberators and builders who work together to get the whole work done. So Jesus' message wasn't just about evangelism and setting people free and it wasn't just about the pastoring and teaching of people. It was both. And here's the main point that stands out to me as an accidental apostle, the people who do the rebuilding work are the people who've been liberated. The growth of the kingdom is self-supporting and self-propagating because when the seed of the gospel is planted it grows fruit and then this fruit produces more seeds and so it goes on. Throughout nature the creator has built in the potential for multiplication and replication. It's a shame we've thrown this out of His church.

"THEY will rebuild the ancient ruins"
Isaiah 61:4

In this book I am calling for an entire change to the mindset that prevails in the church and amongst us as disciples of Jesus. It's not us believers who do all the work as we show endless love and charity to the poor, helpless sinners who can't do anything. We are to liberate people through the power of the gospel and then to help them obey Jesus as our new co-workers. We are commanded to help people understand and act on the truth that through repentance and faith in God we become a new creation where Christ then starts to transform everything about us from the inside out. The great secret we have for the world is not how to find success in business, how to become rich or how to live a perfect life! These things may or may not happen to us as we obey Jesus! The great secret we have and are called to proclaim is that Christ in us is the hope of glory (Colossians 1:27) As people grow in their understanding and obedience to Christ they will rebuild their ruined life and the ruins around them.

You can neatly package this into Jesus' words in Matthew 28:19-20 when he said,

"Go and make disciples of all the nations, baptizing them in the name of the Father and the Son and the Holy Spirit. Teach these new disciples to obey all the commands I have given you."

However it's anything but neat and it is a work that is hard and costly.

Paul's message

Jesus called people to repent and to turn to God as His kingdom was near. What was Paul's message?

"When I first came to you, dear brothers and sisters, I didn't use lofty words and impressive wisdom to tell you God's secret plan. For I decided that while I was with you I would forget everything except Jesus Christ the one who was crucifed. I came to you in weakness, timid and trembling. And my message and my preaching were very plain. Rather than using clever and persuasive speeches I relied only on the power of the Holy Spirit. I did this so you would trust not in human wisdom but in the power of God"
1 Corinthians 2:1-6

Here we have an insight into what Paul said and did when he helped to form the church in Corinth. He follows in the footsteps of Jesus, the 12 and the 72 and relies on nothing but the message of the kingdom. Paul says that his message was unimpressive and simple and his one goal was to see people trusting in the power of God instead of human wisdom.

I have been trying to plant churches and make disciples for a few years now and I can rejoice that there has been some fruit. But I have to say that,even as I write this book, I sense that there is so much more to learn about how to lead people to trust in the power of God and not in human wisdom. Paul's way of doing things led to churches growing in his absence. This is like the holy grail for accidental apostles, how do we see disciples, churches and leaders multiplying without us? So much of what we do revolves around our own ability to lead, encourage, push and influence others. And so little of what we do is about providing a pattern or foundation that others can build on, and the person who can achieve it through them! I can influence others to do things through my zeal, enthusiasm and by simply going on at them all the time! Believe me I have done it. As long as you are constantly present (in person, online or through communication) then you can get things done. However if your strategy is basically YOU then you'll hit a problem!

If all the initiative comes from your wisdom and drive then if you're removed then everything stops. Similarly, ministry in this scenario becomes all centered around you so those you're discipling won't do anything when you're not there because they're used to you doing it all for them. Both scenarios lead to a lack of growth and fruitfulness.

So here we see Paul talking about how he came in humility and weakness and laid the foundation of Christ into that embryonic church. His message and the way He did things allowed others to carefully build upon His ministry. And that is one of the keys to understanding the apostle's call. It is the call to lay unseen foundations that others can build on. Unfortunately today, so called apostles have become like superstars rather than humble servants. There is nothing spectacular about the foundations of a building and as it gets built you actually lose sight of it. True apostles rejoice when the work of others is recognized and honoured and lay themselves down like living foundations in the new churches and ministries they are birthing.

Paul's simple and unimpressive message was Jesus Christ and his crucifixion. If you've ever attempted to plant a church then you will appreciate the wisdom in what Paul did. The gospel of Jesus and life of Jesus is the foundation for the church. A Christ centred community cannot be founded on good ideas, strategies or models. Only by embodying the grace of Jesus Christ will a church grow and be fruitful. Without that, relationships will tear apart and there will be no foundation to build upon!

So Paul preached the message of the kingdom of God and pointed to the work and life of Jesus Christ as the blueprint for life! He constantly pointed his spiritual children back to the example and attitude of Christ when he waded through relational and pastoral issues with them. And for Paul, ministry could be encapsulated by the life and death of Jesus who poured himself out like a drink offering for God and others,

"As for me, my life has already been poured out as an offering to God. The time of my death is near. I have fought the good fight, I have finished the race, and I have remained faithful"
2 Timothy 4:6

Father God is looking for people who will joyfully pour out their lives for Him and others. And there's good news. You don't need to go to a seminary, Bible college or spend years training how to do it.

You can start right here right now. Training and study may help, but the main thing that God is looking for is a sacrificial and servant heart and those are things that cannot be taught in a classroom.

"Every time I think of you, I give thanks to my God. Whenever I pray, I make my requests for all of you with joy, for you have

been my partners in spreading the good news about Christ from the time you first heard it until now. "
Philippians 1:3-60

I always love reading this scripture from Philippians 1 with teams and pioneers. It gives us such a big insight into the way Paul thought. Paul understood that the Father's heart for the nations was so big and that his own ability was so small. When you have a revelation about God's huge heart for the world and an honest evaluation of your own inadequacy to do anything - it forces you to start mobilizing and empowering others to do the work of ministry instead of relying on your own efforts.

For way too long I tried to rely on my own ability to get things done. Ministry was about where I was going to plant a church, who I was discipling and what God was saying and doing in my life. I had a lot of energy and was enthusiastic about the Gospel so naturally I just started to "get things done"! And I did get some things done. Lots of people got baptized and some churches got planted. But it killed me and it affected my family and those around me. Sure I was influencing a few other pioneering types around me, but I wasn't seeing healthy teams, churches and leaders developing. So God told me to stop and think about it.

I began to realise that being a pioneer is not about how strong you are or what you are able to do. If you're anything like me, it's easy to slip into thinking that you're going to save the world yourself and you only have 1 day to do it!

Paul was successful not because of what he did, but because of what others did as a result of what he did. The test of our ministry is not how busy we are or the amazing things that God does through us in the people around us. The true test of ministry is how well we have equipped and encouraged people to obey Jesus in our absence and to pass this onto others. This is why Paul gloried in his weaknesses and preached unimpressive messages, because everything was about honouring and empowering others rather than himself. Paul wasn't just saying to the church in Corinth that they were his partners because he wanted their money or support. He genuinely meant it, since the day they heard the gospel they had become part of the work entrusted to Paul and anyone else who was willing to lay their lives down for it. The work was so extensive that it was literally all hands on deck and Paul knew it! If you're an accidental apostle in the making I want to encourage you to think about the spiritual legacy created through your ministry. Take a moment to think beyond yourself and what you're doing and to reflect on what others are doing as a result of what you've done. Are you still running around reliant on your own energy and effort or have you discovered the same thing that Paul did?

In 2 Timothy 2:2 Paul wrote the following to Timothy his spiritual son,

"You have heard me teach things that have been confirmed by many reliable witnesses. Now teach these truths to other Trustworthy people who will be able to pass them onto others"

When Paul spoke and acted, he was thinking about his spiritual great grandchildren!

Timothy was Paul's spiritual son. The trustworthy people Timothy would teach were Paul's spiritual grandchildren. And those discipled by Timothy's trustworthy people were Paul's spiritual great grandchildren.

The harvesting work in the nations is so great that we need a complete mindset shift! We need to multiply disciples, churches and leaders that can be fruitful and reproduce without us! We need to see those we are discipling as workers who need mobilizing, not as people who will support our ministry and vision.

The work is too great to do anything else.

Am I a disciple of Jesus?

How could my life be more focused on the 99% of people who don't know Jesus?

Chapter 3

Appointed by God to do His work

Acts 13:2

The Holy Spirit appoints men and women to do His work.

I'm just reminding us all because we seem to have forgotten this key foundational truth. In Jesus' kingdom, people are not appointed by committees, leaders or popular opinion. It is the Holy Spirit's job to appoint people to the work of transforming the nations, not ours,

"One day as these men were worshiping the Lord and fasting, the Holy Spirit said, "Appoint Barnabas and Saul for the special work to which I have called them." So after more fasting and prayer, the men laid their hands on them and sent them on their way. So Barnabus and Saul were sent out by the Holy Spirit"
Acts 13:2-5

On our own journey, I've come to the conclusion that the Holy Spirit wants to appoint and send people out to do kingdom work far more than we do. God wants to transform the nations and yet it so often feels that we (the church) act as a spiritual bottle neck rather than a spiritual springboard to all people! So we do well to keep close to the spirit and what He is thinking, feeling and doing.

As we've wrestled in prayer and searched the scriptures over the years I wanted to share with you some things that might be helpful to you when we think about 'the work' that the Holy Spirit wants to appoint people to. And remember I'm writing to accidental apostles who have a passion to see whole villages, towns, cities, nations and people groups transformed. And please also remember that we are not working in a settled church environment with people who've been believers for years (That world has its own challenges!) We're working in the messy harvest fields with new disciples and churches. What we are doing is a glorious work in progress!

You've probably been involved with a church for a while now and benefit from the pastoral safety, risk assessments and clear structures and processes that are no doubt in place. And all of these things are good, helpful and maybe necessary when a church reaches a certain stage of maturity and when you have the manpower to do it.

As you read this book however you may start to ask questions about things like 'leadership' and 'accountability'. These are questions I often think about as well and I hope that some of your thoughts or concerns are answered in this book.

If you still have unanswered questions or concerns however, then I can offer two suggestions…

1) Some questions and concerns can only be answered over time as the work that we and others are doing directly in the harvest matures and developes. So bear with us on those points and pray for us as we continue to apply the scriptures to the disciples, churches and leaders that are growing up around us.

2) Some questions and concerns arise from our fondness of churchianity and mindsets that need to be challenged. In that case I'd encourage you to seek God's wisdom through searching the scriptures with prayer and fasting

Within any family, team or church you always get a range of different opinions. These are all needed and God has planned it this way. Some on our team here in Somerset go to sleep when we talk about strategy and planning, others come alive at that point. Others thrive on spontaneity and the feeling of going with the flow, while some feel very unsure or lost without a clear plan. I feel I am kind of in the middle. A god given strategy and plan is needed to keep us on course and yet should allow for spontaneity and creative licence at the same time. The things I will share in this chapter about the work are more practical and I hope will offer some kind of framework for others who feel called to build the kingdom of God in the harvest. They are not commandments from God and shouldn't be seen like that. At best, they are reflections from a missionary who has seen some fruit but longs to see so much more. When I was thinking about writing this book I felt God say to me that the book was to be 'pragmatic. I've often heard this word but could not really explain its meaning. I presumed it just meant to look at things more practically. According to google, the word 'pragmatic' means,

"dealing with things sensibly and realistically in a way that is based on practical rather than theoretical considerations."

Enough of the theory and information. It's time to get our hands dirty with Jesus in His harvest fields.

What is the work?

God has created us all to do good works (Ephesians 2:10) and in 1 Corinthians 12 Paul explains how there is one Spirit but different works and activities. So in a very real way we all have our own special work to do from the Lord. But Paul makes it clear that all of our special gifts and work are given to us from God for the sake of others in the body,

"A Spiritual gift is given to each of us so that we can help each other"
1 Corinthians 12:7

If we're being honest, lots of us are still on a journey to deeply understand this truth. I can think of so many times where I have used the gifting and calling I have received freely from God to build myself up rather than others. It's very easy to forget that God has put us in His body to work together with others. Let's not spend our whole lives trying to find our ministry and calling and miss the whole point that it's for the benefit of others anyway.

Our whole perspective on life is influenced by our calling and part in the body. Yes God may speak to us clearly, but He also calls us to consider others in the body and to listen to their perspective. God is busy building His body and we need to be mindful of what is needed, and when. For example it would be pointless to try and use the pastoral gift when you're starting the work in a pioneering field. A pastor is no use when there's not even any disciples to shepherd and care for yet!

Likewise, when a work needs establishing and strengthening, the apostolic gift needs to be *rationed out* so other parts of the body can develope and come into their own. God is all about teamwork and bringing the right people onto the building site at the right time. There is no room for pride, competitiveness or superstars! It's His house we're building not ours! What a privilege it is to help build God's spiritual dwelling place amongst all the nations and peoples of the earth. This is the work:

"So now you Gentiles are no longer strangers and foreigners. You are citizens along with all of God's holy people. You are members of God's family. Together, we are his house, built on the foundation of the apostles and the prophets. And the cornerstone is Christ Jesus himself. We are carefully joined together in him, becoming a holy temple for the Lord. Through him you Gentiles are also being made part of this dwelling where God lives by his Spirit."
Ephesians 2:19-22

Paul gives us some clues here about this work amongst the gentiles. God wants to build a people, *his house*, on the foundation of apostles and prophets and on the cornerstone of Jesus Christ. Even as I write this I feel totally captivated by the vision of seeing God's house built amongst the gentiles, where countless numbers of notorious sinners are no longer strangers and foreigners but are being made into a dwelling place where God lives by His Spirit. God's house requires a foundation and I hope that what I share in this chapter will provide you with some foundational principles, truths and stories that will enable you to work with God to build His house with the gentiles you are working amongst.

Many people have such a false view of what it means to be an apostle. I'm sure the devil rejoices when he sees so-called apostles parading around on TV, asking people for money and working to create a following for themselves. May God restore a Biblical understanding of the spiritual gift of apostleship. And to be honest – we'll know this is happening when we start to see the kind of work that I'm talking about in this chapter happening! The fruit speaks for itself!

In a world that craves status, recognition and limelight we have the opportunity through Christ to live in a completely different way and those gifted to be apostles have the honour of laying their lives down first for this quest! (We'll explore this 'honour' in the final chapter!) Paul writes the following in 1 Corinthians 12:27-29,

"All of you together are Christ's body, and each of you is a part of it. Here are some of the parts God has appointed for the church; first are apostles, second are prophets, third are teachers, then those who do miracles, those who have the gift of healing, those who can help others, those who have the gift of leadership, those who speak in unknown languages"

Clearly we understand that Paul is not listing these people in order of importance as in this same letter Paul goes to great lengths to explain that every part of the body is important and to give honour to everyone. What I believe it shows though is the order that is needed to build God's house (Which let me remind you again is not a building but a people where he dwells by His Spirit) Paul says apostles are *first* in the body and this corresponds with the idea that apostles lay the foundations for church planting and Christ's body formation amongst a people or geographic location.

Quite simply, those called to be apostles are first on the scene when it comes to laying a foundation for God's church in an area. Whether they go first themselves (like Paul often did) or are called onto the scene (like Peter and John in Acts 8) apostles lay themselves and the foundation of Christ into a group of disciples so that they become the church of Jesus Christ and continue to grow and multiply in the apostle's absence. This ministry flies in the face of hundreds of years of churchianity and from personal experience is often totally misunderstood and ridiculed by those in the body with other giftings.

However the truth remains that God has, and continues to, call men and women to the ministry of apostleship so that churches are planted amongst every tribe and tongue and Jesus is glorified in the nations. And this book is an attempt to mobilize more of them!

We've been 'giving it a go' in the harvest fields for a few years now. At times it's felt like we've not known what we're doing. Sometimes it's felt like God has shown us just enough so that we can make the next step in the work. If you'd have asked me a few years ago what the work was when I was in a season of evangelism and gospel sowing then I would have given you a very different answer to the one I'd give you now. We are (hopefully!) as people continually growing and developing and things that seemed so urgent at one point in our lives are not so urgent now. My hope though is that our pioneering effort will make it easier for others coming behind us so they can go further, deeper and faster. I can look back now on 10 years of work here in our region and see that God was building according to His plan, even if at the time it didn't seem like it. Through our obedience to Him, God has been able to lay some foundations that others can build on. Do we have lots of regrets, yes! Have we made lots of mistakes, yes! But we can say with Paul,

"Because of God's grace to me, I have laid the foundation like an expert builder. Now others are building on it"
1 Corinthians 3:10

When I think about the work God has called us to here in Somerset (a county of the UK with around a million people) I immediately think about the following verses from Acts 14:21-28,

"After preaching the good news in Derbe and making many Disciples, Paul and Barnabus returned to Lystra, Iconium and Antioch of Pisidia, where they strengthened the believers. They encouraged them to continue in the faith, reminding them that we must suffer many hardships to enter the Kingdom of God. Paul

and Barnabus also appointed elders in every Church. With prayer and fasting they turned the elders over to the care of the Lord, in whom they had put their trust. Then they travelled back through Pisidia to Pamphylia. They preached the word in Perga, then went down to Attalia. Finally they returned by ship to Antioch in Syria, where their journey had begun. The believers there had entrusted them to the grace of God to do the work that they had now completed. Upon arriving in Antioch, they called the Church together and reported everything God had done through them and how he had opened the door of faith to the Gentiles, too. And they stayed there with the believers for a long time"

To me these verses tell us a lot about the work and also what the church's thoughts were about when this work was completed. Paul and Barnabus had been sent out to complete the work and now they returned with news of that completion and that God had opened the door of faith to the gentiles. They brought stories about how they had preached the good news, made many disciples, strengthened these new believers and appointed elders in every church. Because they had done all of these things they concluded that their work was completed, that God had opened the door of faith to the gentiles and that it was time to return to base!

Let me speak from my heart.

I long for the day when we can say our apostolic work in Somerset is completed and we can conclude that God has opened the door of faith to the gentiles. We will know that has happened when we see healthy churches taking root and starting to multiply across all the towns and villages here and we have appointed elders amongst every church. We are building with the end in mind! I remember when I visited Taunton, the county town and administrative capital of Somerset. As I prayed that day I was led to visit the county council headquarters and saw the official motto of

Somerset, *"Sumorsaete Ealle"*. It's an anglo saxon phrase which literally means *"All the people of Somerset"*. As I read this I immediately felt God's heart for this part of the south west and dedicated myself to the work of seeing Jesus known amongst all the people of Somerset. The only way this can happen is through a miraculous multiplying movement of fearless disciples, churches and leaders that is able to replicate and self-sustain itself.

There are encouraging signs as we see some churches beginning to form and some leaders emerging. But if often feels like we have so far to go with this work that often appears so fragile on the ground but is so strong through the eyes of faith! My hope for this book is that will help in some way open the door of faith to the gentiles again in our generation and in the generations to come!

It's not necessarily for my contemporaries in the church who may just want to argue and discuss some of the points I make for the rest of their lives. It's for the few who God is choosing to break with the status quo in order to prepare what is needed for a whole new army of disciple makers who are at the moment a million miles from Jesus.

When I look back over our journey I can now see that the Lord of the harvest took us through different seasons. With hindsight we are now able to put everything we have learned together, but at the time it was like following the pillar of fire through the wilderness like Israel did in the book of Exodus. It's not until God brings you to a time of resting and reflection that you are able to see the bigger picture and take a step back from the challenges right in front of you. At the time, what God was showing us in that particular season seemed 'the most important' thing. But looking back you realise that everything is the most important thing!

Similarly we all see things through the lens of our calling and gifting. Unless you're mature and able to laugh at yourself, we all tend to think and act like what we see needs doing is the most important thing! The pastors insist that loving people is the most important thing. The prophets won't stop wielding the sword as we have to come into alignment with what the Spirit is saying. The teachers don't understand why everyone is not in the word 24/7 and believe the answer to this problem is more teaching! The evangelists, well they are aren't even around long enough to even explain to people what the problem is because the fact that everyone is not going to the lost shows that they don't even love Jesus! And the apostles…well I suppose they keep on banging on about the things I'm writing in this book.

I believe there are some key phases and seasons that need to be worked through in order to 'complete' the work just as the workers did in the New Testament.

From Acts 14:21-28 we see these key areas of the work, preaching the good news, making many disciples, strengthening the believers and appointing leaders. I would also add the area of prayer and honouring the Holy Spirit which is present at the start and then throughout the ongoing building work! They are all as important as each other and like us, the Lord may lead you through all of them or you may find yourself working as a team on one or more of these phases. It's not important who does what, what's important is that the work gets done, that God causes the increase. and that precious souls in the harvest field come to know their loving heavenly Father and become workers.

As Paul says,

"It's not important who does the planting, or who does the watering. What's important is that God makes the seed grow. The one who plants and the one who waters work together with the

same purpose. And both will be rewarded for their own hard work."
1 Corinthians 3:7-9

This year as I've tried to stop and reflect more than I usually would, my mind has been taken back to the season where we learned about how to give ourselves to prayer and honor the Holy Spirit. So that is where we'll start.

What is the work that God has called you to do for Him?

What people or places is God calling you to work amongst?

What is stopping you from doing this more?

Chapter 4

Honour the Holy Spirit

Acts 16:9-11

The Holy Spirit was never spoken about when I was growing up and it was not until I went to university where I had my first encounter with Him. I remember going to see a friend from the christian union who was discipling me. I turned up at his house one evening and his living room was full of people talking in tongues. I sat down and took it all in. Nobody explained to me what was happening and after the meeting finished I left the house with more than just a few questions about what I had just experienced.
I began to read the Bible verses about the Holy Spirit and what happened when people were filled with the Holy Spirit. A wonderful new world opened up which seemed to bring color to my conservative evangelical bible based heritage! But still I felt like someone looking in on this strange world of being filled with the Spirit.

I became very involved with the christian union at university and we did loads of events and projects in our hall of residence. It was great fun. I remember we had planned one event and I was thinking about how we could publicize the event to everyone in our hall of residence. As I was thinking about this, the thought came into my head that literally everyone in my hall of residence (around 200 people) would be in the dining room at 7pm that evening for dinner. Having argued with God for a while about this, I eventually resigned myself to the idea that God was leading me to stand up during that evening's meal time and to say something about the event. To say I was scared about this would be an understatement.

Before I walked back to my halls of residence that afternoon, a walk that took about an hour, I bumped into a friend and we talked about what I was going to do that evening and how I was pretty scared about it. All I can remember her saying to me was *"As you walk back to your hall of residence you need to pray in tongues all the way"*

There's always a point that Jesus leads you to where you have enough information and it's now the time to act and obey. This point is different for all of us. Some need more information before they step out and obey. Some require less information before obeying. And some are prepared to obey when they know hardly anything about what lies ahead. It's a complex mix of faith, maturity, gifting and also whatever is needed at that time. No-one is right or wrong and we're all different, but the important thing is knowing when you've reached that point and getting on with it instead of engaging in more pointless information gathering. Regarding the issue of the Holy Spirit and speaking in tongues I had reached that point. So on the walk home I just did it.

I had read all about the Holy Spirit and it was now time to invite Him to literally take over my life and to fill me with the supernatural power and boldness I needed to stand up in front of 200 of my fellow students. I remember walking next to the busy road starting to make what sounded like baby noises. After a few minutes I was shouting in a new and strange language and something was happening inside me. It wasn't that the feeling of being scared was going away, but something else was rising in me. I asked the Holy Spirit that afternoon to give me the boldness to preach the gospel and the words to say to the people that evening.

That evening I stood up on my chair in front of 200 fellow students and pretty much preached the gospel. Many of them didn't know what to make of it as I talked about eternal life and how Jesus can transform their lives. I also remembered to invite them to the event we were organizing. As I sat down you could have heard a pin drop. What made it more challenging was that for some reason that night I found myself sat on a table with some of the older, more senior, students and this made me feel even more scared and intimidated. But Jesus needed a job doing and I had to do it. Some of the students sat on my table had tears in their eyes as I sat down and continued to eat my food. By the way the event we did a few days later was packed out and a number of students received prayer afterwards.

When I think about this story it makes me think about two things.

Firstly I wish that I'd had a vision for church planting when I was at university instead of trying to take my friends to well-meaning churches in the local area. Maybe some of you reading this book are being called by God to plant churches on university and college campuses that can multiply through the whole student world across the globe?! Lord raise up workers for that ripe harvest field!

Secondly I experienced how the Father loves to pour out his Spirit to empower people to preach the gospel, demonstrate His kingdom and to obey Him courageously. I'd read in the Bible how that so often the Holy Spirit filling people led to them preaching with boldness and doing supernatural and extraordinary things in the name of Jesus! I don't understand the idea which I've heard in many churches that the Holy Spirit is given to us to make us feel good. There are believers in Jesus around the world hiding away in homes and buildings who are crying out and waiting for the Spirit to fill them, but they have no intention of pouring out what they have received to those who are hungry and thirsty around them. These people are going to have a long wait.

It's the same with healing and miracles. We often see healings and miracles in the work we are doing. It's not due to our ability or because our team have mastered the way to pray for healing. It's because we're constantly in situations where we are praying for sick lost people. God loves to demonstrate His kingdom through signs and wonders as we His people preach the gospel.

I often meet believers who ask me the question, *"Why doesn't God heal people?"* I used to try and engage in a theoretical discussion about this to try and help them understand that God does want to heal people. That's what you do in churchianity, talk about the subject and come to a theological answer. However I've learnt that the kingdom is not a matter of talk and arguing it's about power. (1 Corinthians 4:20) I began to realise that a lot of people believe the theory that God can heal people, but all they do with that theory is to occasionally pray for other people in their church when they have the flu. So now when I get asked that question I do what Jesus did and reply with another question! The conversation goes a little like this:

(Christian) "Why doesn't God heal people? I believe he can but I never see it happening?"

(Me) "When was the last time you put your hand on someone who is sick and doesn't know Jesus and commanded the sickness to go in Jesus' name?"

(Christian) "Oh I've never done that"

Things usually go one of two ways after that. People either look for a quick way to exit the conversation because they don't want to face their fear and lack of faith in God, or they come and join us for a day and lay hands on the sick, see them get healed and then do it more because they now actually believe that God still heals today. Faith is demonstrated by what we do, not what we say!

I had to learn that God gives us His power through the Spirit in immeasurable ways when we are living fearlessly and sacrificially for others. So stop waiting for the Spirit to come and go and make disciples! You'll find Him filling you and empowering you just like He did on that evening at university and has done on a daily basis since then.

"After this prayer, the meeting place shook, and they were all filled with the Holy Spirit. Then they preached the word of God with boldness."
Acts 4:31

Just as the gift of apostleship is first in the church, so prayer is first before everything else! Prayer is the basis for everything, it's where we pour out our heart to God, receive direction, instruction and correction and are filled with supernatural ability and power.

At the start of our work I went through what felt like an endless season of prayer. I'd quit my job to literally give myself to prayer and I had to learn how to pray and how to honour the Holy Spirit and walk with Him. For months I had to learn about doing nothing. I'm someone who likes to be active but I had to learn that action without direction is pointless. I learned more on a daily basis how to grow in walking in the Spirit and how to follow His leading and prompting. Often He'd gently pull me away to go for walks in the countryside alone with Him. Sometimes I'd be driving somewhere and He'd ask me to stop and talk to people at a certain house. There were many times where I just ignored his leading because I was too focused on getting to where I was heading to or because the things I

felt He was asking me to just seemed too crazy. I'd grieve the Spirit
many times and each time I would come back to Him and repent of
my selfishness and unwillingness to do whatever he led me to do.

Over time I learned to honour the Holy Spirit and even though it
feels like we now have a much clearer vision of the work God has
called us to, the most crtitical thing is still to give ourselves to
prayer and honor the Holy Spirit as the basis of everything we do. I
am inspired by men and women who have surrendered their whole
lives to Jesus and made themselves wholly available to the work of
the Spirit. One quote from Henry Martyn has stuck with me,

*"The Spirit of Christ is the Spirit of missions. The nearer we get
to Him, the more intensely missionary we become"*

This man gave his whole life to the work of spreading the gospel in
India and Persia. Henry Martyn was an ordinary man just like you
and me, but he became *'intensely missionary'* as he grew nearer to
God. May that be true of us as well.

Sent to China

As this time of prayer and honouring the Holy Spirit continued I
began to understand that what I was learning was the basics of
being a disciple, to hear and obey Jesus! I'd been a christian church
goer for a relatively long time but I couldn't really say that I was a
true disciple. I was learning how to hear Jesus through the
scriptures and the Spirit and how to obey Him immediately and
whole heartedly. It felt like a very different way of life than what I
had experienced in churchianity, where there was a lot of talk but
not much action. Following Jesus had now become an exciting

dynamic adventure. As I spent my time in prayer and asking the Spirit to lead me, I began to feel an incredible burden for China. As I look back on it, it's still hard to understand how this begun to happen. But all I know is that it did. It wasn't like a bolt from the blue where I woke up one morning thinking about it. But as the days went by I seemed to be thinking about that country more and more and becoming increasingly emotional whenever I read anything about China or saw anything on the TV about China. It was a strange and yet wonderful time.

It was like I was carrying something from the Holy Spirit for this country of over 1 billion people. I'd be talking to Catherine my wife and then suddenly China would come into my mind and I'd start weeping. It got to the point where I started to ask the Holy Spirit whether I was supposed to be doing something with this burden. After a week or so of asking this question I felt like the Spirit was showing me that He had given me this burden because He wanted me to go to China. This presented some challenges to me. We were not receiving any wage or payment for the work of prayer we were currently doing, so where would we get money to go to China from? And I didn't even know anyone in China so what would I even be going there for?

I sensed the Spirit's leading so strongly though so I talked with Catherine about it and we started praying about where should I go and when. It was a strange scenario. On one hand we were starting to make plans based on the unseen leading and will of the Holy Spirit. But at the same time I also had very real concerns that I was going crazy.

I couldn't afford to go to China, I didn't know anyone there and actually it would be illegal for me to do any kind of ministry there. I'm not sure this particular project would have passed a risk assessment but I'd given over the reigns of my life to the Holy

Spirit so how could I resist His leading? I felt drawn to a specific city in China and as we prayed with open diaries we began to settle on a date. I'd plan to go in a few months.

The increasing sense I had was that God was sending me to encourage my Jesus-family in China. This significantly raised the bar because it meant I wasn't just going there aimlessly. I was being sent there with a purpose and I believed that somehow God was going to connect me with my brothers and sisters in Christ there. I can remember a couple of dreams I had where I saw the faces of Chinese men. I made a note of these, in case I found myself meeting these people on my trip. Through research into the situation in China it was very obvious to me that the only way I would be able to encourage my family there would be to find those gathering together in underground churches. So we continued to pray and wait for God to piece the plan together!

It was one month before the date we had felt I should travel to China. I went out for a walk because I was feeling very unsettled about the whole situation. Through the eyes of faith it seemed that God was leading me so clearly, yet with just 4 weeks to go I had no air ticket, no money and no real plan for the trip! As is my normal habit in situations like this, I went out for a walk to be alone with Jesus. I felt I needed to know that day whether this was actually going to happen or whether I was losing my mind completely. When I got back home an hour or so later we had received a cheque in the post for around £1000. I was going!

I booked my air tickets and two nights in a hotel so I didn't look too suspicious when I arrived there. My intention was to arrive and then ask the Spirit to direct me to the home or place where my brothers and sisters would be meeting. It was exciting and also scary. It was also a very sobering time for us as a family as we were well aware of the religious and political situation in China and what the consequences would be for me and also those I met with if the authorities discovered what I was believing God to do there.

Two days before my flight I went to an evening prayer meeting and decided it would be a good idea to share about the planned trip so that people could pray for me. One lady at the meeting had been carrying a prophetic word in her heart for a number of years and when she heard me talking about my trip she felt the word was for me. God had given her a picture of a child carrying a small flame to a distant country. When this child reached the country many people came to that child and the flame was spread to them. Then they went and spread it to others. The prophetic word strengthened my faith but didn't really answer any of practical concerns. One couple came to me at the end of the meeting and suggested I contact a friend of theirs who had been to China. I wrote down the phone number but to be honest had no intention of calling this lady until after my trip. However when I returned home I felt like I needed to call this lady and I'm glad I did. She came over to see us the next morning quite amazed because I was going to the same city in China she had been too and she'd actually been wanting to send some documents to someone she knew in that city. That morning she asked me if I could take these documents to her friend in the city and whether I could arrange to meet him when I arrived at the hotel where I planned to stay. In that moment I felt God's peace so I agreed and sent an email to this man in China who replied and said he'd meet me at the hotel when I arrived.

The next day I found myself stood in the lobby of a Chinese hotel waiting for a man who I'd never met. I didn't even know what he looked like. We eventually found each other and he took me out for a walk and a meal. I said very little and listened to what this man was saying. I was very suspicious and cautious that he may report me to the secret police that I had read about before my trip. I told him nothing about my intentions and why I had come to China.

I gave him the documents this lady had asked me to pass to him and we shared small talk. Towards the end of our meal together he became quieter and then looked me in the eye and asked,

"Why have you come to China?"

In that split second I looked to God. What should I say to him? I immediately felt God encouraging me to tell this man everything. I am someone who is fairly confident, but in that moment I felt so vulnerable. But I acted on how I felt the Spirit was leading me.

I shared with the man how God had called me to give myself to prayer and how He had been giving me a burden for the China. I explained how I felt Jesus was sending me here to encourage my brothers and sisters in Christ and that I intended to look to the Holy Spirit to lead me to them.

The man showed no outward reaction to what I had said and just replied that I would not be allowed to do this with any of the government controlled churches so I'd need to find brothers and sisters in the underground church. Which I already knew. We walked back to the hotel and the man said he would come and meet me the day after tomorrow and then left. I prayed and went to sleep.

The next day I wondered around on my own. I was in a city of over 10 million people and I knew nobody, let alone any brothers and sisters in Christ. It was a lonely day but also an amazing day as I wondered the streets of this city smiling at the locals, trying to speak Mandarin and praying my heart out for the millions of unreached people around me. I felt a rollercoaster of emotions that day, which strangely enough was also my birthday. There was a certain irony for me, on a day when I could have been at home receiving lots of well wishes and being the centre of attention, I was in a strange place feeling slightly alone but also feeling I was right in the centre of God's will. As an accidental apostle it's one of my favourite places to be. I was walking according to faith and not by sight. I felt like Noah who built a boat when no-one had ever even seen rain before. I felt like Abraham who left his home when he didn't even know where he was going. Walking by faith has nothing to do with whether people agree or disagree with you or whether they praise you or slander you. It's about pursuing a heavenly vision rather than bowing to popular opinion. As Paul said to King Agrippa in Acts 26:19,

"And so, King Agrippa, I obeyed that vision from heaven"

Are you obeying a vision from heaven?

The following day the man returned briefly to the hotel with another man and then he left without talking to me. I was left with this second man who said he was going to show me around the city. The Holy Spirit said to me to go with him so I did.

As we walked through the city together this man began to explain more about who the first man was and what He did. The first man and his wife had been secretly helping people to meet in homes to be real believers in Jesus. 7 years ago they had started a small group in their home and now it had multiplied to around 30 groups all across the city and surrounding areas. Because of security concerns the first man had told no-one about this outside of the growing team he was working with and it would also be unsafe for him to be seen in public with me. The lady back in England who'd connected me with him had no idea about this secret church planting work either. The second man said that they wanted to invite me to visit all the meetings and churches during my time there in the city. I said that was why I had come and felt in complete awe at what God was doing.

For 12 days I was literally taken from house to house to preach, teach and encourage my Jesus family across that city. I'd be whisked in a car from place to place, often not even knowing if I was supposed to be preaching at the next destination. Some days I was asked to teach and preach at 3 different meetings and only found out when I arrived at the house or meeting place. To be really honest I can't even remember much of what I said because it was the Holy Spirit speaking through me. I'd normally have a translator which gave me a bit more time to think between my sentences which was helpful. The thing that seemed to encourage people the most, was how this ordinary young guy with no special training had come all the way to China because the Holy Spirit told him to do. I appealed to these underground Churches to follow this child-like example and to do whatever it would take to see the gospel spread to all their countrymen. I saw how a network of churches was multiplying across a city through homes and amongst new disciples. It was incredibly informal but also highly organized and intentional. Probably the highlight of the whole trip was gathering with 20-30 leaders one Friday night in a 10th floor apartment. All of these people, mostly couples, were gathering churches in their homes and reporting back on who had been baptized and how their churches were developing. I was asked to speak and teach them. It was one of the most deeply humbling and yet most exciting situations I have ever been in and what I experienced on that trip has shaped much of what we are now doing.

The prophetic word that the woman shared with me had been fulfilled. A child had gone to a far off country with nothing but the flame of the gospel and this flame had passed to people in that country. On the flight home to the UK I had a long time to think about what had just happened and I made a decision that I could never go back from here, I must give myself unreservedly to the

Holy Spirit no matter what. I was excited but also scared of what He might ask me to do next.

I had not shared about the trip with many people because I thought the plan was too crazy for people to understand. I didn't even understand it myself. When I returned I was asked by the leaders of the church we were then part of to share about the trip. I prayed about what I should say and as I stood at the front of that Church all I could say was about how amazing the Holy Spirit is and how amazing things happen when you obey Him. Part of me was tempted to talk about all the things that happened on the trip because some in the church had questioned the trip and whether it was God's plan or my imagination. But it was an opportunity to glorify God instead of myself so I chose to speak of Him who deserves all our honour. It was His work and not mine and that is why we must give ourselves to prayer and honour the Holy Spirit.

A flash of light

I must confess that I get a bit twitchy around people who talk the talk but don't walk the walk. I meet a lot of people who talk about church planting, mission and making disciples. I hear a lot of people use terms like disciple making movements and other fashionable phrases. Whilst all these things are good, the nearer you get to Jesus the more you realise the disconnect between what is in our heart and what often comes out of our mouths. I cringe when I look back on some of the grandiose things that have come out of my mouth. At the time I was well meaning but there was so much immaturity and pride in my heart. Our vision statements are great, but they are just that! Statements and words. What's really important is the work of Jesus in our hearts which leads to fruit in our lives and work. Unfortunately I believe this disconnect between what we say and what we actually do has reached epidemic proportions in the body of Christ. God is gracious with us all of course, but the Holy Spirit wants to bridge this gap in our lives so that we hear and obey Jesus and become true disciples who bear much fruit.

We never set out to plant churches or do anything other than to hear and obey Jesus. We realized that we personally had fallen so far from what it means to be a disciple of Jesus that really all we could do was focus on trying to obey Him ourselves and help our own 4 children to do the same.

During this phase of prayer our constant cry was "Holy Spirit we want to honour you". As we thought about what we were being called to do He began to put main two things on our heart. You are probably much cleverer than I am so bear with me on this.

The Holy Spirit was on one hand giving us a great and painful burden for lost people. People who didn't know Jesus and were not in any way connected with, or even bothered about what was happening at any kind of church. From what we knew we called this kind of work 'evangelism'.

On the other hand the Holy Spirit was showing us the importance of building up and gathering those who were already 'christians'. At that time we called this kind of work 'discipleship'.

I'm realizing more and more how the Holy Spirit loves to lead us down paths that often seem to strange and obscure. We often resist Him because we don't understand what He is doing. It either feels too difficult or He doesn't seem to be answering what we think are the main questions. All the time though, He is leading us down a path which is going to address what the real root issues are that inform all the smaller questions which we seem to obsess about.

So here we were being pulled in two different directions. And they couldn't be more different. The Holy Spirit wanted us to do what we thought was evangelism and yet we also felt the same burden for discipleship. This became a constant wrestle for me as I couldn't work out what we were supposed to be doing. Should we remain in the church we were part of but do evangelism around the fringes? This would fit what the Spirit was wanting to do through us amongst lost people, but we felt it wasn't an option because we couldn't envisage inviting these people to the church we were part of. Or was God wanting us to commit even more to the church, and through discipleship help to push out the church to lost people? That also didn't seem the answer as I had enough sense to realise that the church would never embrace the outward missional thrust we felt so painfully in our hearts.

Instead of reading books and gathering more information I went to the Bible with prayer and fasting. Weeks went by and it felt like these two opposite pulls were going to rip me apart. I devoured the New Testament, looking again at what Jesus and the early church did to try and discover something new that I was missing.

And then one night the answer was revealed to me.

I was sat on the floor of the living room in our small cottage and quite frankly felt like giving up. I could not go on any longer trying to honour the Holy Spirit when it felt so impossible and difficult. I began to go over in my head again about how we could do both evangelism and discipleship and how we should or shouldn't be involved with the church we were part of. Suddenly I saw a flash before me. It was very quick and I don't think anyone else in the room at the time saw it. In that flash I suddenly received a revelation that changed my whole understanding. I had been trying to live out what the Spirit was saying to do through my current understanding of church and ministry and it wasn't possible. You could say that I was trying to put new wine into an old wineskin.

(A word of warning – maybe you are having difficulty understanding what God is asking you to do at the moment because actually - like with us - he's trying to lead you into a completely different way of thinking which goes far deeper than Church models and ministry names. Maybe God is wanting to give you a revelation that will change everything and call you into a new way of being and doing?)

In that moment I realized that all my paradigns had just come crashing down. A paradigm is a model or pattern of thinking and we have paradigms for everything in our lives. Jesus had just smashed my paradigms about Church and ministry and life in general. I had received a revelation that the work that Jesus did and that He has now entrusted to all His disciples was the work of 'making disciples' and this involved both an outward dimension to new people and an inward dimension with those already recruited to the ranks. My whole understanding of church and ministry changed in an instant. I now saw the church as an ever-expanding movement of disciples that could multiply and self-replicate exponentially until it filled the whole world. There was no evangelism as we knew it and no discipleship as we knew it. There was one thing and that was making disciples. That one thing is the work that will see the Gospel being taken to every tribe and tongue so that Jesus is worshipped by every people group on the planet.

When Jesus said to make disciples he was instructing his disciples to do what He did, to find lost people, help them to become obedient to Jesus together in a community and then to teach these people to do the same with people they knew. This was the work God was calling us to do and it was exactly what the Spirit was putting on our hearts. It would impact those in the harvest as they would come to know Jesus through the preaching of the gospel. But then these new disciples would grow in obedience to Jesus and love for each other as they gathered together to be church in a way that was more simpler and informal. We would train and give ourselves to help these new disciples grow and become the leaders of this movement so that it could continue to spread and multiply through all the towns and villages of Somerset.

It all sounded just like what Jesus had done and taught His disciples to do and I felt a bit foolish that I had not worked this all out a lot sooner. But with hindsight I'm glad that we received this heavenly vision and gave ourselves to it, rather than reading about it in a book and then giving up when things got hard. 10 years down the line I've seen many other people come and go as they search for answers to questions like "what is church" but I feel this question has nothing to do with the core missionary task God has called us to. If you're doing what you're doing because you've read it in a book, think it's a good idea or are secretly looking for the magic formula to plant churches and make disciples then I predict that you won't last more than a year or two.

The only thing that keeps us going is knowing that God has called us to build this work amongst the gentiles. It doesn't matter how we feel, whether things look good on paper or what our friends and family say. We will continue to be obedient to the calling that the Holy Spirit has given us until we have fulfilled the heavenly vision and completed the work!

The man from Macedonia

"That night Paul had a vision. A man from Macedonia in Northern Greece was standing there, pleading with him, "Come over to Macedonia and help us!" So we decided to leave for Macedonia at once, having concluded that God was calling us to preach the Good News there."
Acts 16:9-11

The work we are doing is the Holy Spirit's work not ours.

Increasingly we are experiencing how He can lead and direct our efforts if we are prepared to wait on Him and hold our agendas and plans lightly.

In this story from Acts 16, the Spirit gave Paul some direct guidance and the travelling pioneers made an interesting conclusion about it. All too often in churchianity we are taught to spiritually pass the buck. If we receive a revelation like this we are conditioned to believe that it must be for someone else so we just pray about it. Or we believe that this revelation belongs on the shelf for us to think about for the rest of our life. When will we as disciples of Jesus conclude that a revelation from God requires our obedience 'at once'? Paul concluded that the Spirit had shown him the man of Macedonia and the only logical conclusion for them was that they should immediately go to that place to preach the good news. How I long for the day when believers in Jesus come to the same logical conclusions.

I can't emphasize enough that doing the work of Jesus is not rocket science. If you are willing to be obedient to Him no matter what the cost then it's His joy to empower you and use you to extend His kingdom work.

In a later chapter we will look at houses of prayer and how important this regular rhythm of prayer is for the work we are doing. But for now it is enough to say that without Jesus Christ we can do nothing (John 15:5) so before we do anything we must be found on our knees in prayer.

Here are a few stories from my life as an accidental apostle to encourage you to honour the Spirit every day. If I can do it then trust me, anyone can do it.

"Omul de langa mine" (The man next to me)

God had led me to visit Romania. To some around me it was another apparently foolish trip built on a tenuous relationship that didn't really exist with someone I didn't really know.

I was excited about it!

I arrived in the town where I was going to be training a group of believers who wanted to meet as 'simple churches' and make disciples of people who didn't know about Jesus. Halfway through the training we had a break and I asked a few of the people there some questions and filmed their responses. One older guy who was there started to talk and talk. He seemed quite animated but I had no idea what he was talking about. When he finished someone translated what he had said and it was quite amazing. This old guy was recounting a vision that the church had received in prayer. In this vision they had seen a man coming to them with a bag of seed for them which they could then go and plant. They had been prayerfully waiting for this man to come and the man concluded joyfully that this random ordinary man from the UK (Me!) was in fact a messenger sent by the living God! It was comforting to know that I was clearly in the right place and that I wasn't crazy!

"Sunetul de broaste" (The sound of Frogs)

On that same trip to Romania I was praying one evening with three brothers and all I could hear in my mind was the sound of frogs croaking. After a while I shared this with the brothers and asked them what they thought it meant. We didn't really get anywhere so I asked the question, "Is there somewhere near here where you can hear the sound of Frogs croaking?" One of the brothers answered quickly and explained how there was a valley on the outskirts of the town where the sound of Frogs croaking rings out every evening.

What happened next was interesting.

I had already come to the conclusion in my mind and heart that we should go to this valley at once to pray and see if God opened up any opportunities to meet people. But I asked these brothers (having just trained them all weekend!) what they thought it all meant and their response was like a downpour of fear and apathy. Just moments earlier we had felt the Spirit amongst us so strongly but as these brothers began to share their thoughts it felt like the Spirit had been sucked out of that room. I didn't need to hear the translation to know that they were speaking out fear and reluctance because I could see and sense it in their hearts.

Whether you're in Romford, Romania or Rwanda, the excuses and reasons not to obey Jesus immediately are always the same! That night my Romanian brothers came to these conclusions,

"We can't go to the valley now it is too late in the evening"

"There is a gypsy community there and it won't be safe"

"The people there won't want to know about Jesus, they have a lot of problems"

In that moment I had a big dilemma.

Should I bow to popular opinion, be a polite guest and go along with the crowd. Or should I lovingly challenge these brothers and try and pull us all up to a new level of faith and obedience.

What would you do in that situation?

I haven't always been the boldest person and often feel fearful about people rejecting me if I speak my mind and it offends them. More and more though God is helping me,

"Obviously, I'm not trying to win the approval of people, but of God. If pleasing people were my goal, I would not be Christ's servant"
Galatians 1:10

That night I chose to serve Jesus Christ instead of pleasing people. I gently challenged my brothers and insisted that we should drive to the valley right now to at least pray for the area. Eventually we got into the car (albeit rather reluctantly) and we headed to the valley. When we got there I instinctively wound my window down, partly to see if I could hear the frogs and partly because I wanted to hear and sense what God was wanting to do in this community. My friends fearfully asked me to put my window back up because it wasn't safe in this neighborhood. I politely (but very firmly) said that I wanted to hear the frogs and left it open. We drove around and eventually my friends in the car began to loosen up a bit and we were actually able to pray passionately that God's kingdom would come amongst this community and that He would send workers in. I had a sneaking suspicion what would happen after we all prayed this, but I decided that my Romanian brothers had overcome enough challenges that night and didn't need their minds and hearts stretched any further.

I returned home to the UK and a few weeks later I heard from these Romanian brothers and guess what had happened?

The week after my departure, God had led them to go back to that community in the valley to pray for people and search for people of peace. They'd found a whole extended family of gypsies who wanted to start a church in their house and a baptism party was being planned.

"I can't believe you're here?!"

Me and the team were in a town in the Midlands, UK. We were searching for a house of peace in a council estate (an area of poorer housing, full of ordinary working class people who'd generally never go anywhere near a church) We were knocking on doors and asking people if they needed any healing or prayer. After 1 hour of rejection where we'd been walking in constant rain we stopped to reassess what God was saying to us. We'd felt God had led us to this area when we had prayerfully "spied the land" earlier in the day. But something was not right and we were not finding any households prepared to receive us and the message of Jesus into their networks of friends and families (See more about this in the next Chapter!) I sent a quick message to some friends who were praying for us and asked them to send any spiritual intelligence to us. This might be a scripture, a word, a picture or anything that brings direction to a team of pioneers on the ground.

We waited.

After a few minutes one lady who has a very strong prophetic gifting sent me a message that she saw us like pioneers cutting their way through a jungle. It had been hard work, but the message to us was "keep going and searching for who you are looking for".

Walking through the rain that morning in an area that felt spiritually heavy and unresponsive had felt like walking through a jungle. But we felt encouraged to continue the search like Jesus commanded his first jungle pioneers to do in Matthew 10 and Luke 10! We continued to knock on a few doors but then I felt to stop and pray that God would lead us directly to the household of peace, the people who had been prepared by God. Right at that moment a small red car zoomed past me with 4 people in it. I caught sight of two people in the back and immediately felt God saying to me that they were our people. So I literally ran up the road and around the corner where the car had turned.

We saw the people from the car standing outside their house. They were a young couple and their mum was inside. They asked us what we were doing in the area so we told them. The young man started saying "I can't believe you are here today", he was almost shaking as he kept saying this over and over again. I tried to ask him what he meant but he ran inside the house leaving us to talk with his partner. She opened up about her life and the drug addiction she was fighting. We laid hands on her and prayed for her and then she shouted for her mum to come out so we could pray for her. The mum came out and shared how she had cancer. We laid hands on her as well and prayed for her. Then they invited us to go into their house for a cuppa.

As we sipped on our cup of tea the young man came down and wanted to explain what had happened the night before. He had gone upstairs because he'd heard his partner in their bedroom crying. Everything had become too much for this young woman and she was literally crying for a way out. As her partner entered the room she became quiet and said to him, "I've just done something weird!" He was quite concerned so asked her about what she meant and she replied, "I've just asked God to send us some help. It's the first time I've ever talked to him!"

The very next day two random ordinary disciples of Jesus come running around the corner offering prayer and asking if they want to start new lives with Jesus.

All he could say that whole afternoon while we were with them was *"I can't believe you are here"*

About to kill herself

Before we go out to preach the gospel (see next chapter) we always 'spy the land' and ask the Holy Spirit to show us where to go and what to say. He always shows us what the spiritual strongholds are in those areas (it may be drug problems, fear or mental illness) and we pray against these forces in the name of Jesus. We seek the Holy Spirit about what particular areas of a town or city we should target or what streets on a certain estate. It's not magic, but we have learned how to go to the right places to find houses of peace. It's a mix of being led by the Spirit and generally choosing to go to the areas that most people would avoid.

We had employed this strategy again and the team found

themselves knocking on doors in an area of Nottingham. I was on a hill overlooking the area where the teams were working and my prayers were interrupted by a phone call from one of the team. They sounded really excited and really out of their depth all at the same time. Without really understanding what was going on I knew I needed to go and join them immediately. I ran down to the high rise block they were working in and went upto join them. Here's what had happened.

The team had knocked on a lady's door and after a while she answered it but wouldn't open the door properly. One of the ladies on the team (a particularly forceful evangelist) felt that she needed to somehow get into this house because the lady was literally in the grip of satan. So she literally managed to get her foot in the door. Much of what happens on the mission field is often very politically incorrect and opposite to the polite version of christianity we may have grown up with. The evangelist managed to get the woman to open the door wide enough to get in and then the enormity of the situation had become apparent. This lady literally had a knife in her hand and was about to start slicing her wrists to kill herself. Right at that moment the team had knocked on her door.

The team were able to calm the lady down, pray for her and take her out for a walk. She'd not been out of her house for weeks.

When I look back on that miraculous encounter it wasn't down to anything clever or special the team had done. We simply prayed about where to go and then went there to preach the gospel and set people free.

As we come to the end of this chapter I am reminded of something very sobering. Stories like this are encouraging but it makes me think about the millions of other people around us who are lost in darkness and have no purpose in their life.

What if the team had not gone to that estate that day? What would have happened to that lady?

Few believers are willing and prepared to honour the Holy Spirit and be led by Him to those in the harvest who God is preparing. When Jesus walked the earth he simply asked men and women to follow him. This simple invitation to leave behind everything and to walk after Him cut through all people's excuses, all their great ideas and all their well thought out plans.

Maybe it would be good to take some time to give up your own way and commit yourself again to prayer and honouring the Holy Spirit before we move on?

"If any of you wants to be my follower, you must give up on your own way, take up your cross daily and follow me"
Luke 9:23

How can you give yourself to prayer and honour the Holy Spirit more?

Chapter 5

Preach the good news

Acts 14:21

"The command to witness to Christ is given to every member of his Church. It is a commission given to the whole Church to take the whole Gospel to the whole world. When the Church recognises that it is exists for the world, there arises a passionate concern that the blessings of the Gospel of Christ should be brought to every land and to every man and woman."
(Willem Adolph Visser 't Hooft, Dutch Theologian)

I've been engaged with mission in a number of different countries over the last 15 years. I've seen all sorts of churches, organisations and ministries working in a variety of different settings and contexts. Having experienced all this I am, along with others, convinced that we need a radical transformation in our understanding of what it means to be a disciple of Jesus and what we expect from someone who professes to be such a person.

All the missional talk and conversations about the shapes and forms of church threaten to be a pleasant 'intellectual' diversion from this real issue. As long as our minds and hearts are taken up with clever ideas and plans to simply rebrand the church and re-arrange the chairs from rows to circles, we will never address the critical issue that we face in our generation, which is how do we make disciples of Jesus that faithfully complete Jesus' work to take the gospel to every creature on this planet,

"And then he told them, "Go into all the world and preach the Good News to everyone."
Jesus, Mark 16:15

Jesus called a group of ordinary men and women to sacrifice their lives so completely that they enthusiastically gave their lives to Him and the work of spreading the gospel to every person in the whole world. How far we have fallen. Every single person on this planet who professes to be a follower of Jesus shares the sobering responsibility to give everything they have to complete Jesus' work. To be frank, we have lost the plot and have moved so far away from the normal christian life laid out for us by Jesus.

This is part of the reason why I don't call myself a christian anymore. For the millions of people around us who are slipping to an eternity of darkness the word christian means nothing to them. In fact, on the whole it causes a negative response. People reject our attempts to share the gospel because of what christianity has become, not because they are rejecting our Lord and saviour.

We are disciples of Jesus, called by Him to do greater works than He did and to, through the empowerment of His Spirit and the power of His word, take the gospel to the ends of the earth. That's our work. When Jesus first invited His disciples to join in with what He was doing he said,

"Follow me and I will make you fishers of men"
Matthew 4:19

Your gifting, calling or personal preference has nothing to with the truth that Jesus has called you to personally spread the gospel to every person and to fish for more followers of Jesus. When you meet Jesus one day He is going to ask you whether you did what

He's instructed all His disciples to do? He's going to look you in the eye and say,

"Did you make disciples of all nations?"

"Did you baptize people in my name and in the name of the Father and the Spirit and then teach them to obey all my commandments?"

If you think the boardroom scenes from TV programmes like The Apprentice are awkward then that is nothing to what it is going to be like when millions of self professing followers of Jesus meet Jesus and realise they've spent their life doing everything but the things He commanded His followers to do. You can't piggy back on the achievements of others or the spiritual fruit of your favourite leader. You are responsible!

It's scary being a disciple of Jesus. It is the greatest responsibility in life because you are professing before God and others that you are no longer boss of your own life and you will now strive to serve Jesus and His interests in this world. What's even scarier is that there are leaders of churches all around the world who are not even teaching this to their people. May God have mercy on us all and raise up a generation of disciple makers who are worthy to bear the name of Christ and who will take the gospel to the ends of the earth through great trials and suffering.

A few years ago I was invited to share at a church in our area. By UK standards it was a *'large'* and *'lively'* Church and they had multiple ministries and activities happening all through the week.

I'd been thinking about how I could help the people in this church gathering (there would have been about 150-200 people) to understand that we have an issue with our disciple making. So at the start of my talk I asked the congregation some questions. Here's how it went,

(Me) *"Put your hand up if you are a disciple of Jesus"*
(Response) *There were only 4 people there who didn't put their hand up*

(Me) *"Keep your hand up if you've been baptized?"*
(Response) *75% of the people kept their hands up in the air*

(Me) *"Keep your hand up if you've baptized someone else in the last year*
(Response) *Only 4 hands remained in the air*

(Me) *Keep your hands in the air if those you baptized have Baptized others*
(Response) *Only my hand remained in the air*

From the illustration it was clear that this large Church was made up of people who considered themselves to be disciples of Jesus and 75% of them had been baptized.

Great news right? *Not really.*

When I dug a bit deeper there was a huge drop off between those who'd been baptized themselves and those who'd then gone onto baptize others. It was only me and the core leaders of the church who'd baptized anyone else in the last year.

That reveals a lot.

Digging even further I'd asked who'd baptized anyone and then seen those people baptize other people. I was the only person in the room that morning who still had my hand up.

There was an awkward silence in the room at that point.

This church would be seen by many as very successful but I'm really not sure how effective their disciple making was. They were gathering people who proclaimed to be disciples of Jesus but were not training any of them to do the basics of discipleship. And this goes for fellowships of all shapes and sizes whether you meet in a school, coffee shop or an 18th century Parish Church.

I challenge you to do this exercise with those you gather with and to take the conclusions you come to before God in prayer. If we don't realise and understand there is a problem then we will never see the need for anything different. And I believe there is a huge problem.

Jesus told us to make disciples, not converts or followers. I cannot make it plainer, if we are not all baptizing new disciples, teaching them to obey Jesus and encouraging and challenging them to go and do likewise with others they know, then what the heck are we doing? And this isn't some complicated work that only experienced disciples are expected to do. It's normal for everyone who claims to follow Jesus.

Can you imagine sending your kids to a school that never taught them anything? Each day your children would return home not knowing any of the basic skills they need to function and live in this world. No spelling skills. No basic addition or subtraction skills. How long would you keep sending your children to a school like that? 1 day? 1 week? 1 month? A whole year? If a school did this they would be reported and shut down for failing to do the most basic things that it apparently existed for – to teach children!

"For the time has come for judgment, and it must begin with God's household."
1 Peter 4:17

How patient Father God is with the church (you and me!) that bears His name but doesn't teach anyone to obey His commands. One day we will face Him and give an account for our lives and what we have done in His name.

When we had this sobering revelation around 10 years ago we had to ask ourselves some honest questions. All our friends were church-goers and we had no contact with people who didn't know Jesus. We felt this was inconsistent with our claim to be a disciple of Jesus who said he came to seek and save the lost (Luke 19:10) so we had to radically change everything! I made a decision to not spend any more of my time on anything that wasn't contributing towards making disciples the way Jesus instructed us to.

And I dare you to do the same.

As people who professed to be disciples of Jesus Christ we had to go back to square one and consider how we were going to begin seeing the gospel seed planted across the towns and villages of our area. Because after all, that is what our Master and teacher would do if he we here.

How could we make disciples if we didn't know any non-believers and how could we disciple them if we didn't even know how to share the gospel with them?

It's all about the seed

What Jesus means by *"make disciples"* is often very different to what most churches and christians mean by *"make disciples"*

What Jesus means is that he expects all His disciples to find more people who want to repent and be baptized and then to teach them to obey Him together in spiritual families and communities. God's will is that this movement and body of Christ-filled people self perpetuates and builds itself up through love and obedience until the ends of the earth are reached in His name.

To see this great fruit God has given us a potent seed called the gospel. It is the power of God for the salvation of those who believe and I hope you are not ashamed of it?

God has always wanted His family to fill the earth and subdue it. He said the same thing to Adam and Eve in Genesis 1:28,

"Be fruitful and multiply. Fill the earth and govern it"

But instead of fruitfully multiplying and subduing the earth, our disobedience, rebellion and outright apathy as God's people means we are generally unfruitful, on the retreat and overpowered by the prevailing spirit of worldliness.

No more in the name of Jesus!

As we began to pray for the villages and towns of Somerset I began to get itchy feet and a fearful heart! We were praying and fasting for the towns and villages and for this vision we were feeling God unfolding in our hearts and minds. But I felt God was pushing me to the point where I had to do something about what I was praying about. As we prayed God kept highlighting the parable of the sower to us, but the more I understand God's Kingdom I think this story from Matthew 13 should be called the parable of the seed and soil. I'd heard this story at church millions of times but back then it was merely an intellectual exercise or just another sermon. Now I was reading it from a completely different perspective.

I spent hours meditating on these words that Jesus spoke in Matthew 13:1-24 and Mark 4:1-21. It seemed that in this parable Jesus was sharing some secrets about disciple making with His disciples. Instead of just reading these words and forgetting them, I was engrossed with this glimpse into the heart and mind of Jesus, the ultimate gospel sower and disciple maker. I'd encourage you to read these two versions of the story right now. Put this book down and get your Bible. Re-read these stories asking the question, "What can I learn about the work you have called me to do?"

If you really asked God that question then you will have heard some clear answers and truths from Him that you can now obey and put into practice! (We'll look at this more in later chapters!)

It struck me that this parable is a glimpse into some of the foundational elements needed to see the kingdom of God coming across a whole harvest field. Indeed Jesus even said in Mark 4:13,

"If you can't understand the meaning of this parable, how will you understand all the other parables?"

I was asking God how we could see new disciples and churches springing up in the harvest and He showed me! It's all about the seed. I was looking out upon many villages and towns and it was an empty harvest field. Yes there are good and loving churches in our area – many of which I have had some involvement with. However something different is needed to make a dent in the vast multitudes of lost people around us!

The answer to my question wasn't to recycle an existing group of christians and to gather them under a different name. It wasn't to hope that churches with hundred year old traditions will suddenly make a U-turn and start training all their members to be disciple makers. All of those things may be good and helpful and if God has called you to those things then I'd encourage you to it with all your heart.

But the answer God showed me was to roll my sleeves up and set about planting the gospel into the harvest fields around me.

Around that time a friend from another part of the UK contacted me. I'd been out walking and praying and I got home to receive His phone call. He had no idea that we were on the verge of stepping into this new work. He said he'd been thinking of us that morning and he wanted to share a picture with us that he felt God had given him. As he felt moved to pray for us he'd seen me standing in front of a big field and I was holding a small acorn. He felt he needed to encourage me to stop looking at the size of the field and to get on and plant the acorn. He told me that the small acorn I had in my hand contained all the DNA needed to grow a tree which could bear more acorns which could grow into more trees.

He'd summed up our thoughts on disciple making and church planting in one simple picture and this word was instrumental in us making the step away from the church we'd been part of and giving ourself to the work God was calling us to.

It was time to plant the acorn!

Work at telling others the good news

If Jesus said the parable of the seed was the key to understanding everything then it surely contained some important truths for us as we considered where to start the work in Somerset.

As God opened my understanding to the truths in the parable it became really obvious that we had to start with sowing the seed. Without planting the seed nothing would grow. Many of my friends at the time were criticizing me or questioning me where our church was and what the fruit of our work was. But it seemed to me they were asking questions that were not relevant to this season of seed sowing. We hadn't even planted any seed yet so how could there be fruit!? As far as I could see from the story Jesus told, it all starts with someone scattering the seed which is the word of the Kingdom. As that seed takes root in the right soil we then see growth. We were encouraged with the words of James 5:7-9,

"Consider the farmers who patiently wait for the rains in the fall and the spring. They eagerly look for the valuable harvest to ripen. You too must be patient. Take courage, for the coming of the Lord is near"

I'd prayed for God to send evangelists to us to help us and none had come, so we set off ourselves to scatter the word of the kingdom everywhere,

"Don't be afraid of suffering for the Lord. Work at telling others the good news"
2 Timothy 4:5

Over the next season of the work we were doing I visited almost every town and village in the county. Prayer walking, praying for opportunities to talk with people and trying to be bold. I'd spend most days doing this and would make a note of anything that God seemed to be saying about a particular place. I began to see that I lacked the boldness and ability needed to do this work so I asked God what I needed to do!

As is my habit, I turned to the scriptures and prayer to get some revelation on this matter. As I read the book of Acts two things stood out me.

The first thing God spoke to me about was how the believers prayed for boldness,

"And now, O Lord, hear their threats, and give us, your servants great boldness in preaching your word. Stretch out your hand with healing power, may miraculous signs and wonders be done through the name of your holy servant Jesus." After this prayer, the meeting place shook, and they were all filled with the Holy Spirit. Then they preached the word of God with boldness
Mark 4:29-32

Having read those scriptures I decided to set my phone alarm to go off 3 times a day. Each time the alarm went off I prayed,

"Lord give me boldness to preach the Gospel"

Guess what happened? I began to find myself in countless

situations where I had the opportunity to preach boldly. Most times I did just that.

The second thing I noticed from the book of Acts was that there was a man called Philip who appeared to be fruitful in preaching the gospel and seeing people responding to the gospel,

"Philip, for example, went to the city of Samaria and told the people there about the messiah. Crowds listened intently to Philip because they were eager to hear his message and see the miraculous signs he did. Many evil spirits were cast out, screaming as they left their victims. And many who had been paralyzed lame were healed. So there was great joy in that city"
Acts 8:5-9

So I spent some time thinking about who I knew that was being fruitful in preaching the gospel. I visited friends who were finding ways to connect with people to share the gospel and tried to glean anything I could from them. I experienced a million and one ways to preach and share the gospel and I realized that actually it is often just about doing something however foolish you feel, rather than spending ages trying to find a magic technique or method.

I gave out bottles of water, healed the sick on the streets, preached boldly in town centres and even dressed up as a wise man at Christmas. It was great fun and we had many great encounters with people. But I couldn't help but think there was something more God was wanting to do!

At this stage I want to remind you that these are areas of the work that are required to cultivate a harvest field. It's not a magic formula. You may have teams of people who focus on the preaching of the gospel phase of the work like we do here in

Somerset. But what's important is that the gospel must be planted into people and places if we want to see disciples, churches and leaders growing out of them. Or it may be that God asks you to start this work yourself like he did with us. What's important though is to remember that without any seed going into the ground there will be no fruit. You can pray 24 hours a day 7 days a week but if no-one hears the gospel then no-one is going to be saved. You can run the best charitable/social project in the world but without planting the gospel you will make no disciples.

And I feel it's important to remind people that gathering with a small group of christians for more informal fellowship in a house isn't going to get you anywhere if there is no vision for kingdom multiplication and no seed of the gospel planted into people and places around you. Neither is gathering with 200 believers on a Sunday going to result in the great commission being fulfilled unless every person gathering understands that they are personally responsible to make more disciples and have the basic skills needed to baptize people and then gather and teach them how to obey Jesus.

You see *where* you meet and *how many* you meet with is not the point. The point is whether the gospel is taking root in increasing spheres of people or not and this happens through making disciples and planting churches the way Jesus did it,

"Meanwhile, the word of God continued to spread [or multiply] and there were many new believers"
Acts 12:24

Jesus only needed 12 ordinary people so why do we think we can effectively disciple any more people than that! And why do we think we need more people than that? Let's get back to trusting in the power of the seed which we plant into people and then nurturing that seed as it grows and overflows to others. The right seed in the right soil will bear multiplying fruit. Just like Paul and Barnabus in Acts 16:9-11 – during that time the Holy Spirit directed us in many weird and wonderful ways. And our conclusion at that time was always that, *"God was calling us to preach the good news there."*

So that's what we did!

What was our message?

In many ways this season where we did the work of evangelists was an amazing time. We'd stepped away from the familiar world of churchianity and had been catapulted into a world full of new and exciting opportunities. We'd be in people's houses every day until late at night and it felt like Jesus had thrust us well and truly out into His harvest like He had asked his disciples to pray in Luke 10:2,

"The harvest is great, but the workers are few. So pray to the Lord who is in charge of the harvest; ask Him to send more workers into the field"

We were knee deep in harvest but I had this nagging feeling that we needed to see more about what God was wanting to do. As I reflected on our journey so far it became really obvious that although God had opened many hearts and homes to us, we were the ones doing everything. We'd become really good at finding ways to connect with people but we were the ones saying and doing everything! I began to ask the question, *"Are we making any disciples here?"*

It would have been easy to settle down at this point to be honest. We'd become friends with lots of non-believers and we felt we had been successful in our attempts to become friends of sinners rather than church going christians. Other believers around us could not believe the opportunities God was opening to us and it would have been tempting to rest on our laurels.

In prayer, God showed us that we were taking the good news to people but we were not finding people who were reciprocating our efforts. Quite simply, we were taking the bread of life to people and most were enjoying it. But who actually wanted to share in the bread with us? Something had to change so can you guess what I did?

I turned to prayer and the scriptures for answers and God led me to Matthew 10:1-21 and Luke 10:1-18. Here I found the answer,

"Jesus sent out the twelve apostles with these instructions: "Don't go to the Gentiles or the Samaritans, but only to the people of Israel—God's lost sheep. Go and announce to them that the Kingdom of Heaven is near. Heal the sick, raise the dead, cure those with leprosy, and cast out demons. Give as freely as you have received! "Don't take any money in your money belts—no gold, silver, or even copper coins. Don't carry a traveler's bag with a change of clothes and sandals or even a walking stick. Don't hesitate to accept hospitality, because those who work deserve to be fed. Whenever you enter a city or village, search for a worthy person and stay in his home until you leave town. When you enter the home, give it your blessing. If it turns out to be a worthy home, let your blessing stand; if it is not, take back the blessing. If any household or town refuses to welcome you or listen to your message, shake its dust from your feet as you leave."
Matthew 10:1-21

"The Lord now chose seventy-two other disciples and sent them ahead in pairs to all the towns and places he planned to visit. These were his instructions to them: "The harvest is great, but the workers are few. So pray to the Lord who is in charge of the harvest; ask him to send more workers into his fields. Now go, and remember that I am sending you out as lambs among wolves. Don't take any money with you, nor a traveler's bag, nor an extra pair of sandals. And don't stop to greet anyone on the road. Whenever you enter someone's home, first say, 'May God's peace be on this house.' If those who live there are peaceful, the blessing will stand; if they are not, the blessing will return to you. Don't move around from home to home. Stay in one place, eating and drinking what they provide. Don't hesitate to accept hospitality, because those who work deserve their pay. "If you enter a town and it welcomes you, eat whatever is set before you. Heal the sick, and tell them, 'The Kingdom of God is near you now.' But if a town refuses to welcome you, go out into its streets and say, 'We wipe even the dust of your town from our feet to show that we have abandoned you to your fate. And know this— the Kingdom of God is near!' I assure you, even wicked Sodom will be better off than such a town on judgment day."
Luke 10:1-13

Jesus sent his disciples out to find people who would welcome them into their homes and lives and who would receive their kingdom message. The disciples were sent out to find 'good soil people' who would receive the message they were carrying and produce 30, 60 or 100 fold fruit. They were not looking for people who were just sympathetic or friendly to them, or who were generous towards them. Neither were they looking for perfect people who were already the finished product. But they were commanded to locate and stay with people who had a supernatural desire in their hearts to repent, be baptized and become disciples of Jesus along with their whole households.

As I read these scriptures I had another revelation about what it meant to do mission the way Jesus commands us to. According to Jesus, finding people who are ready to become disciples, obey Him and also help their friends and family becomes disciples is normal. To me at that time it wasn't normal, so God lovingly challenged me whether I was going to base my faith on His word or my experience. He won.

It dawned on me, Jesus wouldn't ask us to do something that we actually can't do. He has asked each one of us to make disciples so if we are not doing that, then it can't be anything wrong with Jesus' power or desire to work in people's lives. Jesus is actually longing for every one of his followers to baptize more people and teach them how to obey him so a movement of His disciples multiplies to the ends of the earth.

So if we are not making any disciples the issue is with us.

I'm convinced that the huge majority of people who claim to follow Jesus are asking completely the wrong question.

We ask each other questions such as,

"What church do you go to?

"Where do you worship?"

"Who are you accountable to?"

"Does your church have good worship?"

"Does your church have good expository teaching?"

All the time Jesus is quietly standing near the exit door of our churches and is asking one question,

"Are you making disciples?"

Church isn't meant to be a back up plan for christians who don't feel called to make any disciples themselves. Yet that is exactly what the prevailing mindset is in most churches that I have ever been involved with, and it's what I thought until 10 or 11 years ago.

So I realized that evangelism wasn't enough. We had to do more than this if we are to be faithful to Jesus and make disciples.

If we think back to Jesus' instructions in Matthew 10 and Luke 10 we see how critical it was that the disciples found a household of peace. If they didn't then they would have no food and no-where to sleep that night. I'm pretty sure if you were prepared to ditch your churchianity back up plan and give yourself wholly to this harvest work then you'd quite quickly start to find people of peace. For me. our whole ministry hinges on whether we are growing disciples, churches and leaders in the harvest and this can only happen if we find people of peace. To me it is a matter of life and death, not just something we do for 2 hours a week when our schedule allows.

Here in Somerset we literally have too much harvest now but it wasn't always like that. We had to focus our time and attention on the work in the harvest. We had to position ourselves in faith rather than take the easy road. There are many times we could have turned back to the safety and relative comfort of a local church, but that isn't the work He has called us to do and we do not have a back up plan. It's harvest or nothing for us. We recently had the opportunity to share and receive prayer at the church I grew up in and which we were part of before God called us to this harvest work. We hadn't been invited to share in the Church since we were sent out to pioneer this work around 10 years ago. It was a very strengthening and encouraging experience but also quite challenging as it had taken 10 years. As I prepared some thoughts I was reminded of these words from Paul,

"My ambition has always been to preach the Good News where the name of Christ has never been heard, rather than where a church has already been started by someone else. I have been following the plan spoken of in the Scriptures, where it says, "Those who have never been told about him will see, and those who have never heard of him will understand."In fact, my visit to you has been delayed so long because I have been preaching in these places."
Romans 15:20-23

I stood up in the church that Sunday morning and said how amazing it was to come and share all that God had done in the 10 years since we were sent out from the church. And I joked that it had taken so long because we were delayed because we were preaching in all the towns and villages of Somerset.

There's no place for bitterness in the work of the gospel. It doesn't matter how you are treated or whether people support you or reject you. All that matters is that you remain faithful to God's call on your life to preach the gospel!

I showed the first few chapters of this book to my Mum as I was working on them. I was interested to hear her feedback. She sent me a message saying that as she read it she could see how we had completely given ourselves to the harvest and she wanted to encourage me. It was an encouragement. God knows that we have endeavoured to do just that, to give ourselves completely to Him and His harvest work among the gentiles. And God cannot be mocked,

"Don't be misled—you cannot mock the justice of God. You will always harvest what you plant"
Galatians 6:7

We were looking for everything we needed in the harvest. Imagine the disciples, they had no food or anywhere to stay unless they found these households of peace in the harvest. Maybe I'm too focused or militant but my conviction is that God has called us to do a work and we are not giving up or letting up until we have faithfully finished this work and poured ourselves out into the lives of the disciples, churches and leaders we have appointed in the mission field. I'm looking heavenward with my family to hear my Father say well done and I'm not too bothered about anything else.

I see a lot of people questioning whether they should continue pioneering or to go back to the churches they came from. People ask me questions like *'How long should we give to this work to see if it works or not?"*

Because of this I now spend much more time trying to listen to what God is actually calling people to do. I used to give out tools and training like it was Christmas. I'd help anyone who came to me and tell them what we had learned and give them some tools to go and try out in their mission field. However I've noticed that people are very eager for practical methods and tools and less eager to consider how deeply they are prepared to sacrifice their lives for a heavenly calling. Knowing what tools to use isn't going to get you there, it's God's calling and power at work in your heart that will give you the patience and endurance you need to fulfil His heavenly vision for your life. Most of the time you won't know what you're doing anyway!

We haven't got to where we are because we knew what to do. We got to where we are because of who God is and because of the people He is transforming us into. And we honestly haven't really got anywhere, but we're keeping on going with it.

As I've said a number of times in this book, we rarely know what we are doing and we've learned to rely on the scriptures in a much deeper way. As we set out to live out what we saw in Matthew 10 and Luke 10 I literally did what Jesus told His disciples to do. I realise that this goes against all our christian wisdom and contextual understanding of scripture, but I was desperate and people needed to know Jesus so I thought I would just do exactly what the scripture said.

I went into houses and said "*peace to this house*" That started some good conversations!

I ate whatever food people gave me and looked for ways to heal anyone who was sick. God did some amazing things.

As far as I can see from the New Testament, the Holy Spirit sent out workers with nothing to find households of peace. These households of peace would receive the workers and then form a church as they repented, were baptized and began to obey Jesus together. If you're still not convinced about this church planting strategy then I'd encourage you take a look at the following stories where Jesus and His followers found people and households of peace:

John 4:1-43
Acts 10
Acts 16:11-16
Acts 28:1-11

I started to ask questions and tried to be very courageous so that my efforts moved beyond just finding people who were nice to me and instead I found people who really wanted to become disciples of Jesus who'd gather their friends and families as well.

As we re-shaped our gospel preaching around the truth that Jesus wants us to find households of peace we began to ask people we met 3 simple questions that helped us to find the people we were looking for:

1) Would you like to know more about Jesus?

2) Who else do you know that you could gather?

3) When and where shall we gather?

I dare you to ask people these three questions after you've prayed for them, shared your story with them or shared the gospel with them. It will change everything and is a critical shift from just seed sowing evangelism to making disciples and church planting.

Here are a few stories from the work we've been doing and how we literally followed Jesus' instructions in Matthew 10 and Luke 10 and found households of peace ready to repent, be baptized and start gathering together as new churches:

Křest strana na ulici
(Baptism party on the street)

I was working with a team and through prayer we'd sensed to go to a certain area to search for people of peace. I'd been training them from Luke 10 and Matthew 10 and had given them some simple tools and questions to go and try out. Having sent them out in 2's into the streets of this neighborhood I began to walk around praying for the area and for the teams. After about 5 minutes I came across a man sitting outside his house. He looked foreign and when I tried to say hello to him it was clear he did not understand me. He went into the house to call someone else out and an older man came out and started questioning me in quite a confrontational way. I responded in my usual forthright way that we were followers of Jesus looking for
people who needed healing and wanted to know about Jesus. This older man asked me to come in and took me into the living room where there was about 10 family members all sitting around looking at me. At that point it felt like I had hit the jackpot and I'd not really even had to do anything super spiritual or outrageous!

I went in and ate and drank with them and through a translator explained the basics of Luke chapter 10 and what our mission was from Jesus in that area. This extended family network were so open. The conversation continued and I called in the rest of the team. I felt it would be good to read some scriptures together so we read Acts 2:36-42 with them,

"So let everyone in Israel know for certain that God has made this Jesus, whom you crucified, to be both Lord and Messiah. Peter's words pierced their hearts, and they said to him and to the other

Apostles, 'Brothers what shall we do? Peter replied, 'Each of you must repent of your sins and turn to God, and be baptized in the name of Jesus Christ for the forgiveness of your sins. Then you will receive the gift of the Holy Spirit. This promise is to you, to your children and to all those far away – all those who have been called by the Lord our God. Then Peter continued preaching for a long time, strongly urging all his listeners, 'Save yourselves from this crooked generation.' Those who believed what Peter said were baptized and added to the Church that day – about 3000 in all."

There is nothing like seeing the word of God at work in people's lives, especially in the lives of people who are encountering it for the first time and haven't grown up hearing and reading the scriptures.

It turned out this extended family were all from the Czech Republic and this scripture clearly had cut a number of them to the heart because in broken English one of the ladies there began to ask the question, "What must we do" I pointed them back to the scriptures and they came to the conclusion themselves that they must repent and be baptized. At that time I carried a paddling pool and pump in my car at all times as we were often in situations where people were wanting to repent and be baptized. I don't know anyone else who does this. Maybe you should start doing this and having the faith that you will need to use it.

What happened next was solely down to the power of God and not any ability or skill in us as a team. One of the ladies who appeared to be an influential member of the family started to take it upon herself to challenge all of her family to repent and be baptized. She then started phoning her friends in the area inviting them to repent and be baptized together with her and others from her family. This lady was clearly a person of peace like we read about in Luke 10 and Matthew 10. We inflated my paddling pool in the street outside their house, much to the wonder of everyone living in the area (including many Muslims who came near to watch the whole thing) and then proceeded to baptize 8 people that afternoon. The team then continued to disciple and strengthen these new believers because Jesus said baptizing people is only the start of the work. we must also teach them to become obedient to all of His commands

Back alley baptisms

I was working with a team in Nottinghamshire and we felt to go back to a small village we'd visited a year ago. On our previous visit nothing had happened, but we felt to re-visit the place to search for households of peace. After 30 minutes of unproductive door-knocking we stopped to pray. We were there to find a household of peace, not just pray or do some evangelistic seed sowing. We walked up a street and came across a whole group of people (mainly rough looking men) standing in a back alley. In the middle of this ex-mining village the prospect of approaching these men felt very intimidating. But at the same time they seemed to be exactly the people we were searching for. So with that strange mix of fear and boldness flowing through our veins we approached them and asked if anyone needed any prayer. After their initial jokes, abuse and expletives, one of them told me quietly that he actually would appreciate prayer for his drug habit. This confession started a domino effect in all the guys stood around and soon we were laying hands on people and praying for them.

We then moved onto talking about repentance and baptism and we read – yes you've guessed it – Acts 2:36-42!

God's word did its work and we ended up baptizing 2 men and a woman that afternoon. The team then continued to meet with these new disciples and others from their network of friends and family to train them as disciples of Jesus and to be a church in that village. As we prayed for this new community that afternoon, God seemed to be highlighting that the lady who'd been baptized was a 'Shepherd' in the community and the person of peace we should stay with in that village.

A man covered in scars

I was with a co-worker and we were working with a team in the North of England. My co-worker had become a disciple of Jesus through the work we were doing in Somerset. He was a notorious sinner and well known in our area for being a violent drug addict. But he became a beloved brother to me and others on the team, he's now with Jesus but his example lives on amongst those we are working with. For the weeks leading upto our trip I had been trying to help this brother to discover a more deeper walk with the Holy Spirit.

During this trip we were staying at the home of some friends and one morning this brother shared over breakfast that he'd had a dream. In this dream he'd met a man covered in scars and he'd washed the man's body and his scars had been healed. He didn't know what it meant.

It seemed fairly obvious to me what the dream meant, but instead of giving out answers to people I've learned that it's better to help people find answers themselves. So I reminded him that he'd been asking God to speak to him and encouraged him to think and pray about the meaning. Thankfully this co-worker has not had years of churchianity indoctrination so he quickly concluded that he should pray to meet a man with many wounds or scars in his life and that he should help them this man to be a disciple of Jesus and to baptize him. (It's so refreshing to work with people who simply obey Jesus and take Him and His word at face value. Most christians I know would never even consider a dream like this, let alone conclude that they should act on it in such an immediate and practical way and intentionally look to baptize someone)

Guess what happened later that day?

Whilst searching for households of peace in an estate, this co-worker had found a man who was ready to start a new life with Jesus. Later that day we met the man again to look at Acts 2:36-42 and the man confessed his sin. He'd been a gangster most of his life and had been stabbed and shot multiple times. He pulled up his shirt to show the scars that covered most of his body. I didn't need to say anything, I just looked at my co-worker and smiled. That evening my co-worker baptized this man and trained the man to baptize his housemate who also wanted to repent and start a new life with Jesus.

A modern day legion

Me and a co-worker were in Ireland. The whole trip had been an adventure to say the least. We had already seen God doing some amazing things and, to be honest, endured some testing trials!

We'd arrived in a town and after prayer walking a particularly rough estate we came across a young man. He'd come walking (or staggering!) up the hill towards us and was blind drunk. He started shouting at us, and both me and my co-worker sensed that something was going to happen. We shared the gospel with him but his drunkenness meant we weren't getting anything sensible out of him. We decided to leave him and as he shouted at us we invited him to come with us. He stood still and continued to shout at us as we walked off down the hill. My friend needed the toilet so as he went to find a local toilet I felt God show me to go and sit in the centre of the town. I'd been sat there for no longer than a minute when the same young guy came running around the corner and straight towards me. He stood before me and was now completely sober. Just minutes before he'd been out of his head.

He said to me that he wanted to start a new life with Jesus and I felt to take him over to an area of grassland. Interestingly the young man explained how a young person had recently hung himself and committed suicide on the exact same patch weeks earlier. My co-worker had rejoined me by now and we led the young man through some steps of repentance. Quite early on in our conversation with this man we both felt reminded of the story about when Jesus met the man with a legion of demons in Mark 5:1-20. So we had that 'word' in the back of our minds as we talked with this young guy.

As I asked him some direct questions about Jesus, he started to give some very strange answers. We've learned to recognize when you are dealing with someone who is possessed by demons, and this guy certainly was. Instead of trying to talk and reason with the young man we begun to take authority over the demons in him. Eventually I put my hand on the young man (he was very upset about this) and said, "I command you to come out in the name of Jesus" He immediately jumped backwards and with wide eyes he shouted, "*What have you just done to me?!!?*"

We explained what we had just done in Jesus name and this young guy who had been literally off his face around 30 minutes before through a cocktail of alcohol and demons was now very much in his right mind.

He looked at us and said he wanted to leave everything and to come with me and my co-worker. We could tell he was very serious about this. In that moment the Holy Spirit reminded me of the story from Mark 5:1-20 and particularly these verses,

"As Jesus was getting into the boat, the man who had been demon possessed begged to go with him. But Jesus said, "No, go home to your family, and tell them everything the Lord has done for you and how merciful he has been." So the man started off to visit the Ten Towns of that region and began to proclaim the great things Jesus had done for him; and everyone was amazed at what he told them."
Mark 5:18-21

So I gave this young man my Bible and said to him that instead of coming with us he should go back to the estate where he lived (which was actually the estate we had prayer walked earlier) and tell everyone about what Jesus had done for Him!

Community Talent Show

As a team we felt to hit a certain area of Bridgwater. We tend to go to the places that most christians would avoid, so we found ourselves in an area that would be classed as 'deprived'. (It never ceases to amaze me how our Lord and saviour was called the friend of notorious sinners yet most of His 'followers' never venture anywhere near anyone remotely notorious) We've seen that community events are a great way to find people of peace as you gather a whole crowd in one place to sow Gospel seed and search for spiritual seekers.

We spent a few days in the community inviting everyone to the community talent show. They are not christian events but a way of connecting with a whole community and to bring in spiritual seed in a way that is culturally relevant and appropriate to that community. At the event people from the community perform, sing, dance, rap and share whatever talent they have. Meanwhile we have a 'spiritual readings' table offering prayer, healing and prophetic words and throughout the night team members share a simple story about how Jesus has changed their lives. It is all highly un-religious, very raw and I think Jesus loves it!

That night a number of people indicated that they would like the team to visit them as they wanted to know more about Jesus. One young lad had come to perform a rap that he'd written about his sister who'd died tragically just 2 weeks before. I ran after him when the event had finished and managed to scribble his address down before him and his gang of mates disappeared on their bikes.

We turned up at this young guy's house the following Friday evening and then began to meet regularly each week to have church at his house. This young man, an unlikely person of peace, introduced his family and friends to Jesus and got baptized. His family have sinced moved away to another part of the country but we are still in touch with him and have visited them.

It's not the whole story though

Preaching the gospel, demonstrating God's kingdom and baptizing whole households is powerful and very exciting! There is nothing like seeing people set free from the power of the devil. For the evangelist it is everything. And we desperately need more of it.

But this is only the start of the work if we are to see the door of faith opened to the gentiles as we see in Acts 14. Once we find God-prepared people, Jesus tells us to stay with them and to teach them to become obedient disciple makers themselves. We are not just wanting to see some initial conversions, decisions or a few small groups meeting in homes. We want to see the kingdom multiplying through whole people groups and places. And that can only happen as we grow and multiply disciples, churches and leaders who carry the weight and responsibility of taking the kingdom to more people in our absence. We're wanting to leave a kingdom legacy on this earth when we are long gone. Well I do anyway, you can decide for yourselves what you will leave here.

Jesus' instructions in Matthew 10:1-21 and Luke 10:1-13 are what we need to know in order to start the work. It's how we establish those first few household churches that will act as a spiritual beachhead in a city, area or region. It's how we find our first co-workers and partners in the mission field but it is far from the whole picture.

To finish this chapter we are going back to look at Philip and the story from Acts 8:1-26. It highlights the critical necessity for the work of preaching the gospel but is also an important reminder that this is not the whole story,

"But now the people believed Philip's message of Good News concerning the Kingdom of God and the name of Jesus Christ. As a result, many men and women were baptized. Then Simon

*himself believed and was baptized. He began following Philip
wherever he went, and he was amazed by the signs and great
miracles Philip performed. When the apostles in Jerusalem heard
that the people of Samaria had accepted God's message, they sent
Peter and John there. As soon as they arrived, they prayed for
these new believers to receive the Holy Spirit. The Holy Spirit had
not yet come upon any of them, for they had only been baptized in
the name of the Lord Jesus. Then Peter and John laid their hands
upon these believers, and they received the Holy Spirit."*
Acts 8:12-18

We need more Philips who will preach the gospel, drive out
demons, heal the sick and lead people to repent and be baptized.

But we also need those who are 'apostolically minded' (hence why
I wrote this book) and will move things beyond evangelism and this
initial groundbreaking work. People need to be set free from the
bondages of satan. But then they need to be rebuilt and to
become rebuilders themselves like it says in Isaiah 61.

When the apostles in Jerusalem heard what was happening in
Samaria they sent Peter and John. Why? Because the work isn't a
quick flash in the pan, it's about establishing the kingdom through
new disciples, churches and leaders. But let me say again, the point
of this is not for us to find satisfaction in a job title or label. It's to
ensure that God's work is completed. That's all that counts and
quite frankly it's all hands on deck if we are to see all the nations
discipled like Jesus has commanded us to. As this chapter comes to
a close let's remind ourselves of Paul's thoughts on this from the
book of 1 Corinthians. Paul wasn't speaking about some
theological point here, he was talking about the nitty gritty of life
working in the harvest with others,

"I planted the seed in your hearts, and Apollos watered it, but it was God who made it grow. It's not important who does the planting, or who does the watering. What's important is that God makes the seed grow. The one who plants and the one who waters work together with the same purpose. And both will be rewarded for their own hard work. For we are both God's workers. And you are God's field. You are God's building. Because of God's grace to me, I have laid the foundation like an expert builder. Now others are building on it. But whoever is building on this foundation must be very careful. For no one can lay any foundation other than the one we already have—Jesus Christ.
1 Corinthians 3:5-12

How often do you share the Gospel with people who don't know Jesus?

What's stopping you from sharing the Gospel more?

What do you need to do about it?

Chapter 6

Make many disciples

Acts 14:21

It has often been said that the most important teaching or command that Jesus left with His disciples before He left the earth was to make disciples of all the nations,

"Jesus came and told his disciples, "I have been given all authority in heaven and on earth. Therefore, go and make disciples of all the nations, baptizing them in the name of the Father and the Son and the Holy Spirit. Teach these new disciples to obey all the commands I have given you. And be sure of this: I am with you always, even to the end of the age."
Matthew 28:18-20

I don't want to get caught up in an argument about what is the most important thing that Jesus taught, but my personal conviction is that the command to make disciples encompasses everything that Jesus wants, expects and commands from anyone claiming to belong to Him. It is the 'core calling' out of which all other attributes, callings and giftings grow, we are disciples of Jesus who obey all of Jesus' commands first and foremost. If we can help, encourage, train and admonish people to become disciples of Jesus then we've given them what they really need in this life and the next. It is the flower bed out of which all the fruits of the Spirit grow and flourish. Jesus gave a very simple explanation about how His first disciples were to disciple the nations.

They were to baptize people and teach them to obey Him.

That's it!

It's ridiculously simple but not easy!

You can boil down Jesus' master plan for global kingdom transformation into these few verses at the end of Matthew!

Jesus' great plan is that people will grow in loving obedience to him and help those they know to also fall in love with Him as well. This domino effect will reach into every place and people group until the end comes. It's the same multiplication effect that God has woven into the whole of creation with seeds and plants replicating after themselves. Yet we so rarely see it in our churches or missional endeavors!

Before we jump to the "how to" let us meditate for a while on what it means to be a disciple of Jesus. As we've discussed already, tools and practicalities come a distant second behind what is going on in our hearts!

In Psalm 111:6 it says,

"He has shown His great power to his people by giving them the lands of other nations"

In another version it says that he has given the nations as our inheritance. God has called us to join with Him in the work of transforming the nations, but he only promises that to His people, those who are obedient and trustworthy disciples. We've made being a christian about going to a church for 2 hours on a Sunday, sitting down and listening to more and more information every week and generally trying to live a 'blessed life' on this earth. While we pursue job security, friends, money and finding a church that fits us, we forfeit our invite to join in with God's global spiritual transformation work.

To me when I read these verses from Psalm 111 I think about Adam and Eve who were invited to be fruitful, multiply and subdue the earth,

"Then God blessed them and said, 'Be fruitful and multiply. Fill the earth and govern it.'
Genesis 1:28

And I think about Abraham who was promised a spiritual heritage that would number more than the stars in the sky,

"Then the Lord took Abram outside and said to him, 'Look up into the sky and count the stars if you can. That's how many descendants you will have."
Genesis 15:5

I also think about the promise to us as the people of God,

"Now all glory to God, who is able, through His mighty power at work within us, to accomplish infinitely more than we might ask or think. Glory to Him in the Church and in Christ Jesus through all generations forever and ever! Amen"
Ephesians 3:20 & 21

I am desperate to see God accomplishing infinitely more than I might ask or think. If that doesn't happen in and through me then what does that say about my faith and discipleship? I want to live according to God's plan and power, not my own. Are you committed to denying yourself, taking up your cross and following Jesus every day?

If you are not, then you are not one of His followers,

"If any of you wants to be my follower, you must give up your own way, take up your cross daily, and follow me."
Luke 9:23

Is it time to give up your own way?

We can only make disciples if we are a disciple ourself and have learned to obey Jesus and serve others in our own lives. Otherwise we are a fake and those around you will run a mile. I'm convinced that God is wanting to do a great work in our times but we could not cope. I've become a little cynical about the cries for 'Revival' that echo up and down this land. If we're not even disciples ourselves so how can we expect God the Father to entrust the nations to us to disciple? If we cannot manage our own affairs then God isn't going to entrust anything greater to us.

So if we hear the Prophet's cry for revival let's also hear the apostle's call to prepare and build. You can't have one without the other as Paul writes in Ephesians 2:20,

"Together, we are his house, built on the foundation of the apostles and the prophets. And the cornerstone is Christ Jesus himself."

God's house is built on prophets who hear and see what God wants to do, and apostles who have the building instructions. And Jesus said that to build His work we must make disciples of the nations!

If you love me, obey my commandments

"Not everyone who calls out to me, 'Lord! Lord!' will enter the Kingdom of Heaven. Only those who actually do the will of my Father in heaven will enter. On judgment day many will say to me, 'Lord! Lord! We prophesied in your name and cast out demons in your name and performed many miracles in your name.' But I will reply, 'I never knew you. Get away from me, you who break God's laws. Anyone who listens to my teaching and follows it is wise, like a person who builds a house on solid rock. Though the rain comes in torrents and the floodwaters rise and the winds beat against that house, it won't collapse because it is built on bedrock. But anyone who hears my teaching and doesn't obey it is foolish, like a person who builds a house on sand. When the rains and floods come and the winds beat against that house, it will collapse with a mighty crash." When Jesus had finished saying these things, the crowds were amazed at his teaching, for he taught with real authority—quite unlike their teachers of religious law."
Matthew 7:21-29

Take a minute to chew on Jesus' words.

It amazes me that having grown up in the world of churchianity, sung songs from the Bible and listened to hours of sermons and messages, I was never really taught how to obey Jesus or how to teach others to obey Jesus. Yet this is basic entry level into Jesus' kingdom.

If you do not listen to the words of Jesus AND obey them then your house will collapse when the storms hit. We do so many things in our churches and meetings, except the very thing that will help people to build the houses of their lives, families and dreams! 10 years ago I was faced with this same challenge. I could stand up in front of a crowded church and deliver inspirational and challenging messages, but was I actually making any disciples? And by 'making disciples' I mean the way Jesus did it, finding lost people and helping them to become obedient disciple making disciples themselves who in turn train more disciple making disciples!

Are you making disciples of Jesus Christ?

I can't emphasize enough how asking that simple question changed the whole course of our lives and ministry! As I mentioned already, I made a decision before God that I would not give my time and resources to anything other than making disciples of Jesus Christ the way that God was showing us from the scriptures.

It's hard because there is a lot of 'good work' out there and a million and one things to fill my time with. There are also many good church-based activities that appear to be 'missional' but actually they are not part of a disciple making plan. The word disciple is linked to the word discipline, and following Jesus is about being disciplined, not doing whatever you want or feel like doing.

I'm not at all interested in building a following for myself or building up Ben Taylor ministries. I'm not concerned how big our churches are or how many people I've baptized. My concern in everything is whether I am being faithful to Jesus and teaching, encouraging and admonishing people to obey all of Jesus' commands. By doing that I hope to receive a spiritual inheritance of people from all nations who are obeying Jesus and making more disciples. On my deathbed my hope is that like Abraham I will be able to see my natural family and spiritual children, grandchildren, great grandchildren and beyond, busy being fruitful, multiplying and subduing the earth with God's kingdom.

God loves you of course. But if all you think about is yourself and your own needs then you won't have the desire to make disciples because making disciples is about looking to the interests of others before yourself. That's the real reason why most churches are not making any disciples. It's not because of a lack of prayer, training or resources. It's because people don't want to do it! Making disciples essentially means sacrificing youself for others,

"Don't look out only for your own interests, but take an interest in others, too. You must have the same attitude that Christ Jesus had. Though he was God, he did not think of equality with God as something to cling to. Instead, he gave up his divine privileges, he took the humble position of a slave and was born as a human being. When he appeared in human form, he humbled himself in obedience to God and died a criminal's death on a cross. Therefore, God elevated him to the place of highest honor and gave him the name above all other names, that at the name of Jesus every knee should bow, in heaven and on earth and under the earth,and every tongue declare that Jesus Christ is Lord, to the glory of God the Father."
Philippians 2:4-12

Being a disciple of Jesus means to grow like Jesus in every way. Paul encourages us to have the same attitude as Christ Jesus had. He left his privileged position, took the humble position of a slave and humbled himself in obedience to His Father. Sounds a lot like what Jesus asks His followers to do in Luke 9:23 doesn't it?

So in the work we are doing we teach everyone to do this. Everyone is a disciple and therefore also a disciple maker.

People often accuse me and those on our team of baptizing people too quickly and lowering the bar of what it means to be part of the church of Jesus Christ. For a lot of people they just cannot understand how people can follow Jesus without a vicar, Sunday service or the same traditions week after week. To be completely honest I (along with many we work with) sometimes wonder how people can follow Jesus within traditional forms of church.

That's not to say that we shouldn't consider leadership, accountability and church discipline just as any other church or network must do. But it is sad to see how many so called followers of Jesus are married to a form of tradition or religion rather than to Jesus himself,

"Some Pharisees and teachers of religious law now arrived from Jerusalem to see Jesus. They asked him, "Why do your disciples disobey our age-old tradition? For they ignore our tradition of ceremonial hand washing before they eat." Jesus replied, "And why do you, by your traditions, violate the direct commandments of God?"
Matthew 15:1-4

We believe that baptism should happen immediately and is the first step of obedience when someone wants to become a disciple of Jesus. Scripture clearly teaches this. Public repentance and baptism , not raising your hand or saying the sinners prayer, is the sign of salvation. I always remember a quote from a friend who said,

"We need to lower the bar of what it means to do church and raise the bar of what it means to be a disciple of Jesus"

What my friend means is that we need to simplify how church works so it can grow and multiply in the hands of ordinary people without the need for great buildings, budgets and superstar leaders.

But at the same time we need to get back to what it really means to be a disciple of Jesus instead of watering everything down to please people and spiritual leaches who don't want to count the cost or obey Jesus.

Anyone who gets baptized through our work understands what it means to repent, surrender their life to Jesus and that their calling is now to make more disciples through living a life of obedience to Jesus. Are we perfect, of course not! But we believe our work is to find people who want to sacrificially obey Jesus and help others they know do the same. Being a disciple is a high bar to attain to, and may God have mercy on us for reducing it to simply attending a meeting or saying a prayer.

If we look back to the story Jesus told in Matthew 7:21-29 it always interests me how similar the two builders are.

They are both builders and they both build a house. When they finished, the two houses may well have looked the same from the outside. They may have had the same number of rooms and you could live in both of them.

However when the storms came it revealed a major difference. When the storms beat against both of the houses and the waters rose around them, one house remained and the other was washed away. The only difference between the two houses was the unseen foundations, which is the most important thing in any building!

Jesus looks at people who claim to follow Him and churches that claim to worship and he sees beyond all the things that we think are important. He looks past attendance figures, worship style, preaching series and mission trips and he looks for one thing.

Obedience.

Quite simply, Jesus wants us to obey Him,

"If you love me, obey my commandments"
John 14:15

Most churches I know believe they are making disciples. We can
all trot out our mission statements about making disciples. But from
what I have seen and experienced we actually have no idea how to
make disciples of Jesus. And I include myself in this!

I fear that Jesus is saying the following about us believers,

*"Their worship is a farce, for they teach man made ideas as
commands from God"*
Matthew 15:9

In the work we are doing we teach, model and expect every disciple
of Jesus to do exactly what a disciple of Jesus is meant to do.

We're not clever so we do what Jesus told us to do, we baptize
people and teach them to obey Jesus. These new disciples
understand that their calling is now to grow in their loving
obedience to God and to make more disciples. It's not something
they do a few years down the line when they feel like it, when they
are mature enough or when the leaders give them their blessing.

Some of those new disciples we have baptized have gone onto
baptize and start discipling more of their friends and family in a
matter of weeks. While I see christians meeting to be blessed or
endlessly searching for a church that meets their needs,
people considered notorious sinners are entering the kingdom and
giving their lives sacrificially for the sake of others straight away.

This is nothing new though,

"But what do you think about this? A man with two sons told the older boy, 'Son, go out and work in the vineyard today.' The son answered, 'No, I won't go,' but later he changed his mind and went anyway. Then the father told the other son, 'You go,' and he said, 'Yes, sir, I will.' But he didn't go. "Which of the two obeyed his father?" They replied, "The first." Then Jesus explained his meaning: "I tell you the truth, corrupt tax collectors and prostitutes will get into the Kingdom of God before you do. For John the Baptist came and showed you the right way to live, but you didn't believe him, while tax collectors and prostitutes did. And even when you saw this happening, you refused to believe him and repent of your sins."
Matthew 21:28-33

Jesus isn't bothered about your religious label, denomination or spiritual status. He's just looking for disciples who will obey Him and do what they say they are going to do.

I've been in so many embarrassing situations where I've had a group made up of brand new disciples and also others who'd be considered mature believers. The so called 'mature believers' often act in such immature and religious ways and I've watched the new disciples who've come out of the harvest having to correct and teach them.

I remember one occasion when we were in a café with the team and a church leader came in. We started talking to this leader of a local church and he begun to ask one of the team (a new believer who'd come from a background of drugs and crime) about why we didn't go to church or gather in a building on a Sunday. It was quite apparent this church leader was not really wanting a meaningful discussion and just wanted to justify himself so I began to feel a little protective of the new believers on the team.

But I felt God telling me to sit back and watch as it would be a good test of how effectively I was really discipling these new guys.

After a few minutes this new believer nervously started to answer the church leader and talking to them about making disciples and how the church met from house to house in Acts 2:42. He gently instructed this leader from the scriptures while the leader became increasingly hostile. I was so proud of Him, and felt a mixture of sadness and anger towards the church leader.

Jesus doesn't care about positions, titles, ministries or organizations, he's searching for those who will just obey him through faith,

"When the son of man returns, how many will he find on the earth who have faith?"
Luke 18:8

Being a disciple is how you find your calling. That's part of the reason for writing this book. I meet many people who claim to be called by God or aspire to positions of leadership and responsibility, but to be honest they don't even appear to live like disciples of Jesus. They are trying to climb the ministry ladder instead of falling to the ground and dying. They are trying to lift themselves up instead of humbling themselves and allowing God to lift them up.

I believe that if we will obey Jesus and do whatever is needed in His kingdom then we will accidentally find our calling. I never set out to be an apostle or church planter. I set out to obey Jesus and surrender everything I have to Him. A lot of time and money could be saved in churches if instead of trying to identify leaders and people's gifting we just focused on making disciples. When someone starts to obey Jesus faithfully it's easy to see their calling and gifting,

"The following day John was again standing with two of his Disciples. As Jesus walked by, John looked at Him and declared 'Look! There is the lamb of God!' When John's two disciples heard this, they followed Jesus. Jesus looked around and saw them following. 'What do you want?' he asked them."
John 1:35-39

Making disciples is about getting to the heart of the matter. Jesus asked His first disciples what they wanted and maybe he is asking you the same question now?

Maybe He wants you to ask those you are training and discipling the same question? Jesus is more concerned with inward attitudes and motivation than outward acts and ceremonies.

Take a minute to think about this question.

What do you want?

Disciples of who?

It's easy to forget that we're supposed to be making disciples of Jesus and not building a following for ourselves.

To be honest, many times I have found myself in situations where I seem more concerned about my own reputation amongst people rather than Jesus' reputation amongst them. If my desire is to see Jesus glorified then why do I get so concerned when my feathers get ruffled? May God help us to rejoice when all manner of trials and tribulations come our way because they are opportunities for Jesus to increase and us to decrease. If we have selfish ambition hiding in our hearts then our concern will be to build our own kingdom and not Jesus' kingdom. We will seek to win people to our cause through any means possible, rather than to speak the truth to them and help them to be disciples of Jesus,

"For we speak as messengers approved by God to be entrusted with the Good News. Our purpose is to please God, not people. He alone examines the motives of our hearts. Never once did we try to win you with flattery, as you well know. And God is our witness that we were not pretending to be your friends just to get your money. As for human praise, we have never sought it from you or anyone else. As apostles of Christ we certainly had a right to make some demands of you, but instead we were like children among you. Or we were like a mother feeding and caring for her own children. We loved you so much that we shared with you not only God's Good News but our own lives, too."
1 Thessalonians 2:4-9

Many churches up and down the land talk about being 'sending churches' and talk about the great commission. But very few do it and I'm convinced it's because really the so called leaders are more concerned about how many people are following them rather than how many people are following Jesus,

"Even some men from your own group will rise up and distort the truth in order to draw a following"
Acts 20:30

When this work does happen in a church it's because there are servant leaders who are prepared to make disciples of Jesus and to hold people with open hands. As far as I'm concerned I'm trying to work with Jesus to see Him increase in people's lives and to see them become more obedient to them. I'm not concerned about how many people look to me for leadership or how many people are in our church or network. God has entrusted people to me so that I can help them obey Jesus more, not to make me feel more successful or influential. My prayer is that those I am discipling will grow and leave home (just like our own natural children) to start their own spiritual families and legacies.

How will we see the nations discipled if you keep all your disciples for yourself? It might make your church appear successful but I wouldn't want to be in your shoes when you meet Jesus,

"One day as these men were worshiping the Lord and fasting, the Holy Spirit said, "Appoint Barnabas and Saul for the special work to which I have called them." So after more fasting and prayer, the men laid their hands on them and sent them on their way."
Acts 13:2-4

One of the things that I always say to the team we are working with here in our region is that we want to be a network that sends out our best people rather than one that holds onto them. I have a feeling God will test this, but I hope we will continue to see that those in our care our disciples of Jesus and they should obey Him.

Paul describes his work among the Thessalonian disciples as being like a mother caring and feeding her own children (1 Thessalonians 2:7) I have witnessed my wife be a mother to our 4 children and I can tell you that it isn't a 9 to 5 job where you turn up do your work and then go home and rest. It's a 24/7 commitment to invest your life into your children. And making disciples is no different. Yes it's about teaching spiritual truths, but it's far more about sharing your whole life with people and forming a spiritual family and community with them. Making disciples is actually being prepared to make the ultimate cost, just as raising children is the ultimate sacrifice. But it's all worth it to see your children and disciples growing and developing and then passing onto others what you've taught them. If I can be honest, I've struggled with the difference between preaching the gospel and making disciples. Preaching the gospel is all about power and seeing God do amazing things in a moment. People are healed, set free, repent and are baptized and there is great joy. Making disciples however is quite the opposite! It is slow work that requires patience, wisdom and endurance.

For a long time I wondered whether I was just meant to be doing the work of an evangelist all the time because I found it hard to switch from the "go fast" mentality of an evangelist to the "go slow" mentality needed to stay with people and disciple them to obey all of Jesus' commands. I knew all the tools and right things to do, but God had to change some deep rooted things in my life before I could really learn to make disciples and grow in the patience needed for this part of the work. I had to develope and mature as a person so that I found joy in not only starting things but also seeing things develope and finish. And I had to learn to work with others who see different parts of the whole process.

On our team there are those who lean towards the preaching of the gospel work and that's great. And there are those who lean towards the development and teaching work that comes afterwards, and that is also great. It's all desperately needed and it's all part of making disciples, but God forbid that we think any part of the work is more important than the other parts. That's why the work is to preach the gospel, make many disciples, strengthen the believers and appoint leaders. It requires teams of people working together wholeheartedly and humbly. Over the years my role here in our area has developed. I used to be the one leading the charge into the harvest. I'd be pioneering into estates while it felt like everyone else was sat at home just discussing what we should do. Over time though God has developed a team who think and act in very different ways but who all share a common vision and purpose. I find myself now spending a lot of my time thinking about the team, what is needed for different areas of the work and teaching and modelling about honouring and loving one another. I no longer need to be the one pioneering into new areas because there are people on the team who now do that. And I no longer have to be the only one who deeply cares and agonizes for the new disciples and churches as there are others who also carry this burden with me. Whilst there are lots of difficulties and challenges working with others, it's such a joy to be part of a body of people committed to being a big family on mission together.

Making disciples is hard work that requires great patience. I believe the degree of fruit you see is directly linked to the level to which you are prepared to sacrifice your life. Paul said to His disciples in Thessalonica that he was pleased to not only share the good news with them but also his whole life. Here is the example of how we make disciples. Another translation of this scripture says that Paul was happy to "impart" his life into these people and not only the gospel. Paul wasn't just being nice, meeting needs, doing friendship evangelism or being relational. He was making disciples! He literally imparted all that Christ was in him, into the lives of his disciples,

We loved you so much that we shared with you not only God's Good News but our own lives, too."
1 Thessalonians 2:4-9

We've had the privilege of following Jesus into the harvest with teams and pioneers across the UK and beyond. Everywhere we go the harvest is plentiful but the laborers are few. It's not a theory from the Bible, this is the reality. As the work has developed we've begun to ask very different questions. In the early days our questions revolved very much around how to preach the gospel and have baptism parties because that is what we were wanting to see breakthroughs in. After some time these things became normal because our faithful actions had caught up with our hopes! So then you start to ask different questions like, "how will these households who have baptized receive ongoing training so they learn to obey all of Jesus' commands?"

When I prepare to visit an area to lead a training or to work with a church one of the first questions I now ask is, who is part of the disciple making / church planting team and what time commitment are they giving each week? An evangelist doesn't even consider that question. It's great to go out, preach the gospel, heal the sick and baptize households of people.

But it's better to have a plan to make disciples and plant churches and a team who are committed to doing this.

If you're a pioneer then, like us and Paul, you can grow your team out of the harvest. Either way the work of disciple making requires prayer, thought and wisdom, otherwise your gospel sowing efforts will simply be like *'pissing into the wind.'*

Making disciples is about working to see Christ formed in people. It takes hard work, time and much prayer,

"Oh my dear children! I feel as if I'm going through labor pains for you again, they will continue until Christ is fully developed in your lives"
Galatians 4:19

I often receive criticism for the work we are doing. Normally it's from fellow believers who have concerns about the work and who believe that what we are doing is wrong. I always listen, try to be gracious and enter into conversations where appropriate.

But it's a very lonely and painful life being an accidental apostle. I feel like I carry a great unseen burden for God's people who are not yet His people. I feel labor pains for the new disciples and churches. I have sleepless nights of prayer and face hardships on every side. It feels like a lot of fellow believers I know are motivated entirely by their own comfort. Their questions come out of these desires that are in their heart. Jesus has called me and my family to this great work amongst the gentiles and we're giving ourselves to that. I am inspired by others who have sacrificed themselves for the gospel and ultimately by Jesus who came not to be served but to serve,

"For even the son of man came not to be served but to serve others and to give his life as a ransom for many."
Mark 10:45

I guess you could say that everyone called to be a pioneer or leader would also have these same challenges. But because we are focused on working in the harvest I feel the enemy gives us a little more attention!

To be a disciple means to live according to the will and commands of Jesus rather than according to the world. If you are not prepared to upset those around you and look foolish then this life is not for you! Being a disciple of Jesus means to patiently endure and to continue in obedience to God no matter what,

"So do not throw away this confidant trust in the Lord.

Remember the great reward it brings you! Patient endurance is what you need now, so that you will continue to do God's will. Then you will receive all that He has promised."
Hebrews 10:35-37

If the goal of preaching the gospel is to see households baptized and receiving Christ and His kingdom. Then the goal of making many disciples is to see all people presented to God perfect in their relationship to Christ,

"And this is the secret; Christ lives in you. This gives you assurance of sharing his glory. So we tell others about Christ, warning everyone and teaching everyone with all the wisdom God has given us. We want to present them to God, perfect in their relationship to Christ. That's why I work and struggle so hard, depending on Christ's mighty power that works within me."
Colossians 1:27-29

Jesus has commanded us to make disciples so our responsibility to people is far deeper than just to get them saved or converted. That would be like giving birth to a child and then leaving it to fend for itself. We need wisdom from God as we warn everyone and teach everyone to obey Jesus!

Many think that making disciples is about slotting people into a programme or giving them a book to read. Children are born into families, not programmes or classrooms, and this is no different in making disciples. We don't make disciples through the sharing of information, but through the impartation of the gospel and our lives. God is looking down on earth to see who is willing and prepared to do the great and costly work of making disciples. And Paul helps us to understand how deep this is,

"For even if you had ten thousand others to teach you about Christ, you only have one Spiritual father. For I became your father in Christ Jesus when I preached the goods news to you. So I urge you to imitate me."
1 Corinthians 4:15-17

Making disciples is something so deep and sacrificial. When I look out on the landscape of churchianity I see tens of thousands of teachers who know about theology and can tell people how they are wrong. But I see very few spiritual fathers and mothers who are literally giving their lives sacrifically to make disciples amongst the gentiles. My hope is that this book will in some way change this landscape and that an army of people will begin to take responsibility for the gentiles around them.

Jesus didn't make disciples by sending teaching down to earth from his pulpit in heaven. He came and lived with ordinary men and women and empowered them to imitate Him. He promised to do the same with anyone who obeys Him,

"Those who accept my commandments and obey them are the ones who love me. And because they love me, my Father will love them. And I will love them and reveal myself to each of them"
John 14:21

In another translation it says that Jesus and His Father will come and make their home with those who obey Him. When people obey Jesus He comes and reveals more of Himself to them!

I had a great revelation about this a few years ago when I was reading the book of Revelation. We tend to ridiculously over-spiritualize and complicate everything for some reason. It stops us from entering into the kingdom ourselves and prevents others from entering also.

Jesus, however, tends to simplify things,

"Look! I stand at the door and knock. If you hear my voice and open the door, I will come in, and we will share a meal together as friends."
Revelation 3:20

The reward for hearing Jesus' voice and acting on it is that He will come in and share a meal with us together as friends. When I first began to think about this it seemed a bit strange. Sharing a meal with Jesus didn't seem that special or very spiritual. I mean where was the time of worship? Where was the sermon or the time of ministry? Isn't the christian life much more important than just eating with people?

However as God began to humble me and help me to understand His ways and His work, I began to see how precious it is to share a meal with Jesus. Imagine how much of His life could be imparted to us if we sat across the table from Him and could ask him anything we wanted! It's actually no different from what Jesus did for 3 years during his public ministry. He went into homes and shared meals with people. That was His 'work'. He imparted the good news of the kingdom and His whole life into some ordinary people and then asked them to do the same with others! When we read Matthew 10 and Luke 10 , Jesus sent His disciples out to find people who'd welcome them into their homes (houses of peace) and then to eat with them. That was how to plant a church and make disciples of all nations!

It's ridiculously simple and yet costs everything because it takes time, hard work and your whole life. It's more about who you are than knowing what to do! You can't do it from the safety of a pulpit or through the anonymity of a meeting!

Anyone can do it and it can happen anywhere.

That is making disciples and it's the work all those who claim to follow Jesus are commanded to do.

Come and see

"Jesus looked around and saw them following, 'What do you want?' he asked them. They replied, 'Rabbi (which means "Teacher") where are you staying?' 'Come and see' he said. It was about 4 O'clock in the afternoon when they went with him to the place where he was staying, and they remained with Him the rest of the day. Andrew, Simon Peter's brother, was one of these men who heard what John said and then followed Jesus. Andrew went to find his brother, Simon, and told him, 'We have found the Messiah.'
John 1:38-42

Some people think that the most important thing about making disciples is knowing what to do with people after they get saved. I have an issue with this on a number of levels. Firstly we are not trying to get people saved and then disciple them, we are making disciples from the very beginning. And secondly the most important thing is that you are prepared to open your life to people.

I've met so many people who are tooled up to the max but they are not prepared to sacrifice their time to invest in those they are discipling. Making disciples isn't something to fit into your diary for one evening a week.

If Jesus was a christian then the conversation above would have been very different. Here's two options that I often see played out:

"Jesus looked around and saw them following, *'Do you want to become a christian?'* he asked them. They replied, *'No thanks – we're not religious.'* Jesus replied, *'OK well if you want to find out more come to my church on Sunday at 10:30am.'*

OR

"Jesus looked around and saw them following, *'Do you want to become a christian?'* he asked them. They replied, *'Yes we want to find out more.'* Jesus replied, *'OK come to my church on Sunday at 10:30am.'*

I see these two scenarious happening everywhere I go and neither option has anything to do with making disciples. Let's learn some lessons from Jesus.

Jesus invited these men into his life immediately, not to say a prayer or come to a meeting in a few days. That is making disciples. The men went to see where Jesus was staying and then they hung out for the rest of the day. Straight away one of the men recruited his brother and the next day it continued as Jesus met Philip and then Philip went to find Nathaniel (John 1:43-47) Whether you invite people to your home or are in a household of peace, it's about sharing your life with people and starting a domino effect that leads to more and more people being added to God's kingdom.

What if your conversations with people were more like this. You can insert your name if you like,

"…….. looked around and saw them following, *'Do you want to find out more about Jesus and faith?'* …… asked them. They replied, *'Yes we want to find out more.'* …….. replied, *'OK let's go for a coffee now and talk some more or meet up in the next few days? When and where is good for you and who else could meet up with us as well?"*

I dare you to have conversations like this!

When I felt God challenging me to go beyond evangelism and to find people who had the desire to obey Jesus I decided to read the gospels to see what I could learn from Jesus.

It was a good move.

I learned so much about what was going on behind the scenes and what was in Jesus' mind when he was asking questions and doing things with people. It bothered me that Jesus seemed so concerned that people were like lost sheep but he was not slow to challenge people and raise the bar of discipleship in a way that turned people away. I wrestled with this apparent contradiction for a few weeks wondering why God was pointing this out to me. Eventually my eyes were opened to an important truth about making disciples which totally takes the pressure of our shoulders,

"But Jesus replied, 'Stop complaining about what I said. For no-one can come to me unless the Father who sent me draws them to me, and at the last day I will raise them up. As it is written in the scriptures, 'They will all be taught by God. Everyone who listens to the Father and learns from him comes to me."
John 6:43-46

Don't you love it when Jesus throws out these nuggets of truth that completely transform what you are doing! I was working really hard to find people who want to be disciples and was using up a lot of energy and finding very few people who wanted to obey Jesus. When I read this one day it dawned on me that people literally

won't want to come to Jesus and obey Him unless God the Father is
teaching and drawing them.

What a relief. Finding people who want to be disciples of Jesus
isn't my work. It's God's work and we just have the privilege of
joining in a bit. I had a change in my heart and mind and this
resulted in a change in my behavior. I simply decided that I would
ask people some questions to see if God was drawing them to Jesus
or not. My conclusion was that if God wasn't drawing their hearts
then no amount of time, arguments and me trying to encourage
them would change their hearts. It became clear to me that this is
why Jesus was not so concerned about offending people or
challenging people with the cost of discipleship. He wasn't trying
to make friends and please everyone, He was on a mission to find
those who were listening and learning from the Father and who
would come to him. Once he found those people He would stay
with them and eat with them. Even I could do that.

I asked everyone I met whether they wanted to know more about
Jesus. Pretty quickly it showed me who was being drawn by the
Father to Jesus and who wasn't!

So asking questions like Jesus did is a great start when finding
people who want to be His disciples. I already mentioned 3
questions that will create a whole new headache in your ministry
and work but here they are again:

1) Do you want to know more about Jesus?

**2) Where and when can I meet with you and others to find out
more?**

3) Who else do you know that could gather with us?

Asking these three questions along with desperate prayer and obedience to whatever God shows you will get you knee deep in harvest! And that will lead you to ask certain other questions that I attempt to begin answering later in this book!

Teach these new disciples to obey all the commands I have given you

So having found some people who want to know more about Jesus, how do you start teaching them to obey Him?

Well what you don't do is start giving them loads of christian books, information and ideas! If you want to make disciples you need to give people two things:

1) **A person** – the Holy Spirit

2) **A pattern** – what to do when they gather and how to hear and obey Jesus

As a church planter and disciple maker I've come to realise that my work is about laying a foundation that people can build on in my absence. I'm not so concerned about making sure that those I'm discipling know everything, but that they know God and know how to discover everything. There's a big difference.

It's easy to shoot yourself in the foot when church planting. In your zeal to make disciples and help people grow you can turn into the christian expert who knows everything and does everything. This unfortunately leads to everyone else doing nothing and being in awe of how amazing you are. If you don't believe me then go to any Church near you this Sunday and you'll see what I mean. A few experts do everything and the majority do nothing.

So when you gather with these new disciples my advice would be to say nothing, take nothing except a Bible and do very little. I think this is similar to Paul's reflections on how he started the church in Corinth,

"When I first came to you dear brothers and sisters, I didn't use lofty words and impressive wisdom to tell you God's secret plan. For I decided that while I was with you I would forget everything except Jesus Christ, the one who was crucified. I came to you in weakness, timid and trembling. And my message and my preaching were very plain. Rather than using clever and persuasive speeches, I relied only on the power of the Holy Spirit. I did this so you would trust not in human wisdom but in the power of God."
1 Corinthians 2:1-6

Thank God we're called to be servants and not superstars.

So the less we take the better because it will help people trust in God and force us to rely on the word and the Spirit rather than our extensive knowledge of theology and churchianity which is often a barrier to making disciples anyway.

We will go into this in more detail in the next chapter, but we've found it really helpful to begin modelling to new disciples right from the start what we do when we gather together as church.

When we gather new disciples together we loosely split up our time together into 3 parts. It's often messy, sometimes chaotic and you have to rely on Jesus and think on your feet. It's important to remember that we are not following a formula or holding a religious meeting, we are bringing the kingdom into the darkness and into the lives of new disciples. It's all about God dwelling more fully amongst the people you are discipling and gathering.

We pass on this simple pattern to people when we meet with them and we always try and share food at every opportunity,

IN – Fellowship and caring for one another
UP – Hearing and obeying Jesus
OUT – Praying for others and practicing what we will do this week

Because God's heart is to see His kingdom coming amongst all people we are wanting to make disciples who make disciples and plant churches that plant churches. This is why it's really helpful to have a basic pattern that everyone can follow. It means anyone can go and plant a church with people they know and they are not reliant on a handful of leaders to do everything. Jesus had a pattern that he handed onto His disciples (Matthew 10 and Luke 10) and Paul also had a pattern that he passed onto his churches and disciples,

"Hold onto the pattern of wholesome teaching you learned from me – a pattern shaped by the faith and love that you have in Christ Jesus"
2 Timothy 1:13

A pattern is something that can be repeated or acts as a guide. We are to lead people to know Jesus and to plant communities with the person of the Holy Spirit at the centre, but a pattern can help and strengthen people's faith and work so that's why we use them.

And because making disciples is about imparting not only the gospel but also our whole lives, a very valuable tool is our lifestyle itself. The best disciple makers are able to say, just as

Jesus and Paul did, *imitate me,*

"That's why I have sent Timothy, my beloved and faithful child in the Lord. He will remind you of how I follow Christ Jesus, just as I teach in all the Churches wherever I go."
1 Corinthians 4:17

So let's look briefly at what we have found works really well when starting to make disciples in the harvest and what we do when we gather,

"All the believers devoted themselves to the Apostles teaching, and to fellowship, and to sharing in meals (including the Lord's supper) and to prayer…"
Acts 2:42

IN (Fellowship)

We spend some time at the start of our gatherings sharing our highs and lows and having fellowship. It's good fun to turn this into a game where people share what has been good in their lives that week and what has been hard. We thank God together for the highs and if someone shares a low we pray for them in a very simple way. Then they pass it onto the next person in the gathering!
If the group is too large then you can split people up into pairs or smaller groups to share their highs and lows and pray for each other. During this time we also report back on how it went obeying Jesus this week.

"When the apostles returned, they told Jesus everything they had done"
Luke 9:10

Remember, we are here to help people obey Jesus so an important part is keeping each other accountable to doing what He says to us! The disciples reported back to Jesus so we build this into what we do. It builds faith and also identifies any challenges that people are facing. And how else will you know if those you are discipling are obeying Jesus unless you ask them about it? Our role is to create a culture of discipleship where it is normal to listen to Jesus and obey Him immediately.

If someone shares a need or challenge then the disciples can pray and then see how they can help and pool their resources and support each other. We call this 'bring and share' it is a foundational principle in everything we do. (We'll come back to this later)

UP (Apostle's Teaching)

Jesus commanded His disciples to teach these new disciples to obey all His commands. So we want to help our new disciples to be doers of the word and not just hearers! Instead of teaching or sharing information we teach disciples of Jesus to obey Him. This is a massively different approach then western christianity has taught us. As a leader and disciple maker my focus in disciple-making is on helping others to hear God, obey Him and share these truths with others. My role becomes more about equipping others than building up my own ministry or role in the body. I'm not so concerned about ticking theological boxes with people, but am more focused on introducing them to the friend of Sinners and savior of the world. Jesus does a much better job at teaching people than I do anyway. A lot of people tend to look at what they're doing themselves as a measure of their success or effectiveness. I choose to look for another measure of success and that is what others are doing as a result of what you have done. That really shows you how effective you are at making disciples of Jesus because what people do when you are not there is the real test,

"Dear Friends, you always followed my instructions when I was with you. And now that I am away, it is even more important. Work hard to show the results of your salvation, obeying God with deep reverence and fear."
Philippian 2:12

Typically we have a pattern of teaching we take disciples and communities through (see next chapter), but we also are open to any diversions that the Spirit throws in! The point is though that we are working to lay a foundation into the lives of the disciples and the life of the church. The most important thing we do is pray for the new disciples and churches. Out of that we get a sense of what Jesus is wanting to do amongst them. First we teach the new disciples to obey the basic commands Jesus gives to all his followers (we call these the 7 commands of Christ) and then we continue to strengthen them and the church through further scriptures and truths and through our lives!

Because the goal is obedience to Jesus rather than just head knowledge we try and use good questions to help people discover what God is saying to them and what they need to do about it. If you've been involved with churchianity then your default setting is to discuss everything rather than to obey anything. This is not the way of Jesus and it is not how to teach people to obey Him.

Jesus shared some important truths about the Kingdom and

disciple making in Matthew 13:1-24 and Mark 4:1-21 and as we've already seen, according to Jesus if we don't understand this parable then we can't understand anything else,

"Then Jesus said to them, 'Don't you understand this parable? How then will you understand any parable?"
Mark 4:13

Take a minute to read the story yourself!

What I learn from this story is that there is a type of person who, like the good soil, receives and understands the word, perseveres through hardships and worries and bears 30, 60 or 100 fold fruit. My purpose in life is to be that type of person and to train others who are like that.

I want to suggest that the goal of preaching the gospel is to find these good soil people, and I believe the New Testament would support this. Disciple making is then 'staying' with good soil people (or people of peace!) to train and teach them and their households (your new co-workers!) to obey all of Jesus commands and to lay the foundation for a disciple making movement amongst that whole people group or geographic region!

Jesus talks more about being a fruitful disciple in John 15,

"Yes, I am the vine; you are the branches. Those who remain in me, and I in them, will produce much fruit. For apart from me you can do nothing…When you produce much fruit, you are my true disciples. This brings great glory to my father….You didn't choose me, I chose you, I appointed you to go and produce lasting fruit."

So when we find people who are potentially good soil people we want to help them hear, understand, obey and share God's word so they are fruitful!

When we read a scripture or consider a dream or prophetic word together we ask ourselves these questions:

1) What is this saying?

2) What does it mean?

3) What do I need to do about it?

4) Who can I share it with?

We re-tell the story in our own words to make sure people have heard it. Then we talk about what it means to see if people are understanding what Jesus is saying to them. We then move the conversation along and help people to share what they need to do about it this week.

This is the real test of discipleship, are people prepared to move beyond discussion to obedience? Then we help people to think through who they could share this with and who they can begin to disciple themselves.

It's always messy and never happens as easily and clearly as we may hope for, but the idea is that we help everyone to hear and obey Jesus and prepare them to share what He is saying with others.

OUT (Prayer and multiply)

Jesus calls His people to follow him and to fish for more people so an important part of what we do is to equip those we are discipling so they can personally make more disciples themselves,

"Jesus called out to them, "Come, follow me, and I will show you how to fish for people." And they left their nets at once and followed him."
Matthew 4:19-21

The first thing we do is to help people write down their name list or their mission list as we sometimes call it. Straight away we create an expectation that God wants to transform these people's friends and families. They write down the names of the people they live with, work with or know and start to pray for them and look for ways to start discipling them. Like Peter did, we literally say to them that this message is for you, your family and those you know and others who might seem far away from Jesus,

"Peter replied, 'Each of you must repent of your sins and turn to God, and be baptized in the name of Jesus Christ for the forgiveness of sins. Then you will receive the gift of the Holy Spirit. This promise is to you, to your children and to those far away – all who have been called by the Lord God."
Acts 2:38-40

Secondly we train these new disciples to share their Jesus story by asking them to tell the group what their life was like before they met Jesus, how they met him and what their life has been like since then. And we train them to share the gospel using a simple tool called "The 2 Kingdoms" (google that!) Other people use different tools but the point is to train them in a gospel sharing tool that is fruitful (leads people to repentance and baptism) and that can multiply (they can train others to share it and so on)

Finally we always lay hands on each other and pray that we will be filled with the Holy Spirit and with boldness,

"And now, O Lord, hear their threats, and give us, your servants, great boldness in preaching your word. Stretch out your hand with healing power; may miraculous signs and wonders be done through the name of your holy servant Jesus." After this prayer, the meeting place shook, and they were all filled with the Holy Spirit. Then they preached the word of God with boldness."
Acts 4:29-32

The 7 commands of Christ

So with the above pattern in our hands and the love of Jesus in our hearts we begin to teach new disciples to obey all the commands of Jesus. From many years' experience and through seeing and hearing what is bearing fruit amongst the harvest work, here are the 7 basic scriptures and themes that we teach new disciples. Remember, we are not just trying to convert people to christianity. We are working to help people obey Jesus and that starts from the first moment you meet them and it will never end!

Here are the scriptures and a few notes, but the point is that the scriptures will speak for themselves so go and introduce your disciples to them and ask the questions above. They can be used each week or more often and they are living and breathing truths and attitudes that God wants to grow in us rather than a checklist.

So have some fun and be creative in helping those you are

discipling to understand and obey these foundational truths. There's nothing more boring than a dry bible study.

Read the stories with your people and ask them what it is saying to them, what it means, what they need to do about it this week or what impact this truth will have on their life and then who they can share it with.

1) Change (Repentance)

The first thing Jesus commanded people to do was to repent so that's where we start,

"From then on Jesus began to preach, "Repent of your sins and turn to God, for the Kingdom of heaven is near."
Matthew 4:17

A great story to read on this theme of change and repentance is Luke 19:1-10.

2) Water (Baptism)

According to scripture the sign of repentance and faith is public baptism of whole households.

Try reading Acts 2:36-42 with your people and see what God says to them!

3) Fire (Filled with the Spirit)

In the scriptures people were filled with the Spirit when they repented and were baptized.

A good story to read on this truth is Acts 8:12-18 as it explains how to do it. We would encourage people to speak in tongues immediately as we are laying hands on them.

Without the Holy Spirit these new disciples can do nothing! So set aside your long held beliefs, theories and fears about the Holy Spirit and do whatever it takes to see them filled with the Holy Spirit powerfully! It's about them, not you.

4) Tell (Preach the Gospel)

A disciple of Jesus follows Him and fishes for more people. So along with helping people to write their name or people lists we also read a story from the scripture that teaches about sharing the Gospel with others.

John 4:1-43 is a good one and shows how one ordinary 'sinful' woman can lead to a whole village being transformed!

5) Pray (Pray!)

We must teach our disciples straight away the scriptural and appropriate response to challenges, trials and persecution.

Acts 4:23-32 is a good story to use. We stand up and do it with the people!

6) Gather (Fellowship)

We train everyone so they know who to gather and what to do when they gather. Acts 2:36-47 is a great story to use and you can play a good game using this scripture. First of all read out the story and write down what things happened in the church in Acts. Then you can ask the question – are we doing those things in this community and would you call what we are doing together church?

It's always an interesting game to play and is often a great way to help these new disciples to themselves identify what they are doing as church. It also throws up areas that you can strengthen (see next chapter!)

7) Go (Make Disciples)

Hopefully by this point your disciples will know all about going and making disciples through your message and life.

But looking at Matthew 28:18-20 is always good!

I've said it a number of times and will say it again – this is not a formula that you can pick off the shelf and magically make disciples with. It's worked for us because it uses the scriptures to teach and we are teaching people to obey Jesus. It's also not a curriculum, but some key living foundational truths that need to be planted into disciples and churches so that God lives amongst them more and more and it can flourish without you being there.

It's about them…not you!

We're getting towards the end of this chapter but before I tell you some stories I wanted to share some scriptures that have transformed how I make disciples. I'd encourage you to read the scripture first and ask yourself these two questions:

1) What does this say about making disciples?

2) What do I need to do about this, or change, in my life/work?

I'd love to hear what God says to you and how this changes how you make disciples! You can contact me through our website at www.benandcatherine.org

Who's doing the work?   John 4:1-4

Who are your co-workers?   Philippians 1:3-7

Is it about your ministry or theirs?   1 Thessalonians

Planning for spiritual grandchildren?   2 Timothy 2

A Muslim worker

We are meeting more and more Muslims who appear to be very hungry to know more about Jesus. Muslims are in some ways no different from any people group around us. There are some unique challenges about making disciples of Jesus amongst Muslims and we haven't even scratched the surface yet of what God wants do amongst the Muslim world. But through prayer we can engage these people in the same way we would approach any people group. It's amazing when you are prepared to look beyond outward labels and actions and to search for evidence of God's work in people's lives. In some ways it makes no difference to me whether someone calls themself a christian, a muslim, an atheist or a new ager. Man looks on the outward appearance but God looks on the heart,

"The LORD doesn't see things the way you see them. People judge by outward appearance, but the LORD looks at the heart."
1 Samuel 16:7

While the world is busy dividing people up according to their religions, denominations and ethnicities, God is searching the earth for those with hearts of faith and obedience to Him. Are you searching for people who God is calling and teaching or are you just trying to convert people to churchianity?

We were knocking on doors and searching for people of peace in one area and we came across a young man. He opened the door and we asked him if he needed any prayer. He replied that he was ok and that he was already religious. We asked if he wanted to know more about Jesus and he said *"No...because I am a Muslim"* We had exhausted all our questions but this young guy was still standing there in front of us with his door open. I didn't know what to do so I just thought I'd ask him whether he wanted to come with us in the same way Jesus invited His first disciples to "come and see",

"Jesus looked around and saw them following. "What do you want?" he asked them. They replied, "Rabbi" (which means "Teacher"), "where are you staying?" "Come and see," he said. It was about four o'clock in the afternoon when they went with him to the place where he was staying, and they remained with him the rest of the day."
John 1:38-40

This young guy came with us immediately and we trained him how to knock on doors, share the gospel of Jesus and to pray for those who were sick. In between houses I began to talk to him about God's kingdom, repentance and faith.

At one point this young Muslim who'd not publicly repented or been baptized was leading the team into a housing estate, asking people if they wanted to know about Jesus and sharing the gospel with people. It was a wonderful and yet strange afternoon for me. I mean this young guy was obeying Jesus but was he a disciple? It felt like this young guy was working harder and did more for God's kingdom in one afternoon than most other believers have ever done in their lifetime.

I wondered what Jesus thought of this and I humbly asked Him to help transform my understanding of what it means to help people be His disciples.

Rejecting the Disciples of Jesus

A few weeks ago we were at the home of a person of peace in Glastonbury. She welcomed the team into her home and family when they visited her estate. As a team it has been very humbling to see this lady's generosity and love for her family and community. We were sat in her front garden with her family and extended family and she was telling us about her life. It's always heartbreaking to hear stories of abuse and hardship and quite frankly it's amazing this lady is even still alive. But then she went onto tell an even sadder story.

When she was younger she attended a church with her daughter. After a few weeks of being an attender she wanted to serve others and so she got involved with some of the groups and activities. However our friend shared how she felt very different from all the other people in the church. She tried to change how she dressed and how she acted so that she could fit in more with the people around her. After months of this, she finally received an invite to a party from one of the influential ladies in the church. Feeling like this was the opening she had been praying and hoping for she put her best dress on and went with her daughter to the party.

When she arrived at the lady's home, this lady welcomed her, took her to the kitchen and then asked her to do the washing up for the people at the party. She'd not been invited to the party as a guest but as a pot washer.

I can't explain to you how upset and angry I felt at that moment.

Our friend left that church and has not returned to any kind of church since. She also shared stories with us about how some years for her birthday she wanted to gather the whole community for a party instead of just being spoilt herself. So she did it and gathered the whole community for a party.

She is exactly the kind of disciple and person of peace that we (and I think Jesus!) is looking for and she was rejected by the church because she looked, dressed and acted differently. She hasn't been rejected by Jesus though.

Drug addict becomes disciple maker

As a team we started to work in one of towns in our area. After praying where to go we started to preach the gospel and search for households of peace.

The team met a young lady and man outside Tesco's as they were on their way to get their daily drug fix. They offered prayer to this young couple who seemed interested in Jesus and His offer of new life. As a team we then began to meet with these two along with more of their friends each week on a Tuesday lunchtime. We'd look at the 7 commands of Christ each week as we helped these young people to understand and obey God's will for their lives.

The young lady was clearly a person of peace and someone who knew a lot of people in the town. After a few gatherings she stopped using drugs, got baptized along with her partner and another friend. Since then she has baptized more of her friends and is now developing as a leader. Everything we have done and said with this lady is to help empower her to make disciples amongst those she knows. It's not all plain sailing but we're making disciples who are making disciples who are making disciples!

The transformation that Jesus has worked in this young lady's life in just one year is amazing. And what is even better is that she is already working with Jesus to help others experience His power as well!

I'm not a Christian

One of our town's most notorious sinners became one of our most beloved brothers and co-workers. He is now with Jesus but I often look back on His life and am amazed at what he experienced as a disciple of Jesus.

He had the joy of baptizing others and seeing those who he'd baptized doing the same for others.

He trained others to find people of peace and to plant churches. And he saw God heal many people. He had no church upbringing and had a terrible childhood at the hands of foster parents and family friends. But Jesus called Him and this guy followed! I sometimes miss my friend's refreshing simplicity about being a disciple of Jesus. Often he used to silence religious people and church-goers with his stories of obedience. If anyone asked him if he was a christian then he would laugh and ask them not to call him that name ever again. My friend was very passionate about being known as a disciple of Jesus who was making more disciples amongst the gentiles and not a christian who sits in meetings and does nothing.

We've chosen to leave the comfort of churchianity to enter into the world of sinners and build God's home among them. Just like Jesus left the glories of heaven to enter this world and make his home with us sinners! Through making disciples we have labored with

Jesus to see the Gospel spreading to many people who would never believe that Jesus would even want to know them let alone transform their lives and use them for His work,

"Remember, dear brothers and sisters, that few of you were wise in the world's eyes or powerful or wealthy when God called you. Instead, God chose things the world considers foolish in order to shame those who think they are wise. And he chose things that are powerless to shame those who are powerful. God chose things despised by the world, things counted as nothing at all, and used them to bring to nothing what the world considers important. As a result, no-one can ever boast in the presence of God."
1 Corinthians 1:26-30

Let's do it right now!

One night I had a dream about an influential person of peace we'd met in Glastonbury. I shared it with one of my co-workers the next morning and we concluded that we should try and find him that day.

We'd seen him in town a few weeks before with a guy called Andy and had shared a time of prayer and spontaneous worship with them on the streets. I was keen to try and move things deeper with these guys and to begin a discipling relationship with this guy and 'his people'. We managed to locate them at their caravans down by a river on the outskirts of Glastonbury.

After a brief catch up I started to ask this guy about 'his people' and he mentioned that the guy we'd met with him called Andy was going through a particularly challenging time. In fact this guy described Andy as having lots of demons in him and he started to ask us how Jesus could help him.

I shared with the guy that Jesus talked about the role of prayer and fasting in casting out demons and that we should pray for a time to meet Andy and lay hands on Him in the name of Jesus. Our friend started to get excited and said that he had not eaten all that day. I seized the opportunity to model and teach what it means to be a disciple and a person of peace/shepherd to those in our flock. I said, "Let's go and find him right now then".

He didn't need much convincing and he was in the car before me and my co-worker were. After driving for just a couple of minutes I got my Bible out to read Mark 5 (we'll come back to that!) but as I began to read the guy started shouting us to stop. Andy was stood right there, it was almost like he was waiting for us. We took them back to the caravans and began to ask Andy some questions to try and understand where he had come from and where he was going. Two other neighbors joined the gathering and we read Mark 5:1-21,

"So they arrived at the other side of the lake, in the region of the Gerasenes. When Jesus climbed out of the boat, a man possessed by an evil spirit came out from the tombs to meet him. This man lived in the burial caves and could no longer be restrained, even with a chain. Whenever he was put into chains and shackles—as he often was—he snapped the chains from his wrists and smashed the shackles. No one was strong enough to subdue him. Day and night he wandered among the burial caves and in the hills, howling and cutting himself with sharp stones. When Jesus was still some distance away, the man saw him, ran to meet him, and bowed low before him. With a shriek, he screamed, "Why are you interfering with me, Jesus, Son of the Most High God? In the name of God, I beg you, don't torture me!" For Jesus had already said to the spirit, "Come out of the

man, you evil spirit." Then Jesus demanded, "What is your name?" And he replied, "My name is Legion, because there are many of us inside this man." Then the evil spirits begged him again and again not to send them to some distant place. There happened to be a large herd of pigs feeding on the hillside nearby. "Send us into those pigs," the spirits begged. "Let us enter them." So Jesus gave them permission. The evil spirits came out of the man and entered the pigs, and the entire herd of about 2,000 pigs plunged down the steep hillside into the lake and drowned in the water. The herdsmen fled to the nearby town and the surrounding countryside, spreading the news as they ran. People rushed out to see what had happened. A crowd soon gathered around Jesus, and they saw the man who had been possessed by the legion of demons. He was sitting there fully clothed and perfectly sane, and they were all afraid. Then those who had seen what happened told the others about the demon-possessed man and the pigs. 17 And the crowd began pleading with Jesus to go away and leave them alone. As Jesus was getting into the boat, the man who had been demon possessed begged to go with him. But Jesus said, "No, go home to your family, and tell them everything the Lord has done for you and how merciful he has been." So the man started off to visit the Ten Towns of that region and began to proclaim the great things Jesus had done for him; and everyone was amazed at what he told them."

Andy could relate to various points in the story and concluded that Jesus wanted to clean him up big time. The first step in being a disciple of Jesus is to repent and be baptized so we talked the whole group though this. There was a fire lit so I got a few pieces of paper and a pen and encouraged everyone to write down the sins and areas of their lives that they wanted to ask Jesus for forgiveness and repentance in. Andy had a very long list. We then threw our pieces of paper in the fire and prayed for each other.

Over the rest of the evening more people joined the communal gathering. At one point there were 8 or 9 people. And our friend (the person of peace) was boldly inviting the others to repent of their sin and ask Jesus to help them change! At least two of them wanted to be baptized. We left that gathering thankful that we had helped our friend to see that when, as disciples, we obey Jesus immediately then amazing things happen and spiritual families begin to form.

Who are you discipling and how are you discipling them?

How can you be more fruitful as a disciple maker?

Chapter 7

Strengthen the believers

Acts 14:23

We are called to plant churches.

Let me say that again. We are called to plant churches.

According to the New Testament, we are to find households of peace that receive the gospel of the kingdom and then become churches which further propagate the gospel through their regions and networks of friends and family.

Yes we pray, preach the gospel and make many disciples, but the goal is to plant and multiply churches. If new disciples are not gathered regularly into a Jesus centred community of other disciples then they won't survive and there will be no lasting fruit. Satan knows this and it's why the intention to plant churches is a source of such opposition and contention. What seems to be a clear mandate from Jesus has become the source of such discussion and trouble amongst christians and churches.

In my experience, church members can pray, share the gospel and even start to make disciples in some small ways but if they try to do anything more than that then they will be called into discussions with their leaders. Disciples of Jesus everywhere are too afraid or lack the skills to know how to do the most basic things that Jesus has commanded them to do, make disciples and plant churches. My dream is to see every disciple of Jesus making more disciples, planting churches and teaching them to do likewise. Yet I think this would be most church leaders' worst nightmare. It would become an out of control movement and leaders would be forced to their knees in prayer as the work grows at such a quick and exponential rate.

Bring it on Lord.

The leaders of a movement like this would have to be people of vision and faith who are willing and able to mobilise those around them to become the next generation of leaders who pass on the teachings and ways of Christ to more people. Instead of constantly mollycoddling spiritually immature believers who need constant feeding, leaders would be raising spiritual sons and daughters who learn to feed themselves and become leaders who are able to teach others.

Jesus is continually giving these kind of leaders to the church (apostles and prophets) but there's no room for them in the church management programme so they are forced to go elsewhere and the status quo remains safe and sound.

Why are church leaders everywhere not training all their people to make disciples and plant churches? Is it because pastors and teachers are at the helm of the boat rather than apostles and prophets? Has the mission become about serving and meeting the needs of church members rather than reaching the ends of the earth with the gospel? The church of Jesus Christ doesn't grow by bringing in more effective church managers. It grows as every member builds on the foundation of the apostles and prophets and upon the cornerstone of Jesus Christ himself,

"Together, we are His house, built on the foundation of the

apostles and the prophets. And the cornerstone is Christ Jesus himself."
Ephesians 2:20

The goal of most churches seems to be to eliminate risk rather than to grow faith. Instead of growing as white hot passionate followers of Jesus together, churches become spiritual graveyards. I fear that Jesus will spit these churches out of his mouth,

"I know all the things you do, that you are neither hot nor cold. I wish that you were one or the other! But since you are lukewarm water, neither hot nor cold, I will spit you out of my mouth"
Revelation 3:15-17

It's interesting that most of the New Testament is a collection of spirit-inspired messages to different churches that had grown out of the harvest.

When John was on the Island of Patmos he received messages for the 7 churches in Ephesus, Smyrna, Pergamum, Thyatira, Sardis, Philadelphia and Laodicea (Revelation 1-4)

There are 17 letters written directly to churches (Romans, 1 and 2 Corinthians, Galatians, Ephesians, Philippians, Colossians, 1 and 2 Thessalonians, Philemon, 1 and 2 Peter, 1,2 and 3 John, Jude and Revelation)

And 11 letters written to or for workers or leaders directly involved with planting and multiplying churches (Matthew, Mark, Luke, John, Acts, 1 and 2 Timothy, Titus, Hebrews, James and Jude)

The entire New Testament is about how Jesus is glorified through the planting and multiplication of churches amongst people everywhere. And we are invited to finish the story. There is a wealth of revelation and inspiration in the scriptures to help you complete the work ahead of you so you too can conclude that the door of faith has been opened to the gentiles.

God desires a people who grow as His disciples together and who are built together like a well fitting house. God doesn't address a random bunch of disciples and misfits. He addresses the church in that city or His holy people in this region. It is a wonderful and yet sobering responsibility to be called the church of the living God and we must train new disciples to understand and live out these truths.

People don't just become disciples overnight. They need to be trained and taught how to obey Jesus. And it's the same with planting churches. There are some key milestones along the way (like when a whole household is baptized or filled with the Spirit) but generally it takes a lot of hard work, prayer and love to help a group of people become a church. It's relatively easy for them to call themselves a church once they've been baptized and start to meet together. It's a different matter altogether though to help them actually live and function as the church of the living God.

And that's what this chapter is about.

Strengthen

"After preaching the Good News in Derbe and making many disciples, Paul and Barnabas returned to Lystra, Iconium, and Antioch of Pisidia, where they strengthened the believers. They

encouraged them to continue in the faith, reminding them that we
must suffer many hardships to enter the Kingdom of God"
Acts 14:21-23

There are a lot of times in the work where you need to shift gears.
Seasons change and the mission field needs different things at
different times. The apostolic and prophetic gifts recognize these
times where shifts are needed and help the body to act accordingly.

A shift is needed when prayer must turn into preaching.

A shift is needed to make sure that preaching leads to finding
people of peace.

And a shift is needed when you find faithful disciples and they
need strengthening.

As an apostolic worker I move quickly when trying to find good
soil and then slow down when I find it. I believe Jesus has shown
me through the scriptures how he invested his time in people based
on their faithfulness, obedience and willingness to sacrifice. For 3
years He engaged crowds, searched for faithful men and women
and then poured himself into them. It was the parable of the soil in
action. Those who Jesus invested himself in literally turned the
world upside down (apart from Judas!) I see this same pattern in
the lives of workers throughout the New Testament. I've not
always found it easy but I've tried to develope the same pattern in
my life.

Making disciples and planting churches is all about investing your
prayer, time and resources in a strategic way. I spend a little
amount of time with people and test where their faith and
willingness to sacrifice is really at. I then give myself to them in
proportion to that. Those who, over time, become faithful brothers

and sisters are literally in and out of our home on a daily basis, but we don't open our hearts and homes to everyone,

"Because of the miraculous signs Jesus did in Jerusalem at the Passover celebration, many began to trust in him. But Jesus didn't trust them, because he knew all about people. No one needed to tell him about human nature, for he knew what was in each person's heart." (In another version it says that 'Jesus did not give himself to them')
John 2:23-25

Modern day churchianity though is firmly in the hands of the shepherds and pastors and teaches people to do the opposite.

You're considered mean if you don't pour love out to people unconditionally and the common belief is that the world is going to be won through love. Whilst this is partly true, it is far from the whole truth. Many claim that Jesus treated everyone equally when he actually didn't. People find freedom through obedience to Jesus and need love and help to continue when obeying Him gets hard through suffering and persecution. Giving out cheap love to people though will help no-one and certainly won't help to see Jesus' work finished.

I see Jesus sifting through the crowds to find His true spiritual family who would obey Him and give their lives to His cause. When he found them He then literally lived with them and shared His whole life with them. Once he found people like this he then trained them in the ways of the kingdom and strengthened them as they faced obstacles within themselves and persecution from others. I see Jesus deeply loving and strengthening 'his guys' as they tried to fight through on their mission together,

"As Jesus was speaking to the crowd, his mother and brothers stood outside, asking to speak to him. Someone told Jesus, "Your mother and your brothers are standing outside, and they want to speak to you." Jesus asked, "Who is my mother? Who are my brothers?" Then he pointed to his disciples and said, "Look, these are my mother and brothers. Anyone who does the will of my Father in heaven is my brother and sister and mother!"
Matthew 12:46-50

In the work we are doing there are disciples and churches that are learning to obey Jesus through suffering. Many of them face daily ridicule from their friends and families and satanic spiritual attack as they bring the light to some of the most darkest places in our region. Their biggest need is to continue and persevere in Christ and the strength needed to do this.

When you hit this stage in the work it could be time to harness the power of the more pastoral members of your team and network. You'll also find that the evangelists on your team tend to start finding other things to do so you'll need to pray about where next to invade and then point them in the direction of the next town or region.

A lot of wisdom is needed when growing and multiplying a movement and knowing when certain people or gifts are needed. I believe every disciple of Jesus is personally commanded by Jesus to make more disciples, but I also believe that each of us has gifts to use and equip the rest of the body for ministry.

As I've reflected on our journey so far I regret the many times I've tried to make fast people do slow work and slow people do fast work. Whilst I think it's good for people to experience situations that take them out of their comfort zones, there's also wisdom that is needed!

Let me explain.

Having prayed about where to go, you then need fast people who'll go and preach the gospel and find people of peace straight away. It's not a time to discuss or have inclusive conversations about everything. People need to be set free and there is an urgency.

However once people have been set free and a new church has been established, the work becomes very slow and becomes all about sharing everything and making sure no-one gets left behind.

Go fast people tend to be good at getting new disciples on track (Repent, be baptized etc) and seeing people initially set free or healed. They see the value in casting vision and setting a high bar for the new disciples. But they are not so good at developing a deep sense of community and belonging amongst the church that is being planted. Go fast people can sometimes come across as unloving and harsh.

Go slow people, on the other hand are good at fostering community and a sense of belonging because they involve everyone equally and the most important thing to them is love and consideration for everyone. Go slow people are not so good at starting churches though or setting people free. They sometimes struggle to cast vision as really their passion is to make sure the people are OK and they are very sensitive and concerned not to overburden people.

In reality the work needs everyone but it can be damaging to have people who are not aware of their blindspots doing the wrong jobs at the wrong time. I remember one time where I had left a new group in the hands of some people on the team who were very pastoral. I was keen to see the work multiplying so I although my heart was right, with hindsight it was a bit foolish. This new group was made up of 3 guys who all struggled with alcohol and one of them had just been baptized. We'd found them by door knocking and searching specifically for a household of peace. The second time we visited the house, the owner and person of peace said, "I want my home to be a place of peace for people". He had no idea about Matthew 10 or Luke 10 so we were quite amazed that he would say this. After visiting this community for some time I felt I'd done what I needed to do and handed the ongoing development of that group (I'd hesitate to call it a church at that stage of it's development) over to a couple of team mates. I'd worked quite hard to lay down a misional vision in the group and was confidant that these guys knew their calling from Jesus was to gather others in their area who also needed salvation and freedom. I personally stopped going to that house and got reports back each week from the team. I expected the team to share honestly how it was going and to report back on any challenges or obstacles they were hitting. I presumed the team were thinking apostolically and it was a big mistake because they weren't.

They were thinking pastorally and were go slow people!

After a couple of months the team suddenly announced that they were no longer going to the house. I asked why they had stopped and they gave 3 reasons:

1) The main guy doesn't seem to want to give up drinking alcohol
2) There were others who kept coming along making it hard to focus on the main guy and his problems
3) The gatherings are chaotic

I digged a bit deeper and asked a few questions. To me it looked like the household were still very much open but the team were not approaching the opportunity in the way I would. The team lacked the boldness and authority to set the whole household free from the idol of drink and to establish any kind of pattern for gathering together. The team seemed to want to get the main person of peace fully healed and mature before asking him or expecting him to do anything with anyone else. And to be quite frank the team lacked the passion or anguish for these guys which I felt towards them. I learned pretty fast from that mistake. Don't entrust the work into the wrong hands at the wrong time. No wonder the church was not being established in that house! Ultimately it was a reflection on how poorly I had trained the team I was working with at that time as they lacked the mindset and heart attitude needed to do that work.

I've also made the opposite mistake where I have tried to make go fast people hang around in gatherings and in situations that have almost killed them!

As a team we felt to focus on a particular town. After 4 weeks of go fast work (praying, preaching on the street, healings and deliverances etc) we had a list of potential people of peace to build with. In my mind the season had shifted, we no longer needed to find any more people but instead needed to sift through these potential people of peace who appeared open to the gospel and gathering others.

After this shift had happened we'd go to this town each week and I'd ask all the team what they felt God was wanting them to do that day. Most of them said that the work needed was to stay with the people of peace we'd found like Jesus said in Matthew 10 and Luke 10. However one guy said the same thing every week, "I feel to go and preach in the town centre and heal people" To be honest it started to bother me because he was the only one not hearing the message to start building with the people we'd already found.

To me it seemed foolish that we would keep going and preaching in a town when we'd already found potential team mates and co-workers to plant a church with. What I began to understand though is that my go-fast friend was just being true to his gifting and part in the body. We spent a few hours together talking about this and the importance of seeing our blindspots when working together as a team. But since then I have deliberately tried to pour petrol on his evangelistic gift and to focus him on opening up new areas. He sometimes comes with us when we are going to train and strengthen disciples and churches and helps to equip them in the area of sharing the Gospel with others. If you put go-fast people in go-slow situations it's a recipe for disaster unless they know their blindspots and are mature enough to recognize the opportunity for them to train and equip others, which is, of course, much slower than doing the work yourself!

That's why Jesus' instructions for his go fast team in Matthew 10 and Luke 10 are so powerful because it means they are searching for the go slow people of peace within the harvest. The go-fast people bring their parts and the community continues to grow as the go-slow people do their part,

"Because of God's grace to me, I have laid the foundation like an expert builder. Now others are building on it. But whoever is building on this foundation must be very careful."
1 Corinthians 3:10

Strengthening the believers is a go slow work and involves care and patience. It is still exciting but in a different way to the excitement you experience when people are healed or baptized. The work of strengthening the disciples and churches involves seeing deep rooted thought patterns and habits being broken and replaced with the mind of Christ. It involves the deep joy of seeing these new disciples persevering through many trials and beginning to grow in their giftings and calling. A lot of relational issues begin to surface and at times it feels like the devil is trying to do anything he can to try and bring division and disunity in the churches. And he is. But our confidence lies in Jesus' ability to build His church so we can trust Him,

"Now I say to you that you are Peter (which means rock), and upon this rock I will build my church, and all the powers of hell will not conquer it."
Matthew 16:18

Seeing believers and churches strengthened is like the joy a Father experiences as he watches his children grow up and learn to work together in unity,

"And you know that we treated each of you as a Father treats his own children. We pleaded with you, encouraged you, and urged you to live your lives in a way that God would consider worthy."
1 Thessalonians 2:12

It's important to remember who was needing to be strengthened in the scriptures. It wasn't self-indulgent church attenders who were disappointed with life and unhappy because Jesus wasn't blessing them with happy and peaceful lives! And the strengthening message wasn't Jeremiah 29:11 or some other pithy verse about God having a good plan for your life. We need a wake up call.

Most of the disciples in the scriptures faced extreme hardship or death for the sake of the gospel so it's nothing like what happens in most churches today. Here's the message which will strengthen true disciples of Jesus,

"They encouraged them to continue in the faith, reminding them that we must suffer many hardships to enter the Kingdom of God."
Acts 14:22

For most so called Christians in Europe today this scripture probably means nothing. But for those who have committed to follow Jesus no matter what the cost or hardship, they are strengthening and comforting words!

When we first started to train church planters a number of years ago, the training looked very different to what it is now. There have been lots of changes and improvements made along the way as we have monitored the effectiveness of what we are doing. One of the biggest changes is that we would now include much more about how to prepare for, and endure, suffering and hardship.

When we started out we gave people at the training lots of tools and vision. They went away inspired and knowing what to do. However when we contacted them a month after the training we heard the same thing over and over again. After an enthusiastic start these budding church planters faced hardships, suffering and conflicts which had led them to stop the work. As is our habit, we went to God in prayer about this and searched the scriptures. He showed us how Jesus talked about suffering and hardships all the time and prepared His disciples that this was normal in the Kingdom of God. So we started to do this more as well in our trainings.

We noticed a difference.

When we contacted people after the trainings, there were still some people who gave up when they hit hardships, but an increasing percentage of those trained were continuing despite these challenges and trials. We continued to include more of this in our trainings so that the work would continue despite challenges at home, persecution from church leaders or sickness.

We're training people to be disciples of Jesus and to enter the most brutal battle of all time. The devil will do anything He can to try and stop you from obeying Jesus and spreading the kingdom of heaven here on earth. We must prepare our disciples to know what to do in the spiritual battle and strengthen them to continue in the faith when attacks come,

"Finally, when we could stand it no longer, we decided to stay alone in Athens, and we sent Timothy to visit you. He is our brother and God's co-worker in proclaiming the Good News of Christ. We sent him to strengthen you, to encourage you in your faith, and to keep you from being shaken by the troubles you were going through. But you know that we are destined for such troubles. Even while we were with you, we warned you that troubles would soon come—and they did, as you well know."
1 Thessalonians 3:1-5

Love and Devotion

As we've sought to strengthen and build churches and spiritual families we have consistently seen that love is key. When you try and gather any group of people together it's not long before personal differences and opinions can threaten to tear things apart. Strengthening believers and churches is about helping people to navigate through differences, offences and challenges together, and this can only happen if people choose the way of love,

"Love is patient and kind. Love is not jealous or boastful or proud or rude. It does not demand its own way. It is not irritable, and it keeps no record of being wronged. It does not rejoice about injustice but rejoices whenever the truth wins out. Love never gives up, never loses faith, is always hopeful, and endures through every circumstance"
1 Corinthians 11:4-8

You cannot be a disciple of Jesus and not grow in love and community with others. You cannot separate spiritual maturity from loving and serving our spiritual brothers and sisters who often wind us up and cause offence. So as we seek to take disciples of Jesus further along the path of maturity, strengthening the churches is critical to ongoing growth. Being part of a church (a community of people that acts and functions as a spiritual family on mission) is how you grow as a disciple of Jesus and where the measure of your faith is truly revealed. We cannot love God but hate others,

"If someone says, "I love God" but hates a fellow believer, that person is a liar; for if we don't love people we can see, how can we love God, whom we cannot see? And he has given us this command: Those who love God must also love their fellow believers"
1 John 4:20-21

The more I follow Jesus the more I realise that true love for Him isn't really about raising your hands and closing your eyes to your favourite worship song. It is opening your home and the contents of your fridge to your brothers and sisters in need, often when you have very little yourself and don't feel like doing it.

Strengthening believers is all about helping others to continue obeying Jesus despite the cost and suffering to themselves.

Let me share an honest story about how I was strengthened to continue in the faith.

We live as missionaries and have learned to trust God for our financial needs. We receive support from those who are moved to be generous towards us and who believe in our passion and vision. One day I received an email from a lady who was blessing us financially each month. She was informing me that her circumstances had changed and she could no longer commit to supporting us each month. On top of that she also felt she needed to share her thoughts with me about what we were doing. In her opinion we were wrong to be trying to plant new churches and we should instead be taking new disciples to one of the existing churches in the area.

I receive criticism from other believers on a fairly regular basis. Sometimes the criticism is helpful, normally it isn't. I have developed a fairly tough skin over the years and try to respond to people's comments and attacks with the grace that Jesus responded with when he was accused and attacked. However on this occasion the criticism really affected me.

On top of this loss of income and criticism we were also having a challenging time at home and in our marriage. I was not looking forward to sharing with Cath my wife that we were losing our biggest financial supporter at a time when it felt like we needed it the most. I had one of those afternoons that you have now and again and to be honest I wanted to hide away, have a cry and give up.

Thank God for brothers in Christ though. I was with one of my co-workers that day and I shared this burden with him and we prayed together. I felt strengthened and pulled myself together. We're obeying God's heavenly call on our lives I thought, so God will look after us.

We set out into the mission field that afternoon and although the situation was still in the back of my mind, I was using it to inspire me to be even bolder and courageous for Jesus. One of the most important lessons I have learned is that often we receive these kind of attacks or discouragements just before a big breakthrough. From what I can see in the Bible, true disciples of Jesus become even more determined and bolder in the face of opposition and challenges.

That afternoon and evening we gathered for the first time with a group in Glastonbury. It was a powerful time of fellowship where 4 of the men publicly confessed their sin and repented. Tears were flowing and it was one of the most memorable times of real fellowship I have ever experienced. (Two of the men were baptized a week later) As the evening went on I sat there feeling rather overcome at what God was doing and then these new disciples started encouraging me and telling me to keep doing what I was doing so that more sinners could be saved and more churches could be planted with these people.

I thanked them for their encouragement and shared with them how I'd felt like giving up that afternoon but God had helped me to continue in the faith. Logically I knew that the criticism I had received was unfounded and God would continue to meet all our financial needs. But sometimes logic goes out of the window and you just need to push through trials and tribulations and continue in the faith when you don't feel like it. My troubles are nothing compared to what some believers around the world have to endure and it's certainly nothing compared to what Jesus did for us,

"Think back on those early days when you first learned about Christ. Remember how you remained faithful even though it meant terrible suffering. Sometimes you were exposed to public ridicule and were beaten, and sometimes you helped others who were suffering the same things. You suffered along with those who were thrown into jail, and when all you owned was taken from you, you accepted it with joy. You knew there were better things waiting for you that will last forever. So do not throw away this confident trust in the Lord. Remember the great reward it

brings you! Patient endurance is what you need now, so that you will continue to do God's will. Then you will receive all that He has promised"
Hebrews 10:32-37

When I read how believers in the scriptures and also other servants of Jesus in history patiently endured all things for the sake of the Gospel I feel deeply ashamed. May God help us to continue in the faith and to teach others to do the same instead of shrinking back when things become hard.

Even Jesus, the son of God himself, had to learn to obey His Father through suffering so why should we not have to follow the same path,

"Even though Jesus was God's Son, he learned obedience from the things he suffered."
Hebrews 5:8

As people mature and develope as disciples of Jesus Christ they will inevitably face hardships and suffering and we must prepare and warn them about this. Strengthening the believers is such a critical part of the work but it must come at the right time. Trying to strengthen or pour love into people before they've even shown any proveness as a disciple or demonstrated any sacrifice for the gospel lowers the bar and gives people the false encouragement that Jesus isn't really bothered if we obey Him or not. Another thing is that Jesus often deliberately lead his disciples into hardships and challenges to grow their faith and obedience but we will look at this in the next chapter. Instead of rescuing new believers from any hardships or suffering or trying to shield churches from any risk or challenge, it's actually better to strengthen them to continue obeying Jesus in the face of them.

Paul's goal was to present all people perfect and mature in Christ
Jesus. As we know, he didn't just do evangelism,

"So we tell others about Christ, warning everyone and teaching
everyone with all wisdom God has given us. We want to present
them to God, perfect in their relationship to Christ. That's why I
work and struggle so hard, depending on Christ's mighty power
that works within me."
Colossians 1:28-29

Interestingly I had a call this morning from an old friend. He is
someone who I knew a few years ago and we used to spend many
hours praying and wrestling with the whole theme of disciple
making and church planting. We haven't been in contact for a few
years but he phoned me up out of the blue. He is about to become
the leader of the church they are part of and it was on his heart to
call me for a chat. It was great to catch up with this friend who was
now stepping into a position of responsibility amongst the people
he fellowships with. In many ways my friend is already doing this
work amongst the people but it's good when leaders are appointed
and recognized, as we know from the scriptures. As we talked, he
said how he looks out at the people he has been entrusted to care
for and develope and how he sees them as his own children. He
shared how, like being a parent, making disciples often involves
cleaning up crap and picking up your children after they've hurt
themselves. But a good parent is one who gives an appropriate
level of care based on a child's age and development. New
disciples and churches are like children, just as my friend
explained. And this is how Paul viewed the churches he planted,

"Oh, my dear children! I feel as if I'm going through labor pains
for you again, and they will continue until Christ is fully
developed in your lives."
Galatians 4:19

I've known lots of people who've tried to make disciples and plant churches in the harvest. But they've given up when it has got hard or when there seems to be no visible results. So few people seem to continue in the faith when there are challenges. Where are the people with a deep calling to the harvest and a deep care for the disciples and churches that Jesus will grow through their work? It isn't pleasant and often it isn't enjoyable. Most of the time strengthening the disciples and churches we are responsible for is, I imagine, like being in labor pains.

If you're an accidental apostle like me then you're going to need some supernatural patience and endurance to help your disciples and churches mature and develop into the fullness of Christ and you'll need to build a team of Timothys who share in your care for the people,

"I have no-one else like Timothy, who genuinely cares about your welfare. All the others care only for themselves and not for what matters to Jesus Christ."
Philippians 2:20-22

Most of the New Testament is an appeal to believers to live according to the example Christ has given us and to put away the old ways which are contrary to life in the kingdom. We need God's strength ourselves as we seek to help others mature and put away childish ways,

"When I was a child, I spoke and thought and reasoned as a child. But when I grew up, I put away childish things."
1 Corinthians 13:11

As the team in our region sought God about how to develop and strengthen the believers and churches in the work we were doing,

He spoke to us. Actually he reminded us of a passage that was very familiar to us,

"All the believers devoted themselves to the apostle's teaching, and to fellowship, and to sharing in meals (including the Lord's supper) and to prayer"
Acts 2:42

We felt we needed to teach the disciples and churches to be devoted to these 4 crucial ingredients. We asked ourselves what it would look like for people in our movement to be devoted to prayer, fellowship, apostles teaching and sharing meals and the lord's supper. And this is how we tried to do it.

Devoted to prayer

It's easy to forget about the journey Jesus has brought us on. When we began to look at the theme of prayer I thought a lot about what we had learned about prayer in the early stages of our work. At the time you rarely see the importance of the lessons that the Father is teaching you but you can look back and see how God's hand was guiding and shaping all things.

We began to realise again that you can only teach others what you have learned to do yourself. This is both a sobering and exciting thing. It's sobering because it turns discipleship into a dynamic relational work where it's impossible to fake things. If you commit yourself to making disciples instead of entertaining crowds then there's no pulpit or ten point teaching series to hide behind. But it's also exciting as it means the emphasis becomes about passing on what you know. And how much do you need to know to be able to pass something on? That's right, only one thing. It's liberating to know that making disciples is rooted in obedience to Jesus, not how intelligent you are. I cannot emphasise enough how many times I have met people who have a genuine desire to be followers of Jesus but believe they cannot because they don't know enough. It's one of the first lies I dismantle and instead I help people to see that making disciples is simply obeying Jesus and passing on what you know to others who willing to do the same,

"You have heard me teach things that have been confirmed by many reliable witnesses. Now teach these truths to other trustworthy people who will be able to pass them onto others."
2 Timothy 2:2

A lot of believers often have great concerns about accountability in the kind of church planting work we are doing. But I can sincerely say that the degree of godly, loving accountability we experience in our network is deeper than I have experienced in any church I have been a part of. Personally, I lead through the example of my life and this can be quite scary as it means I don't call people to account from the safety of a pulpit or stage, I can only appeal to them through the scriptures and the example of my life. My ability or authority is directly related to the depth to which I submit to Jesus and His work in my own life. Most of my 'work' is done around tables, eating with people and answering hard questions and concerns. Often it feels like there is no-where to hide as any personal or family challenges are on show for all to see. But we wouldn't have it any other way and a lot of those we are discipling have shared how encouraging it is to them to see that me and my wife are not perfect but need Jesus to help us just as much as anyone else.

So when thinking about how we could teach our disciples and churches to be devoted to prayer, I had to face the real question which is "how devoted am I to prayer?" In the same way that our biological children inherit our natural DNA and this informs their characteristics, our spiritual children and disciples inherit our spiritual DNA. It has often been said that discipleship is more 'caught' than 'taught' and I think I would agree with that.

After talking to Jesus about the matter I got some of the team together and I asked everyone the question, "what would it look like for us all to be devoted to prayer"? There was a whole range of responses, ranging from personal prayer to corporate prayer for the work.

One of the things I am continually learning is that every situation is an opportunity for disciple making. We'll look more at this in the next chapter (appoint leaders), but I am realizing more and more that the important opportunities to teach people to obey Jesus happen through sharing life with them, not really through delivering a sermon once a week. Jesus taught on the job (or in the boat) and so I try and look for ways to model and teach how to walk in the Spirit and be a disciple of Jesus 24/7.

I'm also a great believer that the scriptures are more than able to teach and guide people. We can either believe in the scriptures or not. It's our choice,

"All scripture is inspired by God and is useful to teach us what is true and to make us realise what is wrong in our lives. It corrects us when we are wrong and teaches us to do what is right. God uses it to prepare and equip his people to do every good work."
2 Timothy 3:16-17

So through prayer and discussion we decided to all look at the book of Ephesians to see what we could learn and put into practice around the theme of prayer.

Not only would it help the disciples and churches to grow in their devotion to prayer, but it would also develop a deepening reliance on the scriptures!

So for a whole month we encouraged the team and churches to chew on the book of Ephesians and to ask themselves, "what can I learn about prayer?" Whenever anyone gathered it would be the topic of discussion and I (along with a few others who are not afraid to ask hard questions) constantly tried to move the conversation towards practical application and action.

Why don't you try it for yourselves? Read Paul's letter to the Ephesians and ask yourself, "what can I learn about prayer?"

We found it very interesting to see all the things that Paul said he was praying for. For some on the team (including me) it was very helpful to focus our devotion to prayer more on the development and growth of those we are discipling and training,

"I also pray that you will understand the incredible greatness of God's power for us who believe in Him."
Ephesians 1:19

If you're seeing the need to strengthen the disciples and churches you are working with then I'd suggest you turn to the scriptures and to prayer and do whatever God shows you.

As everyone committed to read the scriptures and pray every day we saw people developing as disciples of Jesus. We also started to develope 3 areas of corporate prayer into the work,

1) House of prayer

A once a month meeting specifically for prayer into any issues or strongholds over certain people, churches or areas. Any spiritual intelligence was then shared with those working on the ground. We found that without this strong prayer, often combined with fasting, those working on the ground were often banging their heads against a brick wall. Our house of prayer gives specific direction on what towns or villages to focus on, what issues or areas to teach on in the churches and what are the most urgent tasks to be focusing on in that season.

2) Day of prayer and fasting

As a team we committed to fast and pray every Monday. We invited everyone involved to join us and some of the new disciples did. We encouraged everyone to share anything that God showed them.

3) All night prayer

We started to pray all night. Often we'd gather in a home for the first part of the evening and then go out on location as God leads.

There were some other things that God showed us about prayer that we taught and modelled. But God also showed us to use some stories to teach about prayer.

What prayer isn't

"As evening came, Jesus said to his disciples, "Let's cross to the other side of the lake." So they took Jesus in the boat and started out, leaving the crowds behind (although other boats followed). But soon a fierce storm came up. High waves were breaking into the boat, and it began to fill with water. Jesus was sleeping at the back of the boat with his head on a cushion. The disciples woke him up, shouting, "Teacher, don't you care that we're going to drown?" When Jesus woke up, he rebuked the wind and said to the waves, "Silence! Be still!" Suddenly the wind stopped, and there was a great calm. Then he asked them, "Why are you afraid? Do you still have no faith?" The disciples were absolutely terrified. "Who is this man?" they asked each other. "Even the wind and waves obey him!"
Mark 4:35-41

This is a great example of what prayer *isn't*!

Having received Jesus' instruction to cross to the other side of the lake the Disciples set out with Jesus in the boat. A fierce storm then whips up and the disciples (some of whom were professional fishermen) start to fear for their lives. You have to feel some sympathy for the disciples. The waves were huge and the boat began to fill with water. It was all hands on deck. They were so fearful they shouted at Jesus,

"Teacher don't you care that we're going to drown?"
Mark 4:38

When I was growing up I was taught that if I had a problem then I can ask Jesus for help just as the disciples did. After all that is what prayer is right, asking Jesus to help you when you have problems or challenges. They felt like they were doing to die so they cried out to Jesus.

Why then in this story does Jesus rebuke them for not having any faith?

I want to suggest that Jesus was looking for a faith in the disciples that went beyond just worrying about personal comfort and safety and which enabled them to take authority over the creation around them. Instead of Jesus saying "Well done crew for waking me up and casting your cares on me" he told them off for having no faith.

Prayer isn't a last resort when we're panicking and anxious words thrown out to Jesus are no substitute for faith, Throughout the Old Testament, God's people are encouraged to meditate on God's word day and night, I wonder what this story could have looked like if the disciples had meditated on Jesus word to cross to the other side of the lake? Could they have commanded the wind and waves to be still themselves as they continued in the faith and obeyed Jesus' word to cross to the other side of the lake?

Being devoted to prayer can look like rising early, going up mountains and gathering to pray with others all night. But it can also look like being asleep in a boat while storms batter everything around you.

And what's interesting is that as we read on after this story we see the reason why they faced the fierce storm and why their mission was to cross to the other side of the lake in the first place.

But I'll let you work that out.

What prayer is

"Jesus responded, "Didn't I tell you that you would see God's glory if you believe?" So they rolled the stone aside. Then Jesus looked up to heaven and said, "Father, thank you for hearing me. You always hear me, but I said it out loud for the sake of all these people standing here, so that they will believe you sent me." Then Jesus shouted, "Lazarus, come out!" And the dead man came out, his hands and feet bound in graveclothes, his face wrapped in a headcloth. Jesus told them, "Unwrap him and let him go!"
John 11:40-45

In this story we see how Jesus' devotion to prayer is very different from the disciples lack of faith in the boat!

In John 11 Jesus was also sailing through a storm, but this time the waves were the people around him and all the emotion and drama surrounding the death of Lazarus.

The best thing would be for you to read John 11 yourself so God can show you what you need to see. But here's what we needed to see.

As we know Jesus lived a life of prayer where he communicated constantly with His Father. Much of this was in private. Because Jesus was devoted to prayer He annoyed lots of people. He didn't walk according to public opinion or jump when his friends and family said jump. God the Father had showed Jesus through prayer what He was going to do in the situation with Lazarus and that determined Jesus' steps. To me, the great thing here is not so much that Jesus raised Lazarus from the dead (although that is amazing!), but rather that Jesus was able to see what God wanted to do and this enabled Him to walk in a completely different world to everyone else around him. While everyone else around him was losing their head and running around like headless chickens, Jesus was able to see clearly what God's purpose was is.

Jesus sailed through the storm and called Lazarus out of the tomb. Being devoted to prayer will help us to do the same.

Developing prayer habits

As a sportsman I don't need to be taught about the value of training your body. If you want your body to perform better then you need to train it consistently over a period of time. Often this involves creating new habits. People don't become professional atheletes overnight, it takes hard work and disciplined training habits.

A habit is *"an acquired behavior pattern regulary followed until it has become almost involuntary."*

Being a disciple of Jesus takes hard work and involves changing your habits! In my experience, Jesus has often asked me to do things that I feel unable to do. In these times I have had to change my prayer habits to reflect the change in mindset or outward behavior that I believe Jesus is requiring from me. Jesus spoke about this when He rebuked the Pharisees,

"What sorrow awaits you teachers of religious law and you Pharisees. Hypocrites! For you are so careful to clean the outside of the cup and the dish, but inside you are filthy – full of greed and self indulgence! You blind Pharisee! First wash the inside of the cup and the dish, and then the outside will become clean too" Matthew 23:25-27

When faced with new seasons and challenges in my life I have often set alarms on my phone to remind me to spend a few minutes in focused prayer. It's amazing how changing your prayer habits changes your heart and mindset and this in turn changes your behavior and practice! Here's a few examples.

When God was calling me to do the work of an evangelist and to preach the Gospel across the towns and villages in our region I realized I was fearful of people. I turned to the scriptures and saw how the disciples were also fearful at times and their response was to pray for boldness. (see Acts 4:29) So I set my phone alarm to go off first thing in the morning, at lunchtime and last thing in night. Every time the alarm went off I prayed, *"Lord give me boldness to preach the Gospel and help me to find people of peace"* Everyone says to me nowadays that it is easier for me to share the Gospel boldly because I am not fearful of people like they are. The truth is though that I was as fearful as they are, I just decided to do something about it for the sake of the Gospel!

When we were reading the book of Ephesians as a network God really challenged me about how devoted I was to praying for the development of the disciples and churches in our care. The following verses seemed to jump out to me when I read them,

"When I think of all this, I fall to my knees and pray to the Father, the creator of everything in heaven and on earth. I pray that from His glorious, unlimited resources He will empower you with inner strength through His Spirit."
Ephesians 3:17

I had to confess that my first reaction in any situation is rarely to fall to my knees and pray. Normally my first reaction is to jump to action or to solve the problem in front of me the best way I can. Although action is good, it needs to be Spirit led action that is based on His wisdom and not mine. So God showed me that I had to change a deep rooted habit in my life. Instead of jumping to action and trusting in my own ability or strength to help people or solve problems I needed to be more devoted to pray. So because the verses were from Ephesians 3:15 I decided to set my phone alarm to go off every day at 3:15pm and I would pray for all the disciples in our region and for the team that God would empower them all with inner strength through His Spirit. Because I am a disciple maker I also trained those I am discipling to set their alarms and to pray for their people as well. At our monthly team gathering I helped everyone write down their people list so they could pray for them and begin looking for ways to disciple and gather them.

God recently seems to be opening some doors into the Muslim world so we are stepping through them as a team! We were recently given the security code for a mosque in our area and invited to visit whenever we want. This felt like a significant gesture and as we visited one time I saw the Muslim times of prayer written up on the wall. We worked out that at 1:12pm (UK time) Muslims around the world would all be praying. So I decided to set my phone alarm for 1:12pm each day and pray, "Lord give us spiritual sons and Timothy's in the Muslim world who we can train to multiply disciples, churches and leaders" Sometimes I kneel and pray at this time.

Devoted to fellowship

When we started to follow Jesus into the harvest to plant churches there, we received a lot of criticism. At the time, some of it was deeply painful. With hindsight though, it taught us to wrestle with the scriptures and in prayer so that our convictions and beliefs were robust enough to face upto even the harshest of critics.

Some of my closest friends called me the "anti-church" because we'd made the decision to stop attending the church we had been part of on a Sunday morning. Our whole reason for doing this wasn't because we were upset or dissatisfied with the church, it was because we felt called to model something different for people who were not yet God's people.

I seem to have this same conversation with people almost every week who are considering leaving this church or that church. They see us as people who have made this step and reach out to us for advice. So many believers are living in a world where their decisions are based on whether their needs are being met, how they feel a church is meeting their spiritual requirements and how gifted or loving they feel their leaders are. As I'm sure you understand from this book, all this has nothing to do with the reason why we were sent out of our church. It has nothing to do with whether our needs are being met. It's about seeing churches planted and multiplying in the harvest. People come to us looking for some kind of affirmation that it is ok for them to jump ship whenever things get a bit rough but they don't normally get the advice they want to hear. If people come to me talking about leaving a church or wanting to get back to how church was like in the New Testament (a common phrase I hear) then I encourage them to gather some new people in their home or wherever they can and then to let me know how it goes.

I've spent too many hours of my life talking with disappointed christians who quite frankly should be thinking about who they are discipling rather than moaning about how their church isn't perfect!

Like anyone who challenges the status quo or has a pioneering spirit we were (and still are) labelled as renegades, loose canons and we are constantly sent this well known verse,

"And let us not neglect our meeting together, as some people do..."
Hebrews 10:25

Things were already challenging because we were pioneering, but we could do without the constant stream of criticism from our brothers and sisters. In the early days we would gather as a family and to be honest we had to learn how to even disciple our own children. And I'm not sure we have figured it out yet. Over time though God has added people to our fellowship, but it started at home in our own family. We had to rediscover the lifestyle of discipleship and a way of being church that could multiply in the hands of ordinary people. It's great that believers around us were enjoying fellowship, but how could new people experience this kind of fellowship which would build them up and strengthen them to make disciples of their friends, families and people?

I love the descriptions of the church in the New Testament. There's such life in what was happening,

"A deep sense of awe came over them all, and the apostles performed many miraculous signs and wonders. And all the believers met together in one place and shared everything they had. They sold their property and possessions and shared the money with those in need. They worshipped together at the temple each day, met in homes for the Lord's supper, and shared their meals with great joy and generosity – all the while praising God and enjoying the good will of all the people. And each day the Lord added to their fellowship those who were being saved"
Acts 2:43-47

As we began to think about what it means to be devoted to fellowship, one little verse stood out to me,

"And each day the Lord added to their fellowship those who were being saved."
Acts 2:47

In churchianity, fellowship has come to mean what we do for 2 hours on a Sunday morning and 2 hours on a Wednesday evening. I now see church as being like a family. Imagine what your family would be like if you only saw your kids for 4 hours a week and even then you didn't really talk to them because you were sat in a row, singing with your eyes closed and listening to someone else talk for 40 minutes. As a family we share our lives together. We try and gather every day, and definitely at least once a week. We eat together, rest together and go on adventures together. As a Father I am trying to prepare and train my children for the day they start their own families. We get it wrong a lot of the time and our marriage is far from perfect, but we are trying to have genuine Christ-centred fellowship as a family and with our extended Jesus family.

In this scripture from Acts it says that the Lord added the people who were being saved to *'their fellowship'*. I've come to understand that this means far more than people just joining a church and coming to two weekly meetings.

The believers in Acts were experiencing a way of life that was radically different to everything around them and God was adding people to this daily fellowship every day. It wasn't a model or a thing. It was people living and moving together sacrificially with Jesus at the centre,

"All the believers were united in heart and mind. And they felt that what they owned was not their own, so they shared everything they had. The apostles testified powerfully to the

resurrection of the Lord Jesus, and God's great blessing was
upon them all. There were no needy people among them, because
those who owned land or houses would sell them and bring the
money to the apostles to give to those in need."
Acts 4:32-26

I meet a lot of people and I can tell you that 99.99% are absolutely
sick of church. But they are desperate for fellowship. Instead of our
constant rebranding exercises which change the label on the tin but
don't change the contents, why don't we allow God to cut
everything back to the root so that real life can grow. The world
doesn't want the latest church programmes, it is looking for life.
Let's stop being like the pharisees who focused all their time on
cleaning the outside of the cup and dish but inside they were full of
greed and self indulgence (Matthew 23:25-27) Making disciples
gets to the root of the issues in all of our lives and leads to true
fellowship. If this kind of fellowship we read about in the scriptures
was the fruit of the gospel's work in people's lives then I'd suggest
we need to rethink what we are planting into people. The fruit I see
in people's lives and in my own life doesn't look that great to be
honest. We started to pray about what we would need to plant into
the disciples and churches here in order for this fruit of fellowship
to grow.

We'd looked at the letter of Ephesians to learn about prayer so we
asked Jesus what book we should look at to learn about fellowship.
I was expecting God to ask us to read 1 Corinthians or a book like
that with lots of practical instructions about gathering together.
Jesus knows what His church needs far more and I do though. He
led us all to read the book of Philippians.

So I'd encourage you to read the book of Philippians and ask
yourselves what you can learn about fellowship. I read it myself
personally and made notes around the following questions:

1) What is it saying to me about fellowship?
2) What do I need to do about it?
3) Who can I share this with?

Here are a few things that stood out to us about fellowship.

The attitude of Christ Jesus

"Is there any encouragement from belonging to Christ? Any comfort from his love? Any fellowship together in the Spirit? Are your hearts tender and compassionate? Then make me truly happy by agreeing wholeheartedly with each other, loving one another, and working together with one mind and purpose. Don't be selfish; don't try to impress others. Be humble, thinking of others as better than yourselves. Don't look out only for your own interests, but take an interest in others, too. You must have the same attitude that Christ Jesus had. Though he was God, he did not think of equality with God as something to cling to. Instead, he gave up his divine privileges he took the humble position of a slave and was born as a human being. When he appeared in human form, he humbled himself in obedience to God and died a criminal's death on a cross. Therefore, God elevated him to the place of highest honor and gave him the name above all other names, that at the name of Jesus every knee should bow, in heaven and on earth and under the earth, and every tongue declare that Jesus Christ is Lord, to the glory of God the Father."
Philippians 2:1-12

We looked at this passage from Philippians together when we gathered as a team. It was quite an amazing time.

Some phrases really stood out to us all as we asked God to help us be more devoted to fellowship,

"Is there any encouragement from belonging to Christ?"

"Any comfort from His love?"

"Any fellowship together in the Spirit?"
"Agreeing wholeheartedly with each other"

"loving one another"

"working together with one mind and purpose"

"Don't be selfish"

"Don't try to impress others"

"Be humble, thinking of others as better than yourselves"

"Don't look out only for your own interests but take an interest in others too"

"You must have the same attitude that Christ Jesus had"

"he gave up his divine privileges he took the humble position of a slave"

"Therefore, God elevated him"

The scriptures speak for themselves.

None of this is rocket science of course. It's all there in the scriptures and we just try and respond to what God shows us! If we have any wisdom, it's to rely on God and not ourselves!

After a time of repentance together we briefly looked at how we can practically grow in agreeing with each other, loving one another and working together with one mind and purpose. But all those things seemed to flow naturally after we had gone to the root of the issue and God had challenged us all from His word.

I thought back to times in the past when in my eagerness to get the work done I'd tried to encourage people to love each other and work together but nothing I did seemed to work. Looking back, it was like I was trying to get the outside of the dish and cup clean without cleaning the inside.

Cleaning the inside of the cup is making disciples and teaching them to obey Jesus. It's a lot slower but in the end produces lasting fruit.

You can't just get people to do fellowship, it is the fruit of helping people to be disciples of Jesus and training them to have the same attitude of Christ, who came to be a servant.

I was very challenged about how we were developing a Christ-like attitude in our own lives so one day as a family we sat down together and read this passage from Philippians 2:1-12. I was seeing in my 4 kids that they were getting very good at identifying what they liked to do and what they were interested in. Don't get me wrong, I think it's great for people to know their own minds, but this can soon turn into selfishness. I concluded that maybe they had observed me and Cath doing the same thing, so I felt I needed to try and model another way of living and as usual I looked to the scriptures for help. As we all read the passage these verses seemed to particularly stand out to us all,

"Don't look out only for your own interests, but take an interest in others, too. You must have the same attitude that Christ Jesus had."
Philippians 2:4-6

After we discussed what it was saying and meaning to us all I got a piece of paper and wrote our 6 names on it, Catherine, Ben, Isaac, Hudson, Grace and Elijah. I had a great idea about how we could actually consider the interests of others instead of just talking and praying about it. We went around everyone in the family and wrote down what their interests were. I made sure everyone was listening and attentive to each person and then we committed to trying to help each other to follow their interests instead of just thinking about ourselves. We still have the piece of paper stuck on our kitchen wall, and this is a good reminder to go and have a look at it today to remind myself about the interests of my wife and children.

I've done similar things with our team and it builds a stronger sense of fellowship as people feel that others are taking a genuine interest in them and builds a culture of servanthood and humility. May God help us to do the things that Paul instructs us in his letter to the Philippians,

"Let everyone see that you are considerate in all you do."
Philppians 4:5

Sharing a meal as friends

I was reminded about what God had shown me about fellowship in the book of Revelation. Most of us will know the first part of this verse but until a few years ago I had never heard or read the second part of the verse,

"Look! I stand at the door and knock. If you hear my voice and open the door, I will come in, and we will share a meal together as friends."
Revelation 3:20

Evangelists urge people to open the door to Jesus, but no-one knows what happens afterwards. People are told to be saved but no-one knows how to be a disciple.

What an amazing promise Jesus gives to those who hear his voice and open the door. He says He will come in and they will share a meal together as friends.

Wow.

These words from Jesus have such a massive impact on our understanding of fellowship and how to make disciples. Fellowship and disciple making happens in the context of a meal not a programme or weekly service. It's about sharing lives and food around a table as equals. The God of the universe comes to sit at your table and eat with you. These words sum up the work Jesus did for 3 years. He knocked on doors and ate with those who welcomed him in. There are at least 10 occasions in the Gospels where we see Jesus eating a meal with people and of course act of eating people was central to the church planting training that Jesus gave to his disciples,

"The Lord now chose seventy-two other disciples and sent them ahead in pairs to all the towns and places he planned to visit. These were his instructions to them: "The harvest is great, but the workers are few. So pray to the Lord who is in charge of the

*harvest; ask him to send more workers into his fields. Now go,
and remember that I am sending you out as lambs among wolves.
Don't take any money with you, nor a traveler's bag, nor an
extra pair of sandals. And don't stop to greet anyone on the road.
"Whenever you enter someone's home, first say, 'May God's
peace be on this house.' If those who live there are peaceful, the
blessing will stand; if they are not, the blessing will return to you.
Don't move around from home to home. Stay in one place, eating
and drinking what they provide. Don't hesitate to accept
hospitality, because those who work deserve their pay. "If you
enter a town and it welcomes you, eat whatever is set before you.
Heal the sick, and tell them, 'The Kingdom of God is near you
now.' But if a town refuses to welcome you, go out into its streets
and say, 'We wipe even the dust of your town from our feet to
show that we have abandoned you to your fate. And know this—
the Kingdom of God is near!' I assure you, even wicked Sodom
will be better off than such a town on judgment day."*
Luke 10:1-13

The entire church planting strategy in the New Testament hinged
on finding people of peace who would open their homes and share
meals. Sounds like what Jesus said and did doesn't it? And it
sounds a lot like fellowship.

Jesus said that if we hear his voice and open the door he would
come in and share a meal together with us as friends. So not only
do we get to share a meal with Jesus but we get to do this as His
friends,

*"For God in all his fullness was pleased to live in Christ, and
through him God reconciled everything to himself. He made
peace with everything in heaven and on earth by means of
Christ's blood on the cross. This includes you who were once far
away from God. You were his enemies, separated from him by*

your evil thoughts and actions. Yet now he has reconciled you to
himself through the death of Christ in his physical body. As a
result, he has brought you into his own presence, and you are
holy and blameless as you stand before him without a single
fault."
Colossians 1:19-23

Haven't we made disciple making scandalously complicated. We
were once enemies of God because of our sin and disobedience but
through repentance and faith in Jesus we can become His friends.
Then we continue to obey Him together as we have fellowship and
share meals in the same way Jesus did with us.

"I no longer call you slaves, because a master doesn't confide in
his slaves. Now you are my friends, since I have told you
everything the Father told me."
John 15:15

Fellowship is about friends sharing together and having everything
in common. It is the playing field where everyone gets to play and
bring their part. Can you imagine what the disciples must have felt
when Jesus called them his friends? If Jesus came to my house and
said to me that I was His friend it would change everything. How
empowering it is to call people friends and to share in fellowship.
And we need that as disciples of Jesus because we have some big
battles to fight for the faith.

I don't know where I would be without the fellowship I experience
with the team and disciples here in our region. Life on the frontline
of mission is very hard and to know that I am part of a community
of people who would literally do anything for me is amazing.

I love gathering together to have fellowship with other disciples.
We eat together, share highs and lows, look at the scriptures and

pray for each other. What makes it even more powerful is that a lot of those we are discipling have never had loving stable families so the love they experience is often very overwhelming for them. We then encourage and support everyone to go and gather people they know and to do the same with them. Anyone can do it, if they are willing.

And as we continue to have fellowship together and train everyone in the movement to go and gather those they know do you know what happens? The Lord adds to our fellowship regularly those who are being saved. (It doesn't quite happen daily yet!)

Devoted to the apostles teaching

Acts 2:42 tells us that the believers devoted themselves to the apostle's teaching. There were no Bibles as we know it, no phone apps or televisions so I've often wondered what the apostle's teaching was and how they taught it!

First of all though it's important to think about what the teaching wasn't. It wasn't the pastor's teaching or the prophet's teaching. It was teaching from men, and probably some women, who'd actually been with Jesus and experienced life with him. They would have Jesus' words ringing in their ears,

"Go and make disciples of all the nations, baptizing them in the name of the Father and the son and the Holy Spirit. Teach these new disciples to obey all the commands I have given you. And be sure of this: I am with you always, even to the end of the age"
Matthew 28:18-20

This collection of ordinary men and women had experienced a 3 year mind blowing kingdom experience and, as Jesus left, He told them to go and do exactly the same with others and to grow a movement which would not stop until the ends of the earth are reached and all nations are discipled. The apostles were literally 'sent ones' on the most important mission from Jesus,

"Just as you sent me into the world, I am sending them into the world"
John 17:18

In Jesus' mind, the work had just begun and he was going to be with the disciples through His Spirit until the end of the age. The disciples were to replicate exactly the life they had experienced with Jesus,

"I tell you the truth, anyone who believes in me will do the same works I have done, and even greater works, because I am going to be with the Father"
John 14:12

There's a lot I don't understand about these words from Jesus. I don't know what could be greater than the works Jesus did, but I think He is giving a hint towards the day when, through the Spirit, all disciples everywhere would advance the kingdom of God on earth in just the same way Jesus did. In the gospels it was Jesus and the 12 and 72. But after Pentecost the Spirit filled and empowered a body of people to spread the kingdom to all people everywhere. The floodgates were opened and the church would now multiply into every people and place. Or at least that's the idea!

Unfortunately throughout history men and women have refused to build on apostolic teaching so the movement becomes a monument!

Let's put ourselves in the shoes of the first apostles in Acts and try and imagine what it was like?

None of them were theologically trained in the way we would understand it today so what would they do? Well through the Spirit's power they did what Jesus instructed them to do! They gathered people, baptized them and taught them to obey what Jesus had passed onto them. It's simple but it's not easy. They shared the teachings of Jesus (probably verbally) with people and helped them to obey it. And it was all done in a context of "sent-ness" where everyone understood they were all called to make more disciples and where they faced hardship, persecution and in some cases death.

I can imagine the apostles staying up late at night as some of them wrote down their eye witness accounts of their time with Jesus. Stories and parables Jesus taught them were probably coming to life for them in new and amazing ways. And they were dynamically passing this onto the new disciples and churches as they met from house to house and in the temple. There was no social media, no internet and no modern technology, but the gospel spread rapidly through the apostles teaching in a way that is generally unheard of today. They must clearly have been doing and teaching in a very different way than we do in most of our churches and ministries today!

Let me re-iterate it again. The teaching was apostolic in nature, not pastoral or prophetic. The goal was to equip the church to be apostolic and to continue the work of making disciples, planting churches and training leaders until all nations were discipled. Apostolic teaching trains people to be apostolic and that is why we see the fruit of this teaching throughout the New Testament.

I fear that we have rejected apostolic teaching and the claims it makes on people and have instead settled for a boiled down milky version called 'pastoral care'. Milky drinks are what babies live on and what people have at night to help them go to sleep. It's time for us to grow up and wake up!

Wake up and Grow Up!

Those with an apostolic call are builders. They help to build disciples, churches and leaders by laying a foundation and an example that others can build on,

"Because of God's grace to me, I have laid the foundation like an expert builder. Now others are building on it."
1 Corinthians 3:10

I remember when we were working through our calling and considering whether we should become more involved with our church or seek to be sent out to pioneer. I would regularly visit the pastor of the church we were part of to talk things through. I think we both found it a challenge to try and understand each other. He was approaching the conversation as someone with a strong pastoral gifting and with hindsight I was approaching the conversation from an apostolic perspective (although I didn't have the words or experience to communicate this at the time) One week we met up and God showed me to ask the question, "What is your vision?", so I did.

My friend described the vision he had and it was basically a Sunday morning meeting where a community of believers came together to encourage and build each other up. I encouraged my friend because he was living that vision!

Then my friend asked me what my God given vision was.

I thought for a moment and then answered,

"To see a network of simple churches multiplying across Somerset until Jesus is known amongst every person"

That conversation revealed a lot and I realized that morning that it was pointless trying to persuade my friend to believe in my vision because he just couldn't see it. And that was OK. So I decided from that moment to stop trying to persuade or argue with people about what we are doing and to start building it. It makes me chuckle now when I see some of my team getting into conversations and arguments with other believers who just cannot see the vision God has given us. I've come to a place of peace that there isn't a magic formula for mission or church planting and that the answer isn't big church, small church, house church, simple church or no church. The answer is obeying the vision God has given you. So we're cracking on with it and if others want to work together with us that's great and if they don't then we encourage them to build towards the vision God has given them. And if they have no vision we encourage them to get on their knees and pray.

I came to the reality that I am wired completely differently from someone with a pastoral gift and that is OK. These two gifts can work together if people are willing to humble themselves.

If I walk into a group of people I will act in a completely different way to someone with another gifting. When I meet with any group of people I will listen a lot, ask some questions and quickly assess what is going on. I will pick up on any sense of shared vision and working together and seem to be able to see who potential or emerging leaders are. My wife on the other hand normally homes in on what God is saying to that group or to an individual and also gets a very strong empathetic sense for members of the group who maybe struggling. I'll leave you to work out what our giftings are.

As someone who just wants to do whatever is needed and has accidentally stumbled across their apostolic call I understand the sentiments expressed in Hebrews 5,

"There is much more we would like to say about this, but it is difficult to explain, especially since you are spiritually dull and don't seem to listen. You have been believers so long now that you ought to be teaching others. Instead, you need someone to teach you again the basic things about God's word. You are like babies who need milk and cannot eat solid food. For someone who lives on milk is still an infant and doesn't know how to do what is right. Solid food is for those who are mature, who through training have the skill to recognize the difference between right and wrong."
Hebrews 5:11-14

I must confess that I get easily frustrated with believers who should by now be teaching others, but instead still need feeding. I'm sure this frustration has crept into this book. Most of you reading it will have been believers for some time now and I am not trying to be critical or judgmental. Whether it's someone in a Church who has been talking about gathering some new disciples in their home but never seems to get around to doing it. Or whether it's a new person of peace who's been saying they are going to give up alcohol but doesn't seem to be doing anything about it. I am wired for growth and multiplication in a way that others seem not to be. We're trying to train people to be spiritually mature not perpetual babies and this causes me to have lots of run ins with the pastoral police (as I fondly call them) who simply want to care for people and make sure they are ok. I'm talking a little tongue in cheek here, but it is a real tension in the body of Christ that I feel needs re-addressing.

I often hear people say that the church is like a hospital for broken people, but I'm not sure they have thought through their analogy. In their desire to highlight the pastoral aspects of church I think they have missed the bigger picture. A hospital exists to care for sick people and to get them healthy. The goal of a hospital is get people back out of the door and in today's business-orientated world there is a lot of pressure to get people out even quicker to free up beds for those who really need them.

I wonder if churches share this urgency and passion to get people healed and sent back out?

From what I've seen, churches are more like hospices, offering palliative care to people who are slowly dying.

Apostolic teaching is geared towards growth and life and helps to create an apostolic church that will take the gospel to the ends of the earth. Jesus taught His disciples to know the Father for themselves so that they could continue in the faith without Him when He left,

"At that time you won't need to ask me for anything. I tell you the truth, you will ask the Father directly, and He will grant your request because you use my name."
John 16:23

Apostolic teaching equips everyone to know the Father for themselves rather than to become more reliant on human teachers and fathers. And that is why so much of our teaching is not apostolic. Leaders would rather build dependency on themselves and their ministries instead of doing themselves out of a job! Instead of laboring hard behind the scenes to help people hear and obey Jesus for themselves, leaders tend to spoon feed their flocks each week with great sermons and the latest revelations. But Jesus never told anyone to prepare sermons and disseminate information, he commanded us to teach people to obey the commands of Jesus. And apostolic teaching does just that.

Paul exhorted Titus to encourage the believers to do the teaching because we are making disciples not spiritual sponges who soak everything up but do nothing about it,

"You must teach these things and encourage the believers to do them. You have the authority to correct them when necessary, so don't let anyone disregard what you say."
Titus 2:15

I take the responsibility to make disciples and to teach people very seriously. It is hard and often unseen work as you help people overcome the internal and external obstacles that prevent them from obeying Jesus,

"I solemnly urge you in the presence of God and Christ Jesus, who will someday judge the living and the dead when he comes to set up his Kingdom: Preach the word of God. Be prepared, whether the time is favorable or not. Patiently correct, rebuke, and encourage your people with good teaching. For a time is coming when people will no longer listen to sound and wholesome teaching. They will follow their own desires and will look for teachers who will tell them whatever their itching ears want to hear. They will reject the truth and chase after myths. But you should keep a clear mind in every situation. Don't be afraid of suffering for the Lord. Work at telling others the Good News, and fully carry out the ministry God has given you."
2 Timothy 4:1-5

As we've already seen, Jesus teaches and has fellowship around a meal table, not from a pulpit. And Paul describes to Timothy how he needs to patiently correct, rebuke and encourage his people with good teaching. It takes a lot of time and energy to do this with even a small group of people, which is maybe why Jesus only had 12 disciples. It takes great patience to help people become who they are called to be in Christ, it doesn't happen overnight. Paul was committed to His people long term and labored hard to see Christ fully formed in them. It didn't mean he moved in with them and spent all his time with them. But he labored apostolically for them in prayer and visited when the Spirit led him to,

"Night and day we pray earnestly for you, asking God to let us see you again to fill the gaps in your faith."
1 Thessalonians 3:10

When I'm training church planters it's interesting to see how much of their strategy depends on prayer and apostolic teaching and how much depends on them being physically present with the people to care for them and to motivate them. A few years ago I was basking in the success of seeing churches planted in a number of towns. But my pride was shortlived as I soon realized that really I was leading all the churches and was out every night of the week. It was completely unsustainable as everything was dependant on me doing everything. The work only happened around me. People of peace would gather people if I was there telling them to do it. People got baptized if I was there doing it. And so on. I had to stop and re-assess how effectively I was really making disciples and planting churches and whether I was really laying a foundation that others could then build on. Things had to shift from me doing all the work to others doing all the work with me filling in the gaps where needed. And we'll look at that more in the next chapter!

If, like me, you have a vision to see churches planted in multiple towns and villages or across a whole city you're going to realise pretty soon that your strategy can't involve you being in all those churches. You're gonna need to lay foundations which others can build on. Apostolic teaching is part of that foundation and it will allow you to fade into the background and let others be the leaders of the movement. Apostolic teaching builds the church up so that it can grow and multiply without apostles being physically present and so that every member of the body can play their part in the mission of God to make disciples of all the nations.

More than a message

When you look at the New Testament it becomes very obvious that apostolic teaching is far more than just a 6 week bible study,

"For when we brought you the Good News, it was not only with words but also with power, for the Holy Spirit gave you full assurance that what we said was true. And you know of our concern for you from the way we lived when we were with you. So you received the message with joy from the Holy Spirit in spite of the severe suffering it brought you. In this way, you imitated both us and the Lord. As a result, you have become an example to all the believers in Greece—throughout both Macedonia and Achaia."
1 Thessalonians 1:5-8

The apostles teaching was powerful and obeying it would get you into trouble.

I hear so much talk about whether this church or that church is biblical or whether the latest superstar leader preaches the true word or not. But are we really ready to hear and obey apostolic teaching if we were faced with it.

It's fairly easy to digest a 40 minute sermon that has no practical application to our lives that week. Can you imagine having one of the original apostles living amongst your church or network. Instead of receiving a neatly packaged sermon once a week you'd be thrown into the life of disciple making where every day would be about hearing and obeying Jesus. Would you be prepared to be on the end of loving rebukes and encouragement as you become someone who can teach others instead of someone who is just a receiver,

"Now these are the gifts Christ gave to the church: the apostles, the prophets, the evangelists, and the pastors and teachers. Their responsibility is to equip God's people to do his work and build up the church, the body of Christ. This will continue until we all come to such unity in our faith and knowledge of God's Son that we will be mature in the Lord, measuring up to the full and complete standard of Christ. Then we will no longer be immature like children. We won't be tossed and blown about by every wind of new teaching. We will not be influenced when people try to trick us with lies so clever they sound like the truth. Instead, we will speak the truth in love, growing in every way more and more like Christ, who is the head of his body, the church. He makes the whole body fit together perfectly. As each part does its own special work, it helps the other parts grow, so that the whole body is healthy and growing and full of love."
Ephesians 4:11-17

Movements of churches that are built on apostolic and prophetic foundations, and which are equipped by all the giftings mentioned in Ephesians 4, produce mature disciples who together measure up to the full standard of Christ.

Instead of being tricked with lies so clever that they sound like the truth, we will speak the truth in love. Apostolic teaching 'says it how it is' and equips disciples to become teachers and disciple makers themselves and as Paul says in Ephesians 4:14,

"Then we will no longer be immature like children"

The apostolic gift creates a kingdom culture of faith, obedience and perseverance where disciples and churches obey Jesus and strengthen each other. Looking back I've often put too much focus on what I am 'doing' to train disciples and churches. God gives gifted people to the church to equip them, not tools and programmes. Don't get me wrong I'm the first to look at patterns of teaching, tools and patterns if they are going to help grow the work. But I'm realizing more and more that the most powerful thing I have to offer the body of Christ is actually myself. And that goes for all of us. We all have unique revelations, passions and thought processes which everyone else in the body of Christ needs. We all need each other. When I work with a church or network of people I can somehow see fairly quickly what some of the gaps are in people's faith and practice. It's not because I'm any better or more gifted than anyone else. It's just because that is who I am. I get a kick from listening to people's stories, frustrations and challenges and working with them to find solutions from the scriptures and the spirit. In the same way, people with other giftings quickly see what is lacking from their perspective. I often encourage people that maybe God has shown people a particular problem or challenge because He wants them to prayerfully come up with a solution and action it. Mature believers go away and do it. Immature believers look at me like I am speaking a foreign language because they still think that the answer always lies with someone else. And do you know what happens in the body of Christ when everyone does something about what they see is lacking and brings their part?

"As each part does its own special work, it helps the other parts grow, so that the whole body is healthy and growing and full of love"
Ephesians 4:16

As a family we are going away soon to visit some friends who are leading a church. I'm particularly excited because we haven't seen these friends for a few years now and we used to share many a long night praying and talking about mission and church. They also live in a region that I feel a particular calling to work in. So we're supposed to be going on holiday but it's more like a family adventure. I'm looking forward to seeing and hearing if the church has a clear vision for their region and how they are progressing with it. I'm keen to be amongst the church and to discern those whom God is calling and stirring up. It's not something I try and do, it's part of who I am.

I suspect we may be involved with the church in the future as we help to equip them to make disciples and plant churches. On this trip I hope to get a sense of the overall health of the body in that region and to get a sense of what is lacking and also what we can learn from them. However some people in my family prefer to go with the flow and if I shared all these thoughts with them then it would take all the fun out of our trip. The joy of being in families, churches and teams with people who have different giftings and personalities. Most of all though I'm looking forward to sharing our lives with those in the church there because that is our most powerful tool for training and making disciples. People need more than a message, they need to see apostolic teaching in action on the streets, in homes and in workplaces. That is why Paul imparted not only the gospel to the Thessalonian Church, but his whole life,

"We loved you so much that we shared with you not only God's Good News but our own lives, too."
1 Thessalonians 2:7

I remember when we lived in Australia near Catherine's Mum and Dad. My father in law was an amazing carpenter and builder. He's now with Jesus, but during our 4 years living there I learned quite a few carpentry skills from him. I've never been very good at D.I.Y or anything like that so I was a bit shocked at how easy it was.

My Father in law would show me what to do. Then he'd help me to do it and then eventually he'd trust me to use the saw and other machinery unattended. I even did some carpentry on the house they were building. When we returned to the UK I made a bookcase for our house which I am still quite proud of.

I never thought that I would ever be able to make anything with my hands but as I reflected on the whole process I realized what a good teacher my Father in law had been. To me, making things out of wood was a huge mystery so I had no idea how to even do it. But as my Father in law walked me through things step by step and trusted me more and more I realized that actually it wasn't that hard.

My Father in law could have sent me a link to carpentry videos on youtube or bought me a book on how to build a bookshelf but it wouldn't have been anywhere nearly as effective as what He did. He imparted not only the basic facts of what to do, but helped me to understand so much more. What I appreciated most of all was being able to ask Him about anything as it took away the fear of not knowing what to do.

I try to do the same now when I am training and discipling people. The most important thing I want to do is to build a trusting relationship with people so they feel like they can ask me questions and be vulnerable with people. Yes, I help them to understand the mechanics of how to find people of peace and what to do when you gather disciples together. But apostolic teaching is so much more than just dishing out instructions. It's about helping people to know the living God for themselves and building them up in their faith,

"I may seem to be boasting too much about the authority given to us by the Lord. But our authority builds you up; it doesn't tear you down. So I will not be ashamed of using my authority."
2 Corinthians 10:8

I've met leaders and so called apostles who fly in and fly out and never share anything of their life with people. People may be touched and blessed by their messages, but I wonder how many of these people have been equipped to lead an apostolic life? To be honest every church in the land would say they are making disciples but in reality the vast majority have very little idea how to be a disciple themselves, let alone disciple others. It's not a theoretical work that needs doing, it's nuts and bolts training that can only happen on the job when we show people how to actually make disciples. And after all that's what Jesus did,

"They replied, "Rabbi" (which means "Teacher"), "where are you staying?" "Come and see," he said. It was about four o'clock in the afternoon when they went with him to the place where he was staying, and they remained with him the rest of the day. Andrew, Simon Peter's brother, was one of these men who heard what John said and then followed Jesus. Andrew went to find his brother, Simon, and told him, "We have found the Messiah" (which means "Christ")"
John 1:38-42

You're meant to do something about it!

Those with an apostolic call are compelled by a God-given vision and will get on with the job whether public opinion is with them or not. There has been many times where I've felt I had to choose between pleasing people around me (often those closest to me) or pleasing God. I often think that is why Paul encouraged Timothy to be prepared whether the season was favourable or not (2 Timothy 4:2)

"For we speak as messengers approved by God to be entrusted with the Good News. Our purpose is to please God, not people. He alone examines the motives of our hearts. Never once did we try to win you with flattery, as you well know. And God is our witness that we were not pretending to be your friends just to get your money! As for human praise, we have never sought it from you or anyone else."
1 Thessalonians 2:4-7

In many ways apostolic teaching exhorts us to please God not man and to live free from the need of human praise. It places loving obedience to Jesus, not endless discussions, at the centre of everything,

"The purpose of my instruction is that all believers would be filled with love that comes from a pure heart, a clear conscience, and genuine faith. But some people have missed this whole point. They have turned away from these things and spend their time in meaningless discussions."
1 Timothy 1:5-7

The more I get to know Jesus the more I feel that we spend far too much of our time engaged in meaningless discussions.

When we gather together as disciples and churches we look at the scriptures and treat it as the apostles teaching. It is truth to be obeyed, not just nice ideas to talk about. We engage with the truth found in the scriptures by reading it and asking some questions:

1) What is this saying to me/us?
2) What does this mean?
3) What do I/we need to do about it?
4) Who will I/we share it with?

The scriptures are there to be obeyed!

To most believers I know, searching the scriptures for practical and spiritual guidance and then doing those things immediately is a completely foreign activity. It seems to have become quite a popular pastime for believers to argue and debate the authority of scriptures instead of wrestling with whether they are willing to obey it. As a team, we are very reliant on the scriptures and the Spirit as our source of guidance. We gather together at the start of a day's work to read the scriptures and prayerfully look at how we will obey Jesus that day. We're not reading the scriptures to form theological opinions that have no effect whatsoever on our life. We're hungrily searching for the bread we need that day,

"People do not live by bread alone, but by every word that comes from the mouth of God"
Matthew 4:4

We also turn to the scriptures when we are wrestling with questions and issues. I regularly turn to the Bible and my notebook when I'm praying through an area of the work like how do we effectively raise up leaders or help disciples become mature. In fact most of this book has come out of what God has shown us in private. I normally divide the page in my notebook into two so I can write down what stands out to me on the left hand side and what I need to do about it on the right hand side.

Why don't you try it? Read 1 and 2 Thessalonians yourself and ask the question, what can I learn about apostolic teaching? Down the left hand side of your page write down what God shows you or what stands out. And on the right hand side of the page write down what you're going to do about it this week or in the coming month.

Then you can pass this onto someone else so you're helping them to be devoted to the apostles teaching as well.

The apostles teaching was like the seed behind the growth of the movement in the New Testament. Without seed in the ground nothing will grow. You can water the ground as much as you want but if there is no seed planted you'll just create a muddy mess in your mission field. As you seek to play your part in the discipling of all nations why don't you join Paul and many others in praying the following prayer,

"Finally, dear brothers and sisters, we ask you to pray for us. Pray that the Lord's message will spread rapidly and be honored wherever it goes, just as when it came to you."
2 Thessalonians 3:1

May the Lord's message spread rapidly through your mission field.

Sharing meals (including the Lord's supper)

As we've already seen, eating together and gathering around a shared meal is very important in planting and strengthening churches. Jesus taught around a table and He commanded His disciples to do the same.

In Acts we read that the church was devoted to sharing meals including the Lord's supper (Acts 2:42) It wasn't just a social activity tagged onto the real 'spiritual' life of the church, it was a central part of what it meant to be God's people. We've seen that gathering for meals in homes is such a powerful environment to make disciples and helps to keep our 'spirituality' grounded in real life. Many believers are hand raising their way through life without ever having to confront the questions that Jesus may be asking them from across the table. Worship times, sermons and sitting in rows means that it is fairly easy to enjoy churchianity without the challenge of obeying Jesus or loving others. For a long time our 'spiritual life' existed in a church building and sometimes in our home from 7:30pm-9:30pm on a Wednesday night. But contrary to popular belief God doesn't dwell in religious buildings or temples, but in the homes and hearts of believers who obey Him and love others,

"David found favor with God and asked for the privilege of building a permanent Temple for the God of Jacob. But it was Solomon who actually built it. However, the Most High doesn't live in temples made by human hands. As the prophet says, 'Heaven is my throne, and the earth is my footstool. Could you build me a temple as good as that?' asks the Lord. 'Could you build me such a resting place? Didn't my hands make both heaven and earth?'
Acts 7:46:51

Throughout the gospels, Jesus could be found eating with people in their homes and teaching them to be His followers. This table fellowship continued amongst the believers in the book of Acts and throughout the New Testament,

"They worshiped together at the Temple each day, met in homes for the Lord's Supper, and shared their meals with great joy and generosity"
Acts 2:46

When we first started the work God has called us to we invited people to a bring and share meal at our house. It was very simple and as those we were discipling grew, it allowed us to be devoted to prayer, fellowship, the apostle's teaching and to sharing in meals including the Lord's supper. We felt strongly that we should be building our strategy around sharing meals in homes, not just tagging it onto church life in the way some do.

In the context of a shared meal where everyone contributed something for the table, we were able to model and teach what it meant to be disciples and to be a church. Everyone could contribute to the gathering and for most gathered around our table it was like the family they never had.

We described what we were experiencing as "bring and share". Early on, I made a point of insisting that everyone (unless they literally had nothing, which was sometimes the case!) brought some food to share. Many of those we are discipling have come from very broken backgrounds and have become victims of the system. I felt it was important that people knew that me and Catherine were not going to be doing everything and providing everything every Wednesday. We were teaching the community to obey Jesus and to share everything they had. Instead of us doing the normal christian thing where we offered the poor broken sinners everything they needed and asked for nothing in return. We saw these people as disciples of Jesus who all had something to bring and share. For many of these guys it was the first time anyone had challenged them to bring something rather than to just take things.

Coming from lives of crime and drug abuse, many of our disciples were used to getting what they needed out of life and had become comfortable with hiding behind the victim mentality. I wasn't having any of it (and still don't) and did all I could to help them understand that God had entrusted talents into their hands for them to multiply. Although some drifted away because their needs were not being met, the majority were transformed from excuse-makers into disciple-makers. And by the way, Jesus didn't send us out into the world to make excuses! He sent us to make disciples who obey Him.

Because bringing and sharing food was part of our culture on a Wednesday night, it wasn't that hard when we started to encourage everyone to bring something spiritual to share each week. We began to see everyone coming along with something to share each week. Whether it was an encouraging story, something they were thankful for or a message from Jesus for the whole group. It was the church functioning as Jesus intended it to,

"Well, my brothers and sisters, let's summarize. When you meet together, one will sing, another will teach, another will tell some special revelation God has given, one will speak in tongues, and another will interpret what is said. But everything that is done must strengthen all of you."
1 Corinthians 14:26

I've been in so many gatherings where people are encouraged to participate and share but all there is stony silence or the same voices heard each week. If bring and share is not part of the culture of a church then you can't expect people to suddenly oblige when they are put on the spot one Sunday morning. It's much the same with leadership. If you are not building leadership development into what you are doing right from the start then you can't expect leaders to suddenly appear overnight!

I was not prepared to plant churches where people came expecting to be fed, so what we did and the culture we grew together reflected that. And I believe that if churches are being built around disciple-making and on the apostolic and prophetic foundations then there will be no room for selfishness. As we considered how to train our people to be devoted to sharing meals including the Lord's supper we felt to look at Paul's first letter to the Corinthian church as he had much to say about this theme.

So before I share a few things that we have learned from 1 Corinthians, why don't you read it yourself and see what you and your disciples can learn and put into practice about sharing meals and the Lord's supper.

Love strengthens

Sharing a common meal around the same table really strengthens a community. Everyone feels like they are part of what is happening and has something to share.

When we break bread in our gatherings it is such a visual way of explaining how we are one body,

"So, my dear friends, flee from the worship of idols. You are

reasonable people. Decide for yourselves if what I am saying is true. When we bless the cup at the Lord's Table, aren't we sharing in the blood of Christ? And when we break the bread, aren't we sharing in the body of Christ? And though we are many, we all eat from one loaf of bread, showing that we are one body."
1 Corinthians 10:14-18

According to Jesus, one of the measures of our progress in the faith is our love and consideration for others in the body of Christ. Throughout the New Testament letters we hear how Paul and others are laboring hard to help the churches grow in love for Jesus and for one another,

"I pray that your love will overflow more and more, and that you will keep on growing in knowledge and understanding. For I want you to understand what really matters, so that you may live pure and blameless lives until the day of Christ's return."
Philippians 1:9-11

What really matters when teaching and strengthening churches is love.

I have lost count of the number of times in recent months where I have been trying to help those I am working with to see from a more loving perspective. We so often resort to childish ways that are only concerned with who is right or wrong and don't consider other people's needs or opinions.

As we strengthen churches and help disciples grow in maturity, shared meals and table fellowship provides the perfect environment for getting to the root of many issues in all of our lives!

Paul talked to the church in Corinth a lot about this and he used the shared meal as the basis of his teaching. No wonder Jesus wanted eating and shared meals to be central to the life of His Church. So many issues come up when we try and do it together and it creates so many opportunities for disciple making,

"When you meet together, you are not really interested in the Lord's Supper. For some of you hurry to eat your own meal without sharing with others. As a result, some go hungry while others get drunk. What? Don't you have your own homes for eating and drinking? Or do you really want to disgrace God's church and shame the poor? What am I supposed to say? Do you want me to praise you? Well, I certainly will not praise you for this! For I pass on to you what I received from the Lord himself. On the night when he was betrayed, the Lord Jesus took some bread and gave thanks to God for it. Then he broke it in pieces and said, "This is my body, which is given for you. Do this in remembrance of me." In the same way, he took the cup of wine after supper, saying, "This cup is the new covenant between God and his people—an agreement confirmed with my blood. Do this in remembrance of me as often as you drink it." For every time you eat this bread and drink this cup, you are announcing the Lord's death until he comes again. So anyone who eats this bread or drinks this cup of the Lord unworthily is guilty of sinning against the body and blood of the Lord. That is why you should examine yourself before eating the bread and drinking the cup. For if you eat the bread or drink the cup without honoring the body of Christ, you are eating and drinking God's judgment upon yourself. That is why many of you are weak and sick and some have even died. But if we would examine ourselves, we would not be judged by God in this way. Yet when we are judged by the Lord, we are being disciplined so that we will not be condemned along with the world. So, my dear brothers and sisters, when you gather for the Lord's Supper, wait for each other. If you are

really hungry, eat at home so you won't bring judgment upon yourselves when you meet together."
1 Corinthians 11:20-34

The true measure of our faith is only seen when people are up in our face and we're trying to work out relational challenges with others. Community living is the great leveler for us all! I can stand up and preach to churches from the safety of the stage, but it's when I'm gathered around a table with my family or those I'm discipling where I really see how deeply Christ's love is at work in me. When leaders swap a stage for a shared meal we see how effective they really are at making disciples and equipping others!

The Corinthian 'bring and share' had become a free for all and Paul took the opportunity to help the church to address this issue and grow. Nobody was really interested in the Lord's supper as everyone was concerned with eating their own meal. Instead of a body of people meeting each other's needs, they'd become full of selfishness and independence.

Paul tries to bring them back to the whole point of sharing meals and the Lord's supper,

"For I pass on to you what I received from the Lord himself. On the night when he was betrayed, the Lord Jesus took some bread and gave thanks to God for it. Then he broke it in pieces and said, "This is my body, which is given for you. Do this in remembrance of me." In the same way, he took the cup of wine after supper, saying, "This cup is the new covenant between God and his people—an agreement confirmed with my blood. Do this in remembrance of me as often as you drink it."
1 Corinthians 11:23-26

The bread represented Jesus' body which was given for us and the wine represented Jesus' blood which was spilled for us. Sharing in the Lord's supper is a clear reminder that our master gave himself for others and poured out his blood for us. There is nothing more strengthening to the church than to become more like Christ in our selflessness and service to each other and sharing meals and the Lord's supper is central to this.

Paul also encourages the church to wait for each other. Although such a simple instruction it has such huge implications. Are we prepared to consider the needs of others and wait for others even when our own needs have not been met? I don't know about you, but when I'm hungry I can become pretty focused on meeting this need in myself. Yet Paul encourages us to consider the needs of others before ourselves in the same way as he does in his letter to the Philippians,

"Don't look out only for your own interests, but take an interest in others, too. You must have the same attitude that Christ Jesus had."
Philippians 2:4-6

Waiting for each other and considering the needs of others opens the way for the continued development of spiritual gifts as Paul goes onto talk about in 1 Corinthians 12, but if we cannot even eat together in a loving way then how can we function in our spiritual gifts.

The church in Corinth were having some issues around sharing meals and certain foods. Instead of entering the argument though Paul taught a better way,

"Now regarding your question about food that has been offered to idols. Yes, we know that "we all have knowledge" about this

issue. But while knowledge makes us feel important, it is love that strengthens the church."
1 Corinthians 8:1-4

Whilst the church were arguing about who was right or wrong, Paul teaches them about love and considering others. Love isn't concerned about proving a point, but seeks to build others up. Instead of arguing about whether food is clean or unclean, Paul encouraged them to instead look at the effect that what they were doing was having on others. Sharing meals and the Lord's supper meant these deeper heart issues came up and could be addressed by Paul,

So whether you eat or drink, or whatever you do, do it all for the glory of God. Don't give offense to Jews or Gentiles or the church of God. I, too, try to please everyone in everything I do. I don't just do what is best for me; I do what is best for others so that many may be saved."
1 Corinthians 10:14-33

Imagine a church where everyone commits to not just doing what is best for me but doing what is best for others so that many may be saved!

Who's not eating?

I always find it interesting watching people! You learn a lot by watching and listening to people. In the following two bring and share stories it's really interesting to see what everyone is doing. As everyone is enjoying the shared meal and the Lord's supper there is one person who isn't eating.

Why don't you have a read of the two stories and see for yourself,

"When it was evening, Jesus sat down at the table with the Twelve. While they were eating, he said, "I tell you the truth, one of you will betray me." Greatly distressed, each one asked in turn, "Am I the one, Lord?" He replied, "One of you who has just eaten from this bowl with me will betray me. For the Son of Man must die, as the Scriptures declared long ago. But how terrible it will be for the one who betrays him. It would be far better for that man if he had never been born!" Judas, the one who would betray him, also asked, "Rabbi, am I the one?" And Jesus told him, "You have said it." As they were eating, Jesus took some bread and blessed it. Then he broke it in pieces and gave it to the disciples, saying, "Take this and eat it, for this is my body." And he took a cup of wine and gave thanks to God for it. He gave it to them and said, "Each of you drink from it, for this is my blood, which confirms the covenant between God and his people. It is poured out as a sacrifice to forgive the sins of many. Mark my words—I will not drink wine again until the day I drink it new with you in my Father's Kingdom." Then they sang a hymn and went out to the Mount of Olives."
Matthew 26:17-31

"Before the Passover celebration, Jesus knew that his hour had come to leave this world and return to his Father. He had loved his disciples during his ministry on earth, and now he loved them to the very end. It was time for supper, and the devil had already prompted Judas, son of Simon Iscariot, to betray Jesus. Jesus knew that the Father had given him authority over everything and that he had come from God and would return to God. So he got up from the table, took off his robe, wrapped a towel around his waist, and poured water into a basin. Then he began to wash the disciples' feet, drying them with the towel he had around him.

When Jesus came to Simon Peter, Peter said to him, "Lord, are you going to wash my feet?" Jesus replied, "You don't understand now what I am doing, but someday you will." "No," Peter protested, "you will never ever wash my feet!" Jesus replied, "Unless I wash you, you won't belong to me." Simon Peter exclaimed, "Then wash my hands and head as well, Lord, not just my feet!" Jesus replied, "A person who has bathed all over does not need to wash, except for the feet, to be entirely clean. And you disciples are clean, but not all of you." For Jesus knew who would betray him. That is what he meant when he said, "Not all of you are clean." After washing their feet, he put on his robe again and sat down and asked, "Do you understand what I was doing? You call me 'Teacher' and 'Lord,' and you are right, because that's what I am. And since I, your Lord and Teacher, have washed your feet, you ought to wash each other's feet. I have given you an example to follow. Do as I have done to you.I tell you the truth, slaves are not greater than their master. Nor is the messenger more important than the one who sends the message. Now that you know these things, God will bless you for doing them."
John 13:1-18

Did you notice that in both stories Jesus is not eating while everyone is? Here are three clues for you in case you missed it,

"While they were eating, he said, "I tell you the truth, one of you will betray me."
Matthew 26:21

As they were eating, Jesus took some bread and blessed it. Then he broke it in pieces and gave it to the disciples, saying, "Take this and eat it, for this is my body."
Matthew 26:26

"It was time for supper, and the devil had already prompted Judas, son of Simon Iscariot, to betray Jesus. Jesus knew that the Father had given him authority over everything and that he had come from God and would return to God. So he got up from the table, took off his robe, wrapped a towel around his waist, and poured water into a basin. Then he began to wash the disciples' feet, drying them with the towel he had around him.
John 13:2-6

As this chapter comes to an end and we move onto the next chapter it's interesting to see that Jesus is not eating with everyone else. Instead of feeding himself He chooses to teach others in word and deed. In the first story from Matthew he teaches about the bread and the wine and the significance of the Lord's supper. And in the second story He actually gets up from the table and washes everyone's feet.

Remember this interesting observation as I share a few stories about how we have strengthened the churches we have planted and then we move onto the next chapter about appointing leaders.

The church that met in our house

When we first started the work we gathered people at our house on a Wednesday night. We had a house full of not yet or new disciples of Jesus. We'd deliberately asked God to give us the worst people in our town and God had answered this prayer! Each week people brought food to share and we ate together. We'd go around the table sharing highs and lows, looking at a simple story from the Bible and asking questions about it and then praying for each other.

Most weeks someone in the community would jump up during the meal and had to leave the room as they'd never experienced family like this and were unable to handle the emotion and deep feelings that the fellowship was bringing up. It was a powerful time. A number of the group were baptized, it was chaotic and amazing all at the same time. And it was so different from the church we'd been sent out of a year or so earlier.

One evening I lay in bed reflecting on how Jesus was building a church in our home. It was truly amazing to see how He was at work on a Wednesday night and how the people we were discipling were experiencing God's transforming power and love.

But I felt there was something missing.

All that week I was praying about this and reading the scriptures and then God showed me what it was! Even though the church we were gathering were experiencing Him in amazing ways, I was reminded that Jesus was calling us to fish for more people and to spread the gospel. I felt that there was a missing outward element in our community life and I began to think about how I could encourage and train those I was discipling to begin looking for who they could disciple.

The following Wednesday I got some paper and pens ready for them and at the end of our time together I asked everyone to write down the names of their friends and family who they love and who they could start praying for and sharing Jesus with. After all, I said, Jesus was doing so much in our lives and we want to share this with everyone else we know. Everyone sat around the table agreed. So they all wrote down some names and started to pray for 'their people.' Within 2 weeks one of our disciples had baptized someone from his people list and that guy had also written his people list and was starting to pray and share with them.

I felt that in some small way I had begun to make disciples that could make more disciples and that a movement could multiply across our region of the UK in a way that wasn't dependent on me or anyone else.

Breaking bread in a Pub

We were in Glastonbury and had met a Rastafarian, a new age man and a young lady. I suggested we sat down together and broke bread. I didn't know whether this was the right thing to do theologically but I felt the Spirit was telling me to do it so strongly that I thought I better obey Him.

As we broke bread and talked about the Gospel a Sikh man noticed what we doing and asked if he could join us. I asked the Sikh man (a visitor from Birmingham) if he had any sicknesses and He shared that he had chronic shoulder and neck pain and couldn't raise his arms above shoulder height. We laid hands on him and commanded the shoulders and neck to be healed. The pain went immediately and we watched as he raised his hands all the way up with ease. He couldn't believe what Jesus had just done. We continued to read some Bible together and then went to a local pub. Before the Sikh man left he said that we should go and visit some of the Sikh temples if we ever visited Birmingham as they serve food and would be happy to receive prayer for healing.

After that first gathering we began to meet weekly at this Pub in Glastonbury to break bread and do church with around 4-10 people. After we had broken bread each week we then took bread to everyone else in the crowded pub and offered healing and prayer in the name of Jesus. It was a great time!

(Interestingly - a year or so later I took my son to Birmingham and I remembered the suggestion from the Sikh guy. I took my son into a big Sikh temple and we met a person of peace who showed us around the temple, fed us and then announced to everyone in the dining hall that we had come to heal people in the name of Jesus. I think 5 of the men we prayed for that day were healed and our person of peace explained to them that we were followers of Jesus. He said we should come back on a Saturday because the temple would be full and there would be lots of people we could pray for. The harvest is plentiful but there are just not enough laborers!)

All night prayer

We'd been working in Glastonbury as a team and had found 3 households of peace who we were gathering and training. As we prayed for them it became clear that God was inviting us to do an all night prayer session for the work in that town. We planned to go up the Tor (a famous hill) for sunrise and to pray over the area. All night prayer is something I've often done and it seems to be something that Jesus did as well.

We visited one of the households in Glastonbury the week before our prayer session and one of the ladies shared how she loved going up the Tor at sunrise. So we invited them all to join us. At the time we didn't really understand why we should invite them – but it seemed like God had showed us to do something and there was a way that it could fit with the people. This is an important lesson – the key thing is trying to find common ground with the people we are trying to make disciples and plant churches with and must be prepared to think on our feet and change our plans accordingly. People are infinitely more important than our plans or ideas.

We turned up at their house at 4am and 4 of them joined us in our walk up the Tor. We prayed on top and played music and then their mum cooked a full English breakfast for us all at 6:30am in the morning. Not only did the prayer strengthen the work but it was also a great time of fellowship with these new disciples who seemed quite amazed that followers of Jesus also liked staying up all night to pray and seeing the sun rise. I talked with the team afterwards and we reflected on how great it was that these new disciples were experiencing life with Jesus instead of just sitting in a row on a Sunday morning becoming slowly christianised. We felt it was an honour to be helping these precious people connect with their creator and to understand His ways.

Hold onto the pattern of sound teaching

We've thought and prayed a lot about how to pass on apostolic teaching to those we are discipling. Paul wrote the following to Timothy,

"Hold onto the pattern of wholesome teaching you learned from me – a pattern shaped by the faith and love that you have in Christ Jesus. Through the power of the Holy Spirit who lives within us, carefully guard the precious truth that has been entrusted to you."
2 Timothy 1:13-15

We asked ourselves, what is our pattern of wholesome teaching? What simple framework are we passing onto our people so they can grow as disciples and also teach others who can teach others?

Here is what we have developed so far.

1. Preach the good news
Matthew 10 and Luke 10
(see chapter 5)

2. Make many disciples
7 Commands of Christ
(see chapter 6)

3. Strengthen the believers
Prayer (Ephesians)
Fellowship (Philipppians)
Apostles teaching (1 and 2 Thessalonians)
Sharing meals and the Lord's supper (1 Corinthians)
(see chapter 7)

4. Appoint leaders
1 and 2 Timothy
(see chapter 8)

Obviously within that there is the freedom to look at other issues from scripture as they arise. But this gives a good apostolic framework for people to build on! And of course we read the scriptures and help each other obey them.

What is lacking in the Churches you have planted or are working with?

How does God want to strengthen the Churches you are working with?

What do you need to do about this?

Chapter 8

Appoint leaders

Acts 14:23

As I've progressed with this book, every chapter has felt like the most important chapter. Each part of the work is needed and flows into the next part. They are like living, breathing building blocks needed to piece together a church planting movement amongst the gentiles in the harvest. It would be like asking a farmer what is most important, planting the seed or harvesting the crop. It's a whole process which requires different activities at different stages.

If we do not pray and honour the Holy Spirit then we will not see the abundant fruit Jesus expects from us and we'll lack direction and power.

If we do not grasp the importance of preaching the gospel to those in darkness then all our hopes and theories about making disciples and planting churches are irrelevant because there won't be any people.

If we do not make disciples then our work will come to nothing and if we don't strengthen these believers and build up the churches then there will be no lasting fruit and no workers.

Depending on your calling and what stage of the work you are in, I suspect different chapters in this book will be screaming out to you as most important.

For me, however, this chapter, "Appoint leaders", is in my opinion, the most important of the most important chapters. Maybe it's because I have been living this chapter for the last few years and it's the most freshest in my mind. Maybe it's because this chapter talks about the key to empowering those around us in a way that really leads to multiplication. Or maybe it's because I feel this area is still most lacking in the work we are doing and in other emerging missional networks and movements here in Europe.

What's certain though is that without appointing leaders the work will never be finished and God's heart for the gentiles (the 99% of non church going people in the UK and Europe) will remain in the hands of a dwindling pool of believers and never become the full blown movement He wants it to.

And I am not prepared to see that happen in my lifetime.

"After preaching the Good News in Derbe and making many disciples, Paul and Barnabas returned to Lystra, Iconium, and Antioch of Pisidia, where they strengthened the believers. They encouraged them to continue in the faith, reminding them that we must suffer many hardships to enter the Kingdom of God. Paul and Barnabas also appointed elders in every church. With prayer and fasting, they turned the elders over to the care of the Lord, in whom they had put their trust."
Acts 14:21-24

I long to see God's work pushed even further into the hands of a new generation of disciples in the harvest. It's only when we see leaders appointed from among these new believers who carry real responsibility that this can happen. Here in our region I will know our apostolic work is finished when there are leaders appointed in every town who will continue to build on the foundational work God has given us and the team the grace to do. I am primarily writing this book to people like me. It's an attempt to inspire and mobilise an army of accidental apostles. I'm writing to people who stay awake at night thinking about how to multiply disciples and churches in a way that will transform whole regions and nations. I'm writing to people who know God is calling them but who know their work won't look anything like churchianity. I'm writing to people who's food in life is to do the will of God and to finish His work,

"Then Jesus explained: "My nourishment comes from doing the will of God, who sent me, and from finishing his work."
John 4:34

If you want to finish the work God has called you to more than you want food itself then read on!

Finishing the work

As I've got older I've started to ask myself different questions.

When we started this work I was full of zeal and energy. I'd return home from the latest baptism party or church we had planted thinking that life couldn't be any better. My thoughts and questions were all about how I could become more effective and powerful as a disciple maker and leader. I'd fast and pray all night as I tried to overcome the challenges I was facing and found great joy in inspiring others through my example. I thank God for that season in my life and how I played my part in advancing the Kingdom of God.

But seasons change.

As I've slowly matured (and it has been slow) my outlook on the work has changed,

"When I was a child, I spoke and thought and reasoned as a child. But when I grew up, I put away childish things."
1 Corinthians 13:11

Just as Paul writes to the church in Corinth, sometimes what's needed is a complete shift in thinking. For a while I struggled with the idea that God was wanting to shift my thinking and bring me into a season of greater fruitfulness. My pride didn't want to admit any weaknesses and it was just easier to try and go harder, faster and longer instead of stopping and re-evaulating everything. For most of my life I'd overcome challenges by simply pushing through, being stronger and working harder. But this time I knew God was inviting me to STOP and to experience a major shift in thinking.

I started to think about my life and how I was basically half way through my existence here on earth. I reflected on the first half of my life and although I was thankful to God, I felt like God was showing me that things needed to change. I thought about our biological children and those we were discipling and I began to think about how I could reshape my life around empowering them to do the work and preparing for my departure from this earth. It may sound a bit weird or morbid. But it didn't feel like that. I felt like God was reminding me that things were not designed to be dependant on me and that for the rest of my life I should give everything I had to build a foundation for others to build on. I needed to plan to leave! I decided to put childish and youthful things behind me and to embrace a more mature way of thinking.

I was reminded about the scripture Jesus shared with His disciples which perfectly encapsulated how he discipled those around Him in preparation for his departure,

"I tell you the truth, unless a kernel of wheat is planted in the soil and dies, it remains alone. But its death will produce many new kernels—a plentiful harvest of new lives"
John 12:24

I realized how much of my time and energy was spent on doing the work myself and solving problems or challenges, and how little I helped others to do the same. I desperately wanted to raise up leaders and empower others but there was something about the way I did things that stopped this from happening.

It was during this time that I felt God asking me to write this book and to look again at what it means to live out an apostolic calling just like Paul did.

It became obvious that the approach I'd used up until this point in my life was no longer going to work. Getting on with it on my own had worked when it was time to pioneer, but now the work was too great for me and I was feeling overwhelmed and broken. I'd tried to build teams and develope leaders before, but it wasn't from the heart so it didn't work. You don't develope leaders by following a text book or because it's the right thing to do. Leaders are developed when you love others more than yourself and when you become humble enough to realise that others can more often than not do a better job than you can do.

Any shift or growth that God wants to work in our life is rooted in our heart attitudes. For me, I had to come to the painful reality that although I was passionate about Jesus and His work, there was also selfish ambition lurking in my heart.

God doesn't share his glory with just one person and I had to learn that I can't save the world and I don't have all the answers. In fact I have hardly any answers. I humbled myself before God and began to see a different way of working. God is glorified through His body working together and through teams of leaders honoring each other. Like Paul I experienced the great truth that it is actually in our weakness that we are strong,

"Three different times I begged the Lord to take it away. Each time he said, "My grace is all you need. My power works best in weakness." So now I am glad to boast about my weaknesses, so that the power of Christ can work through me. That's why I take pleasure in my weaknesses, and in the insults, hardships, persecutions, and troubles that I suffer for Christ. For when I am weak, then I am strong."
2 Corinthians 12:8-11

So instead of trying to work harder or do the same thing that I'd aways done, I instead went back to the scriptures and asked God about what we needed to do to finish the work He had called us to do. He showed me some interesting things,

"I left you on the island of Crete so you could complete our work there and appoint elders in each town as I instructed you."
Titus 1:5

I revisited the apostolic call to lay foundations for churches and movements and how saw afresh how Paul's purpose was to equip churches to grow and flourish without him. I saw again how Paul was completely reliant on God but also completely reliant on His co-workers! He left Titus on the Island of Crete to complete their work. Paul was dispensible and so am I.

The work didn't belong to Paul or Titus. It was carried by a team. Paul had laid a foundation but Titus had the amazing responsibility to finish the work. And what was the key to finishing the apostolic work? Paul's view is that when elders were appointed in each town (as He'd instructed Titus to do) then the apostolic work was completed. Paul wasn't just hoping this would happen in all the churches. He'd instructed Titus to make sure it actually happened.

That's why in Acts 14 when Paul and Barnabus returned to Antioch they concluded that God had opened the door of faith to the gentiles. Not because a few people prayed the sinners prayer, but because churches had been planted which now had indigenous leaders appointed from among them. The work could continue without Paul and Barnabus because there were leaders who'd continue the work.

I started to ask another question, "If I died today would the work in our region continue without me?"

I dare you to ask that question and to answer it honestly. It's one of those questions which could radically transform you and what you're doing. It changed me because I realized that if I was taken out of the equation then not much would continue. Back then if someone had removed my enthusiasm, drive and communication from the work in our region I seriously wondered what would be left. So I decided to change how I did things and to think about how I could multiply people like me who could continue the work if I wasn't there.

Instead of asking God about myself all the time I started to ask God how to appoint leaders in the harvest from among the new churches and disciples that were growing. And here are a few things that helped me to do that.

The best thing to do is nothing!

I've come to learn that making disciples is about looking at yourself and being willing to change instead of pointing the finger at others. It's pretty easy to point out other's faults or weaknesses, it's harder to embody in your own life, the change you wish to see in others. But that's what being a disciple is all about, obeying Jesus and bringing your part to the body rather than criticizing the other parts. I've learned this as a Father to our children. When our children act in an ungodly or disrespectful way it's easy to get frustrated and annoyed with them. But more and more God is helping me to see that their lives and attitudes are the fruit of what me and Catherine and others have planted into them. This is both an amazing opportunity and a terribly scary responsibility. Of course they must also take responsibility for their own actions, but the scripture about reaping what we sow does ring true,

"Don't be misled—you cannot mock the justice of God. You will always harvest what you plant. Those who live only to satisfy their own sinful nature will harvest decay and death from that sinful nature. But those who live to please the Spirit will harvest everlasting life from the Spirit."
Galatians 6:7-9

And it's the same with making disciples and the culture we establish amongst our churches and networks. If we're seeing a lack of fruit or an area of weakness in the work and in those we are discipling then yes let's pray for them. But let's also get on our knees and into the scriptures and ask God if there is anything we need to change as their spiritual parents and leaders. It started to really bother me that others around me were not developing in the way I'd hoped and how I still felt like I was carrying everything on my shoulders. So instead of blaming others and thinking it was due to issues in 'them', I asked God to change me first.

"Nor do we boast and claim credit for the work someone else has done. Instead, we hope that your faith will grow so that the boundaries of our work among you will be extended. Then we will be able to go and preach the Good News in other places far beyond you, where no one else is working."
2 Corinthians 10:15-17

As I read Paul's letters to the church in Corinth I began to understand even more about the apostolic call. In these verses above we see that the growth of the work is not dependant on Paul's faith or actions. Paul writes that the boundaries of the apostolic work extend as the people's faith grows.

As an immature leader and pioneer I had adopted the attitude that the work would only extend as my own faith grows and as I do more. Everything was dependant on me and what I was doing and nothing was dependant on those I was discipling and training. In my mind the answer to every obstacle in the work was for me to pray harder, fast for longer and understand the scriptures more. Yet as I did that it was just me increasing and not Jesus increasing. I was trying to be successful and do a good job for Jesus when all the time the real issue was whether I was prepared to become less so He could be more successful. Just like John the Baptist said,

"Therefore, I am filled with joy at his success. He must become greater and greater, and I must become less and less."
John 3:29-31

Ouch!

The answer to seeing the work grow was for me to become less and less and to help Jesus and others become more and more successful. I felt deeply troubled with myself and how deep down I was more concerned with whether others honoured me and viewed me as a success. I made a commitment with Jesus that I would now live to make Jesus and others more and more successful and pour my life out to enable others to lead and pioneer.

Instead of trying to do everything, meet every need and solve every problem, I stopped and did nothing. It was very hard for me. I began to ask myself, "what are the things in our work that only I can do" and I started to only do those things.

I stopped running around doing what I thought were the exciting things like baptizing households, healing people and planting churches. Instead I felt a growing joy about seeing the team and leaders in our area growing and developing. I'm known by many as an "action man" type figure who's always the first to lead the pioneers over the hill into battle. I haven't lost that spirit, but there are now others who can do that job in our mission army so I need to do other things. I came to the realization that until now my main concern was about how I was ordering my own life and family's life around the work I talk about in this book. Now God was challenging me to grow and wrestle with how you order a body of people around this work.

I've stopped so others can start.

I learnt that often what people most need to develope as a leader is space and time. If you are willing to give someone those two things then it shows you are prepared to trust them. I reflected that in my enthusiasm to develope leaders it was like I was constantly standing over them, sharing tools, scriptures and encouragement all the time. When really I just needed to trust my relationship with them and also of course the Holy Spirit's work in their lives.

So I took a step back from those I was trying to develop as leaders and instead of trying to get them to do the things I thought they should be doing, I instead tried to build a loving and trusting relationship with them.

The result was that people started to lead and take initiative themselves and come to me for help or advice without me needing to say anything to them.

The boundaries of our apostolic work were extending through the faith and work of others and not mine. Which was good because I was feeling pretty weak and it allowed me to spend more time praying about opportunities that were opening up to build relationships with others across the UK and beyond. Because I had died and let go of getting the glory in our region, others were able to get in on the fun and I was freed up to start praying and exploring other areas of the work that needed developing. Looking back it all seems so simple and I wonder why I didn't just do it sooner. But there are always heart issues that underpin our actions and as a stubborn pioneer I seem to take a long time to understand this.

Instead of just giving instructions and direction to people, I asked them questions, just like Jesus did. I tried to be disciplined in working to develop people's ability to solve a problem or move around an obstacle instead of solving it for them and giving out quick answers.

If you're looking to develop leaders then I'll let you into a little secret. Here are two of the most important things you should to say to your people:

i) I don't know

ii) What can YOU do about that?

Maybe those around you are not coming forward with answers or solutions because there is no room for them to do so. I'd encourage you to restrain yourself and operate out of a place of genuine weakness and dependence on God and others. Stop dishing out all the answers and vision and start helping your disciples and potential leaders to speak up.

If you're willing to be humble and to change, then you may miraculously see that those you are training will be willing to change as well.

I've started to let things go in the work. Instead of just taking responsibility for gatherings, prayer meetings and everything that happens, I've let it go and am waiting for others to step up and take things on. Although it's quite a hard discipline to learn and can feel like nothing is happening, in the long run I know it will help other leaders to develope. Instead of people constantly following me, others will learn to take the lead themselves. The long term fruit of appointing leaders far outweighs the short term feeling of failure we might feel if we stop doing everything. We talk about trusting God to speak to people, but do we really believe that He is able to speak to all the parts of the body to get them moving?

Make some room for God to work in His body.

At this stage I'm reminded of the need to give ourselves to prayer which we looked at in chapter 4. If our strategy revolves around ourself then we won't be able to multiply disciples or churches. I am deeply challenged by the example of the church in China. I've heard many stories from missionaries who were expelled during the revolution or killed during the rebellions. Their influence was removed through death or deportation. Those that returned to the UK and other countries could only pray. One missionary couple I read about escaped China with only one thing. They had to leave behind all their posessions and clothes and all they brought back home was one photo of the church they had been able to plant during their time there.

For years after their return to the UK this couple would faithfully get that photo out every morning and pray for all of the people in it by name. Day after day. Year after year. I would imagine that this story is the same for many other missionaries who were forced to leave their flocks and entrust them into the care of the Holy Spirit. History tells us that the true Chinese church exploded in the absence of foreign missionaries and through severe testing and persecution. Is this not a lesson for us church planters about what is the most important part of our work? Apostolic workers lay foundations in churches and then move on. The hard work is not what we do when we're with the people, the hard work is carried out in prayer after we've left them,

"Night and day we pray earnestly for you."
1 Thessalonians 3:10

When working with teams I love to ask them questions and listen carefully to the answers I receive. I learned this from Jesus. He discerned what was in people's hearts and minds and asked questions to draw out the real issues. Often what people say or do on the outside is not what is really going on inside them. Some say it is the gift of discernment but from my experience it is more about knowing those you are caring for and praying constantly for them,

"Know the state of your flocks, and put your heart into caring for your herds"
Proverbs 27:23

Whilst many teams I work with say all the right things and talk about planting churches, it is only through questions and conversations that you see and hear what is really in people's hearts. When faced with challenges about how to train new disciples I so rarely hear anyone suggesting an apostolic solution. Most people suggest that they need to spend more time with the people, care for them more and teach them more. Rarely do I hear people suggesting that the answer isn't about us doing more but is actually about relying more on the power of prayer and making sure we are laying a strong foundation which the people can build on. Is our faith in God's work or our work? It always amazes me that Jesus left His disciples after 3 years. How could he entrust His work into the hands of these ordinary men and women? Jesus had such a trust in the Father's work in people's lives that He actually knew it was better for him to go away than for him to stay,

"But in fact, it is best for you that I go away…"
John 16:7

So many people I meet have no understanding of the apostolic call. They get offended at the idea that Jesus can look after His church without 'leaders'. When we train people how to plant a church, lay a foundation and then leave, they look at you like you've asked them to sacrifice their own children or something! Apostolic work goes against everything we are taught to believe in churchianty.

Why do people find it so hard to believe that God can speak to a community of disciples who have been trained to obey Him? If we can't imagine how a group of new disciples can grow without a 'pastor' or a 'leader' parachuted in from somewhere then what does that say about our disciple making and more worryingly about our faith in God?

Then we will be able to go and preach the Good News in other places far beyond you, where no one else is working."
2 Corinthians 10:16

Those gifted to be evangelists are constantly moving onto preach the good news in other places.

Those gifted pastorally are constantly staying in the same place and not moving anywhere.

But those who are gifted apostolically do both of those things but at the same time neither of those things! Apostles go to new places to preach the gospel and plant churches. Evangelists understand that part but pastors don't. They stay with the new believers like a pastor for as long as it takes but, unlike a pastor, they plan to leave, because their job is to lay a foundation which others will build on.

Evangelists are all about going. Pastors are all about staying. Apostles are all about building.

In my more immature days I would be constantly on the move. Starting things in one place, staying for a really short time and then moving on. God has put an unquenchable flame in me for the gospel and I cannot just stay in one place for too long. There was lots of action and excitement but there was not much fruit left in the places where me and the team had been working. Part of the problem was that I moved on too fast but part of the problem was that I misunderstood my calling. I was pioneering into new places and starting to make disciples. But then I'd abruptly move on to new places without training the people or laying a foundation in their lives.

As I talked to those around me I got mixed responses. My evangelist friends encouraged me not to worry about this and to keep "going" because that is what Jesus has commanded us to do and anyway God will care and look after those who've been baptized and become disciples. My more pastoral friends urged me to stop moving on and to stay with those already won because those people had so many needs and God wouldn't want me to move onto find new people if we can't even look after those we've already won. As I wrestled through this in prayer I came to the conclusion that everyone was right so there must be a way of doing it all!

Welcome to what I call *"The church planting dichotomy."*

A dichotomy is a division or contrast between two things that are, or are represented as being, opposed or entirely different. Staying and going are entirely different and opposing things, but in apostolic work we do both. We stay to leave and then leave to stay. Anyone with ears to hear should listen and understand! (Matthew 11:15)

The gift of apostleship enables both to happen because apostles lay foundations that others can build on. They only need to stay for a while because then others continue the work in their absence. When God says to move on, a mature apostle will have already prepared the people to continue the work without him or her being physically present. I've seen people trying to plant churches through finding people of peace and helping them to gather their people. But it often doesn't work because the "christian worker" operates pastorally instead of apostolically. The pioneer starts to meet everyone's needs and begins to lead, instead of laying a foundation that others can build on and then watching to see who emerges as a leader. Unwittingly the "christian worker" becomes the leader and completely shoots themselves in the foot.

Alternatively the "christian worker" does the work of an evangelist (see Chapter 5) and rides off into the sunset as soon as a household is baptized, leaving them with no foundation to build on.

There is another way, and I hope this book begins to explain that. Apostolic leadership makes room for others to lead so churches are built up and apostles can move onto preach the gospel in new places.

When I look at most churches today I see two things happening:

1) Leaders not stopping or moving out of the way and making room for others

2) Leaders desperately scratching their heads about how to raise up leaders

Surely you don't have to be a genius to see what is happening here?

If you're a leader then you're job is help your flock of people hear and obey Jesus and then to move out of the way to let other emerging leaders flourish.

If that doesn't happen then there's a problem with your disciple making or your heart attitude. The work of an apostle is to equip the body of Christ to be apostolic. So not all leaders may be called by God to constantly move on and plant more churches, but every leader is called to be apostolic and to train more leaders for the ever expanding work of mission. It's actually for the church's benefit that apostolic workers leave. It gives room for Father God to develope the church and raise up leaders from amongst them. There's such a great value in the time between planting a church and then going back to appoint leaders,

"Never be in a hurry about appointing a church leader."
1 Timothy 5:22

If the work is so urgent then why does Paul encourage Timothy to not be in a hurry to appoint leaders? Is it because Paul knew the value in letting a church work it out together and growing as disciples together without their influence? Paul trusted that God would be at work in the church without a leader telling people what to do. He trusted in the foundation that he had laid and that over time and with encouragement, rebuke and teaching, faithful disciples would emerge who were able to teach others, show patience with difficult people and solve problems in the church. And do you know what people like that are called?

Leaders.

Feed my sheep

Remember at the end of the last chapter when we saw something interesting about Jesus?

In Matthew 26 and John 13 we see Jesus not stuffing his face with food while all His disciples are. If you want to appoint leaders then I'd encourage you to look at who's not eating when the food is laid out!

In both of those stories Jesus chose to feed others rather than be fed himself. Instead of eating the food before Him, Jesus taught His disciples and gave them spiritual food. As a leader, that's what I do. No-one has to tell me to do this. It's nothing to do with my own cleverness or goodness, it is God's call on my life. Whenever I am amongst a group of people I choose to refrain from meeting my own needs and thinking about myself and my concern is with feeding Jesus' sheep. There seem to be so few others who think like that in the body of Christ. God has called me to live like this and others have encouraged and at times challenged me to develope this calling. But for the work to multiply I have had to learn how to develope more people who think like that and act like leaders.

What do you think I did to try and learn how to develope leaders? Yes that's right, I turned to the scriptures and looked at how Jesus did it.

Take a minute to read the following scripture and ask yourself the question "how did Jesus develope leaders?"

"When they got there, they found breakfast waiting for them - fish cooking over a charcoal fire, and some bread. "Bring some of the fish you've just caught," Jesus said. So Simon Peter went aboard and dragged the net to the shore. There were 153 large fish, and yet the net hadn't torn. "Now come and have some breakfast!" Jesus said. None of the disciples dared to ask him, "Who are you?" They knew it was the Lord. Then Jesus served them the bread and the fish. This was the third time Jesus had appeared to his disciples since he had been raised from the dead. After breakfast Jesus asked Simon Peter, "Simon son of John, do you love me more than these? "Yes, Lord," Peter replied, "you know I love you." "Then feed my lambs," Jesus told him. Jesus repeated the question: "Simon son of John, do you love me?" "Yes, Lord," Peter said, "you know I love you." "Then take care of my sheep," Jesus said. A third time he asked him, "Simon son of John, do you love me?" Peter was hurt that Jesus asked the question a third time. He said, "Lord, you know everything. You know that I love you." Jesus said, "Then feed my sheep. "I tell you the truth, when you were young, you were able to do as you

liked; you dressed yourself and went wherever you wanted to go. But when you are old, you will stretch out your hands, and others will dress you and take you where you don't want to go." Jesus said this to let him know by what kind of death he would glorify God. Then Jesus told him, "Follow me."
John 21:15-20

What stood out to you?

When I read this story I am very challenged by Jesus. He'd recently suffered an excruciating death, been deserted by all his disciples and even after pouring out his life into them for 3 years they still didn't get it. What would your response be if that had happened to you? Be honest. Would you want to prepare a nice breakfast for those who'd deserted you? Here we see Jesus modelling what it means to be a leader and persevering with those he was teaching to be disciples,

"Then Jesus served them"
John 6:13

It wasn't just a "love in" though because Jesus wasn't eating himself, he was feeding His sheep and calling His disciples to a whole new level of commitment. During this gathering Jesus turned his attention to Peter and went to the heart of the issue. If we want to develope leaders we cannot be fearful of asking people the hard questions which others tend to avoid. To appoint leaders we are looking for those people who have a calling from God to serve and lead others. Ultimately leadership development is about prayer and faith in God's work rather than techniques or formulas. Jesus was relating to Peter through the eyes of faith, not just dealing with him on a human level. Through human eyes, Peter was a headstrong man who promised more than he could deliver. He was unstable and unreliable. But Jesus saw something completely different,

"Simon, Simon, Satan has asked to sift each of you like wheat. But I have pleaded in prayer for you, Simon, that your faith should not fail. So when you have repented and turned to me again, strengthen your brothers." Peter said, "Lord, I am ready to go to prison with you, and even to die with you." But Jesus said, "Peter, let me tell you something. Before the rooster crows tomorrow morning, you will deny three times that you even know me."
Luke 22:31-35

Jesus was in prayer for His team and could see how the Father was testing Peter's faith and forming him into a leader. I meet with so many leaders who just cannot see what God is doing in people's lives. They can't see how God is working in people's lives or how He is calling people to be leaders. So it's no wonder they are cannot (or will not) appoint any leaders. They claim the issue is with 'their people' but actually the issue is with them.

If we return back to Jesus' breakfast barbeque we see Him questioning Peter's love and commitment to the cause. Three times Jesus' questions Peter and calls for a deeper and deeper level of love for Him. Here we see Jesus training one of His leaders and getting to the root of Peter's desire to do his own thing in the face of persecution and challenges. After Jesus' death, Peter had given up and returned to his fishing boat. He had thrown away God's calling on his life and was not acting like the rock upon which Jesus would build His church (Matthew 16:18)

Jesus called Peter back to God's calling on his life and exposed the heart issue that caused him to stray away from it.

After the third round of questioning at the barbeque we read that Peter was hurt,

Peter was hurt that Jesus asked the question a third time. He said, "Lord, you know everything. You know that I love you." Jesus said, "Then feed my sheep. "I tell you the truth, when you were young, you were able to do as you liked; you dressed yourself and went wherever you wanted to go. But when you are old, you will stretch out your hands, and others will dress you and take you where you don't want to go." Jesus said this to let him know by what kind of death he would glorify God. Then Jesus told him, "Follow me."
John 21:17-20

Jesus' questions had got to the heart of the matter. When Peter was young, he could do what he liked. When things became hard he could run away. But Jesus was calling him to be a leader who would be prepared to endure suffering and hardship for the sake of the gospel. Jesus was asking him to feed the sheep rather than to seek personal comfort and pleasure.

Are you prepared to challenge potential leaders to be the people God is calling them to be? Are you willing to lovingly 'hurt' your people when required and deal with the painful root issues in their lives?

Jesus asked His disciples hard questions all the time. He didn't gather a group of hand raising super spiritual church goers together who spent all day soaking in His presence. He trained a group of ordinary men and women to live sacrificially and supernaturally. At no point did Jesus teach his disciples that they would be happy or receive everything they needed to live a contented life. He urged them and challenged them to lay down their lives for the kingdom of God. Jesus used the example of His own life to teach His disciples that it is more blessed to give than to receive (Acts 20:35) and he expected them to give everything.

Is that what you are modelling to those around you?

I'm constantly criticized by the 'pastoral police' for asking too much of people and not being caring enough. But I've learned to not be afraid of asking more of people and teaching our people to meet the needs of others rather than doing it all myself,

"Our people must learn to do good by meeting the urgent needs of others; then they will not be unproductive."
Titus 3:14

I want to bear much fruit for Jesus and appoint leaders to take the work deeper and further than I ever could. But that won't happen if I don't intentionally train people to be productive by learning to meet needs and being stretched in their faith.

"Late in the afternoon his disciples came to him and said, "This is a remote place, and it's already getting late. Send the crowds away so they can go to the nearby farms and villages and buy something to eat." But Jesus said, "You feed them."
Mark 6:35-38

We train disciples and leaders by asking them to feed people and watch as their faith rises or falls. It takes discipline to step back and watch others trying to faithfully solve problems.

When we have people coming to visit the work we are doing I ask the team who they can stay with. When we have a need in the work I ask the team who can meet that need. And when people share a problem or question I ask them how they can solve that problem with the team's help. It's sometimes hard watching those you love having their faith sifted and tested. But we're called to appoint leaders not mollycoddle spiritual babies.

If God has called you to build an apostolic work then you need to stop solving problems and create them for others to solve. It goes against the prevailing culture in churchianity to create difficulties for people and of course Jesus took no pleasure in deliberately making life hard for His disciples. But to see greater fruit and harvest in the kingdom you'll need to ask more of your disciples and potential leaders just like Jesus did. I want to encourage you to pray more for your people. Ask God to show you what He is doing in their lives. Work with the Holy Spirit to help those you are discipling push out deeper and experience a new level of fruitfulness in their lives. You'll soon start to see some potential leaders emerging who rise to the challenges and start to feed and care for others.

Peter and the disciples had been out fishing all night and caught nothing, but Jesus encouraged them to continue and go out to deeper waters. And we all know what happened,

"When he had finished speaking, he said to Simon, "Now go out where it is deeper, and let down your nets to catch some fish." "Master," Simon replied, "we worked hard all last night and didn't catch a thing. But if you say so, I'll let the nets down again." And this time their nets were so full of fish they began to tear! A shout for help brought their partners in the other boat, and soon both boats were filled with fish and on the verge of sinking. When Simon Peter realized what had happened, he fell to his knees before Jesus and said, "Oh, Lord, please leave me - I'm such a sinful man." For he was awestruck by the number of fish they had caught, as were the others with him. His partners, James and John, the sons of Zebedee, were also amazed. Jesus replied to Simon, "Don't be afraid! From now on you'll be fishing for people!" And as soon as they landed, they left everything and followed Jesus."
Luke 5:4-12

What would it look like for you to do the same with those you are discipling?

That's how you develope leaders.

Giving an example to follow

The scriptures are full of truth and wisdom about how to appoint leaders. And it's all there for us if we search for it.

A great place to start is to look at the life of Jesus who taught and modelled leadership to His disciples and then expected them to go and replicate this with those they would disciple and train,

"After washing their feet, he put on his robe again and sat down and asked, "Do you understand what I was doing? You call me 'Teacher' and 'Lord,' and you are right, because that's what I am. And since I, your Lord and Teacher, have washed your feet, you ought to wash each other's feet. I have given you an example to follow. Do as I have done to you. I tell you the truth, slaves are not greater than their master. Nor is the messenger more important than the one who sends the message. Now that you know these things, God will bless you for doing them."
John 13:12-18

Because most churches and leaders don't make disciples, there seems a huge gap between a normal christian and a leader. Appointing leaders is some kind of magical myth that is way beyond anything we could hope for. Leadership teams spend lots of time praying and talking about who to select for their special leadership classes and then pull them out from the crowd.

Somehow we are believing that people will go from sitting in a row once a week and doing nothing to becoming a superhuman leader who can do everything.

If the focus is on making disciples, however, then all our churches and communities are leadership training pools. Appointing leaders is simply recognizing those disciples who seem to have a God given ability to persevere through hardship and to teach others. There's not a huge gap between being a disciple and being a leader in some ways and it means you'll be appointing leaders who are actually leading instead of selecting who you think would be a good leader and then trying to turn them into one. I've tried to do this in the work we are doing and it is a waste of time. The people God raises up are often not the people we would select and investing time in someone who shows potential but no proven-ness is foolishness. Make disciples and let God show you who He is raising up. Then appoint those people as leaders with prayer and fasting.

Paul's two letters to Timothy are a great source of wisdom for those seeking to develope and appoint leaders. I've often read 1 and 2 Timothy and written down in my journal what God shows me about training leaders and then what I am going to do about it in the coming days, weeks and months.

Why don't you do it?

It always hits me how Paul imparted so much of his 'way of life' to Timothy,

"But you, Timothy, certainly know what I teach, and how I live, and what my purpose in life is. You know my faith, my patience,

my love, and my endurance. You know how much persecution and suffering I have endured. You know all about how I was persecuted in Antioch, Iconium, and Lystra—but the Lord rescued me from all of it. Yes, and everyone who wants to live a godly life in Christ Jesus will suffer persecution.
2 Timothy 3:10-13

Timothy was familiar with Paul's teaching, how he lived and what his purpose in life was. Do you share your life to this extent with those you are discipling? When I'm beginning to develope a leader I start by focusing on two things,

1) I ask them questions about their purpose

and

2) I look at how they live

Often it can take a long time to help someone to clearly understand and communicate their God given purpose and calling. But stick with it because helping someone to know their purpose is like helping them to stand on solid ground,

"Timothy, my son, here are my instructions for you, based on the prophetic words spoken about you earlier. May they help you fight well in the Lord's battles."
1 Timothy 1:18

Paul's instructions to Timothy were not based on what Paul thought Timothy should be doing. His instructions to Timothy were like Fatherly direction based on what God was saying to Timothy. There is a huge difference between what Paul did and what most leaders do. Paul made disciples who knew how to obey Jesus and he then helped them to do it. Most leaders today suggest, advise and, dare I say it, manipulate their flock in the direction in which they think things should go. One way has an appearance of fruitfulness but produces no leaders. The other way takes much longer but produces leaders. I'll let you work out which one is which.

Take the time and attention to help developing leaders discern what God is asking of them because it will help them to fight well in the Lord's battles. Model to people the importance of knowing God's will and purpose for your life. Often those God is calling to leadership are enthusiastic and commit to lots of things. You need to help them to focus on what God is asking them to do and to give themselves to only what is necessary.

Along with that, take every opportunity you can to share lives together. How do they live at home, at work, with their husband or wife and with their children. Timothy knew how Paul lived. Those I am discipling know how I live because they come to our home and they see our lives warts and all. They see how I treat my wife and my children and how I respond when stressed and tired.

Sharing your way of life with a developing leader is the most valuable thing you can do because it helps them to flesh out what it looks like to build your life around service to God and others. When I am discipling people I want to see how they are growing in every area of their life. It's great if someone has boldness out on the mission field but the real test of their character is how they act at home with their family.

As the apostolic work grew, Paul couldn't be with all the churches at the same time. I hope that sooner or later you might also hit this point! When you do you'll realize the importance of passing on a way of life and not just some teaching points,

"That's why I have sent Timothy, my beloved and faithful child in the Lord. He will remind you of how I follow Christ Jesus, just as I teach in all the churches wherever I go."
1 Corinthians 4:17

Timothy was sent to remind the believers about Paul's way of life. It was the same way of life that Paul taught in all the churches. Giving an example to your teams and churches is critical and provides a pattern for them to imitate and build on. I often hear those I am discipling say to me that when they are in a challenging situation they ask themselves, "what would Ben do?" I ask them what they think I would do and more often than not I am encouraged by the response! Usually they respond by saying that they prayed, looked in the Bible for guidance and asked others on their team for help. Apparently that is what I do!! (It's not always been like that) Remember I told you the story about my Father in law teaching me carpentry skills in Chapter 7? He took away the mystery of working with wood and showed me how to do it. It's the same when you use the example of your life to teach others. I can't tell you how much growth I have seen in others when I have simply shared my life with them and modelled simple things like praying constantly, how to be patient with difficult people and how to respond to trials and suffering,

"Always remember that Jesus Christ, a descendant of King David, was raised from the dead. This is the Good News I preach. And because I preach this Good News, I am suffering and have been chained like a criminal. But the word of God cannot be chained. So I am willing to endure anything if it will bring salvation and eternal glory in Christ Jesus to those God has chosen."
2 Timothy 2:8-11

I'm convinced that we must prepare disciples to courageously endure persecution and suffering for the sake of the gospel.

I remember how one friend modelled to me how to respond to persecution. We were in a crazy situation and I was a bit like a bunny in the headlights. But my friend provided me with an example of how to live in situations like that. I have since been able to pass that onto those I am discipling as well. I will never forget how my friend was able to deal with the challenging situation we were in but still take the time to teach me and serve others throughout the episode! I was just trying to look after myself!

Leaders are those who know and understand that even though they may be chained – the word and work of God is not. Even though life might be hard for them, leaders know that there is a greater purpose for their circumstances than their own personal comfort and well being,

"And I want you to know, my dear brothers and sisters, that everything that has happened to me here has helped to spread the Good News. For everyone here, including the whole palace guard, knows that I am in chains because of Christ. And because of my imprisonment, most of the believers here have gained confidence and boldly speak God's message without fear."
Philippians 1:12-15

To appoint leaders we must first teach our churches to be more concerned about the spread of the good news than with their own comfort. Every obstacle and trial is an opportunity for our faith to grow and for the kingdom to be extended. We must model a lifestyle that seeks to die like a seed that falls to the ground for others and then fearlessly call others to do the same. I sometimes joke with people that in the Bible the mark of leadership was how many scars you had for the gospel. Nowadays it seems you can be leader by sitting in a classroom and writing an essay.

Here's what Paul said to the Ephesian elders when he met with them for the final time in Acts 20. It's a goldmine for those wanting to be more effective in training and appointing leaders.

What stands out to you from his words and what are you going to do about it?

"But when we landed at Miletus, he sent a message to the elders of the church at Ephesus, asking them to come and meet him. When they arrived he declared, "You know that from the day I set foot in the province of Asia until now I have done the Lord's work humbly and with many tears. I have endured the trials that came to me from the plots of the Jews. I never shrank back from telling you what you needed to hear, either publicly or in your homes. I have had one message for Jews and Greeks alike—the necessity of repenting from sin and turning to God, and of having faith in our Lord Jesus. "And now I am bound by the Spirit to go to Jerusalem. I don't know what awaits me, except that the Holy Spirit tells me in city after city that jail and suffering lie ahead. But my life is worth nothing to me unless I use it for finishing the work assigned me by the Lord Jesus—the work of telling others the Good News about the wonderful grace of God. "And now I know that none of you to whom I have preached the Kingdom will ever see me again. I declare today that I have been faithful. If anyone suffers eternal death, it's not my fault, for I didn't shrink from declaring all that God wants you to know. "So guard yourselves and God's people. Feed and shepherd God's flock - his church, purchased with his own blood - over which the Holy Spirit has appointed you as leaders. I know that false teachers, like vicious wolves, will come in among you after I leave, not sparing the flock. Even some men from your own group will rise up and distort the truth in order to draw a following. Watch out! Remember the three years I was with you - my constant watch and care over you night and day, and my many tears for you.

"And now I entrust you to God and the message of his grace that is able to build you up and give you an inheritance with all those he has set apart for himself. "I have never coveted anyone's silver or gold or fine clothes. You know that these hands of mine have worked to supply my own needs and even the needs of those who were with me. And I have been a constant example of how you can help those in need by working hard. You should remember the words of the Lord Jesus: 'It is more blessed to give than to receive.'"
Acts 20:17-36

Trainers not babysitters

Local leaders that have been appointed by apostolic teams continue the apostolic work in a region. Yes these leaders may be more pastoral in gifting and calling but they are still all working towards the same purpose,

"The one who plants and the one who waters work together with the same purpose"
1 Corinthians 3:8

Paul writes to the church in Corinth that the planters and the waterers all work together to multiply disciples, churches and leaders. They are all one team, joined in the Spirit though distant in person.

The work doesn't slow down when leaders are appointed, it continues. Leaders are appointed to continue with the work of making disciples of all nations and to build on the foundation laid by the apostolic team in that region.

Paul exhorts Timothy to continue the work of disciple making and multiplication in 2 Timothy 2:2,

"You have heard me teach things that have been confirmed by many reliable witnesses. Now teach these truths to other trustworthy people who will be able to pass them on to others. Endure suffering along with me, as a good soldier of Christ Jesus. Soldiers don't get tied up in the affairs of civilian life, for then they cannot please the officer who enlisted them. And athletes cannot win the prize unless they follow the rules. And hardworking farmers should be the first to enjoy the fruit of their labor. Think about what I am saying. The Lord will help you understand all these things."

Paul

Timothy

Trustworthy People

Others.

Imagine if your spiritual Timothys discipled other trustworthy people and these trustworthy people discipled others.

That's what we are praying about, planning for, and working towards because there are a million people in our region and the harvest needs an abundance of disciple makers and leaders that multiply themselves.

Leaders teach people to obey Jesus and correct them when necessary. That's the kind of person you're looking for,

"You must teach these things and encourage the believers to do them. You have the authority to correct them when necessary, so don't let anyone disregard what you say."
Titus 2:15

But how do we stop the leaders we appoint from becoming spiritual babysitters who become bottlenecks for the apostolic work? Well we read about a scenario like this in 3 John 5-11 where one leader called Diotrephes wants to get all the glory and be number 1,

"Dear friend, you are being faithful to God when you care for the traveling teachers who pass through, even though they are strangers to you. They have told the church here of your loving friendship. Please continue providing for such teachers in a manner that pleases God. For they are traveling for the Lord, and they accept nothing from people who are not believers. So we ourselves should support them so that we can be their partners as they teach the truth. I wrote to the church about this, but Diotrephes, who loves to be the leader, refuses to have anything to do with us. When I come, I will report some of the things he is doing and the evil accusations he is making against us. Not only does he refuse to welcome the traveling teachers, he also tells others not to help them. And when they do help, he puts them out of the church."
3 John 5-11

This man wasn't welcoming travelling workers to teach and bring what was lacking to the churches in his region. He was cutting off the churches from receiving any help from outside and Paul spoke against his behavior and attitude. Diotrephes loved to be the leader and had become a bottleneck for the apostolic work they were all engaged with. He wasn't concerned about the health of the church, he was only concerned with his own ego and reputation. Maybe Paul had people like Dioptrephes in mind when he warned the believers in Philippi,

"Dear brothers and sisters, pattern your lives after mine, and learn from those who follow our example. For I have told you often before, and I say it again with tears in my eyes, that there are many whose conduct shows they are really enemies of the cross of Christ. They are headed for destruction. Their god is their appetite, they brag about shameful things, and they think only about this life here on earth."
Philppians 3:17-20

For the apostolic work to continue, local leaders need to welcome travelling workers into the churches to teach, model and equip the saints for the work of ministry. It takes humility from both sides.

In our work I constantly remind people that it is not important who does the planting, or who does the watering. What's important is that God makes the seed grow just as Paul reminded the church in Corinth. (1 Corinthians 3:7)

Fierce tests

Jesus prayed for His leaders to come through the fiery trials and so must we!

Throughout the scriptures we see God testing the faith of His people. I'm sure we can all look back at times in our own life where God has allowed our own faith to be tested. Although it's painful at the time, it produces new levels of glory and grace in us,

"For our present troubles are small and won't last very long. Yet they produce for us a glory that vastly outweighs them and will last forever!"
2 Corinthians 4:17

If Jesus learned what it meant to be obedient to His Father through suffering (Hebrews 5:8) then why should we be surprised when God takes us down a similar path,

"Dear friends, don't be surprised at the fiery trials you are going through, as if something strange were happening to you. Instead, be very glad - for these trials make you partners with Christ in his suffering, so that you will have the wonderful joy of seeing his glory when it is revealed to all the world. If you are insulted because you bear the name of Christ, you will be blessed, for the glorious Spirit of God rests upon you. If you suffer, however, it must not be for murder, stealing, making trouble, or prying into other people's affairs. But it is no shame to suffer for being a Christian. Praise God for the privilege of being called by his name! For the time has come for judgment, and it must begin with God's household. And if judgment begins with us, what terrible fate awaits those who have never obeyed God's Good News? And also, "If the righteous are barely saved, what will happen to godless sinners?" So if you are suffering in a manner that pleases God, keep on doing what is right, and trust your lives to the God who created you, for he will never fail you."
1 Peter 4:12-19

God tests us to prove the genuineness of our faith and to see if we will continue through suffering and hardship. We should not be surprised when we face all manner of hardships but rejoice and be glad because it is an opportunity to glorify Jesus even more,

"So be truly glad. There is wonderful joy ahead, even though you must endure many trials for a little while. These trials will show that your faith is genuine. It is being tested as fire tests and purifies gold—though your faith is far more precious than mere gold. So when your faith remains strong through many trials, it will bring you much praise and glory and honor on the day when Jesus Christ is revealed to the whole world."
1 Peter 1:6-8

When God tests people it reveals what is really in their heart.

We should embrace the testing of faith and see it for what it is, rather than shield people from it. If we dumb everything down and keep people in a pastoral wonderland their faith will never grow and they will remain spiritual infants.

According to the dictionary a "test" is a procedure intended to establish the quality, performance, or reliability of something, especially before it is taken into widespread use. You would never release a product or piece of machinery into the market without carrying out vigorous tests on it. And God doesn't release a leader into His work without deeply testing their faith. I've come to realise and understand that the true measure of a leader is not what they say and do from the pulpit during a meeting, but it's how they act under pressure and in the midst of fiery trials. Whilst it's not pleasant or nice to see those you are trying to develope going through tests and trials, we have to remember that it's actually for their own good! We must train them to continue in the faith and not shrink back during these times. So many people I've met talk about serving Jesus but then give up and pull back when it's time to really serve him. It's easy to say we are serving Jesus when there's no cost to us! When you have enough money, food and everyone agrees with you then it's pretty easy to talk about being a leader or a pioneer. Trials, hardships and persecution reveal who you really are though. Real servants of Jesus aren't surprised when they are abused, have nothing and suffer hardships because they are not concerned about being served any more. Meeting the needs of Jesus and His work is all that matters.

I enjoy watching television programmes about how organisations recruit and train their workers. It interests me how they train and instill their values into potential recruits and how they test hopeful candidates to see what kind of people they really are. This is seen most clearly when hopeful recruits apply to join the Armed Forces. It is quite entertaining to watch the instructors take their fresh faced recruits through a selection process which is designed to test them to breaking point. They are trying to see who the recruits are deep down when all the bravado and talk has been taken away. They want to see who the recruits really are before they give them a gun and let them loose in a war zone.

Do you know that Jesus also has a selection process designed to break those who claim to want to be His followers? The process is even harder for those who aspire to be a leader in His army,

"In the same way, deacons must be well respected and have integrity. They must not be heavy drinkers or dishonest with money. They must be committed to the mystery of the faith now revealed and must live with a clear conscience. Before they are appointed as deacons, let them be closely examined. If they pass the test, then let them serve as deacons."
1 Timothy 3:8-11

Maybe you haven't heard this talked about at your Sunday morning social club, but the basic selection process into Jesus' army involves a public initiation ritual that should be done in front of all your friends and family (the bible calls that "repent and be baptized") and then the commanding officer Himself will lead new recruits through a series of tests and trials aimed at helping people to turn their back on this world and their selfish lusts. One of the main requirements of joining Jesus' army is that you immediately start passing on what you are learning onto others so they can start obeying Him as well. That is basic entry level and Jesus calls it "Go and make disciples" In this army you don't move up through the ranks you actually move down. The greatest war heroes and generals in Jesus' army are those who serve others and no-one ever retires or graduates from the process as you join for life. Each day the training consists of carrying a heavy cross and denying yourself.

Is that what you signed up for? Recruits who show great patience with other team members and are able to solve problems under pressure are singled out for an even greater level of testing as the commanding officer is looking for trustworthy people who can take responsibility to teach and lead others in the army.

If this all sounds a bit strange to you then you need to pick up your Bible and read how Jesus taught and trained His disciples and would-be leaders.

Paul encourages Timothy to test people before appointing them as deacons and elders and John warns people to look beyond people's words to test the spirit of a person,

"Dear friends, do not believe everyone who claims to speak by the Spirit. You must test them to see if the spirit they have comes from God."
1 John 4:1

If you're still not convinced then here's a story which shows how Jesus tested what kind of spirit was in his disciples. We'll call it the

"Fierce storm challenge" The challenge was designed to test the potential recruits to their absolute limits and to see if they would remember their training and purpose in life threatening situations. Fierce means physically violent and frightening or strong and powerful.

Let's look at the "Fierce storm challenge",

"As evening came, Jesus said to his disciples, "Let's cross to the other side of the lake." So they took Jesus in the boat and started out, leaving the crowds behind (although other boats followed). But soon a fierce storm came up. High waves were breaking into the boat, and it began to fill with water. Jesus was sleeping at the back of the boat with his head on a cushion. The disciples woke him up, shouting, "Teacher, don't you care that we're going to drown?" When Jesus woke up, he rebuked the wind and said to the waves, "Silence! Be still!" Suddenly the wind stopped, and there was a great calm. Then he asked them, "Why are you afraid? Do you still have no faith?" The disciples were absolutely terrified. "Who is this man?" they asked each other. "Even the wind and waves obey him!"
Mark 4:35-41

In this story Jesus, the commanding officer, asked His disciples to cross to the other side of the lake. He knew they would have to navigate through a fierce storm and remember their training in a very fearful and dangerous situation. It was a test to see if they would remember that the command was to get to the other side and if they would have faith and take authority over the situation.

They didn't.

The commanding officer had to step in and show them what to do.

A leader doesn't lose their head in a storm and remembers what their commanding officer has instruced them to do. In the future these disciples would become leaders who continued to sail through storms and kept their team on track despite the waves of persecution and fear that threatened to drown them. But Jesus had to test them and train them before He left them unsupervised.

What's interesting is that when Jesus and the disciples reached the other side of the lake (which was the goal all along) they met the man with a legion of demons. It's such a great story as well,

"So they arrived at the other side of the lake, in the region of the Gerasenes. When Jesus climbed out of the boat, a man possessed by an evil spirit came out from the tombs to meet him. This man lived in the burial caves and could no longer be restrained, even with a chain. Whenever he was put into chains and shackles—as he often was—he snapped the chains from his wrists and smashed the shackles. No one was strong enough to subdue him. Day and night he wandered among the burial caves and in the hills, howling and cutting himself with sharp stones. When Jesus was still some distance away, the man saw him, ran to meet him, and bowed low before him. With a shriek, he screamed, "Why are you interfering with me, Jesus, Son of the Most High God? In the name of God, I beg you, don't torture me!" For Jesus had already said to the spirit, "Come out of the man, you evil spirit." Then Jesus demanded, "What is your name?" And he replied, My name is Legion, because there are many of us inside this man." Then the evil spirits begged him again and again not to send them to some distant place. There happened to be a large herd of pigs feeding on the hillside nearby. "Send us into those pigs," the spirits begged. "Let us enter them."So Jesus gave them permission. The evil spirits came out of the man and entered the pigs, and the entire herd of about 2,000 pigs plunged down the steep hillside into the lake and drowned in the water. The

herdsmen fled to the nearby town and the surrounding countryside, spreading the news as they ran. People rushed out to see what had happened. A crowd soon gathered around Jesus, and they saw the man who had been possessed by the legion of demons. He was sitting there fully clothed and perfectly sane, and they were all afraid. Then those who had seen what happened told the others about the demon-possessed man and the pigs. And the crowd began pleading with Jesus to go away and leave them alone. As Jesus was getting into the boat, the man who had been demon possessed begged to go with him. But Jesus said, "No, go home to your family, and tell them everything the Lord has done for you and how merciful he has been." So the man started off to visit the Ten Towns of that region and began to proclaim the great things Jesus had done for him; and everyone was amazed at what he told them.
Mark 5:1-21

The disciples are not even mentioned in this story, maybe they were still drying out their clothes from the previous challenge! Having just gone through a fierce storm they were now faced with a fierce man! This man was so fierce that he could not be restrained with chains and he wondered around the hills day and night howling and cutting himself with rocks. I don't know if you have ever stopped to think about this? If you lived in that town you would hear that man screaming and howling over you day and night. He wasn't just a guy with a few 'issues' He was a major demonic stronghold over the entire region.

Jesus was trying to show His disciples that there was a great purpose in crossing the lake and that they needed to remember their orders in times of crisis. Often times of crisis come right before the biggest victories. If they lost their faith then they'd lose the battle. Jesus was there on that occasion to step in, but he wouldn't always be there. That is why He was testing them.

What happened to the man with a legion of demons was, I'd suggest, a big victory.

This man who formerly wondered the hills screaming and howling was now in his right mind and about to be sent as a missionary to the ten towns he'd previously terrorized. I believe Jesus tests us all to prove the genuineness of our faith. Most believers are stuck going round and round on the "Fierce lake challenge". At the sight of any danger or risk to themselves they jump ship and have to go back to the start. They completely forget their orders to get to the other side of the lake and their training which will help them to take authority over the elements in the name of Jesus.

However a few people remember their training and the command from Jesus and they sail through the storm. They persevere with their team and get to the other side to face the next challenge.

The bible calls these people 'approved workers' and you should keep an eye out for them. They are strong candidates for leadership,

"Work hard so you can present yourself to God and receive his approval."
2 Timothy 2:15

"For you know that when your faith is tested, your endurance has a chance to grow. So let it grow, for when your endurance is fully developed, you will be perfect and complete, needing nothing."
James 1:3-5

"God blesses those who patiently endure testing and temptation. Afterward they will receive the crown of life that God has promised to those who love him
James 1:12

Jesus tested His disciples with the fierce storm because the real work was waiting on the other side of the lake. There are tormented people all around us who need setting free and sending in the name of Jesus. If we fail the tests sent our way then we forfeit our place on the other side of the lake where the real action is.

For many of us we still need to be overcomers in our own lives and become leaders ourselves before we can even think about appointing anyone else to lead.

If God is calling you to be a leader then don't forfeit your place in His army. Don't allow your faith to be shipwrecked. Remember the mission. Keep Jesus' words before you at all time. Persevere through hardship. Then the commanding offer may approve you for the real work.

If you've been approved by God then your work is now to train others to become approved workers and appoint them as leaders. You'll need to take people through a selection process which is designed to test their faith, resolve and team work.

Here's some thoughts on how to do that.

Leaders don't magically appear

As the work we were doing began to grow I had a sense that I needed to pray for a Timothy, someone who could share the burden of the work with me and who I could rely on as a faithful co-worker and leader. When God shows us something like this, it's easy to think that somehow the answer is going to fall into our lap. It's like all the talk of revival that I've heard in churches, God may well be promising to pour out His Spirit, but I believe the promise is conditional on our faith and hard work. With hindsight, God was putting this on my heart so that I could learn how to train a spiritual Timothy. It's much the same as making disciples. I've often felt like jumping ship or pulling back from people because it's felt like they've not really wanted to obey Jesus or overcome a certain challenge in their life. Often though these situations have been an opportunity for me to train and teach people about the things that I am seeing in their lives. Instead of using other people's weaknesses or immaturity against them, maybe God is showing us them so we can help them to grow as a disciple! After all, we all have our issues right! Disciples are made, they don't magically appear overnight. And leaders are developed, they don't fall from heaven but are produced through much prayer and hard labor. Instead of looking out at the disciples and churches around us and wondering who was a leader, I decided that I needed to develope leaders. There weren't any because no-one was being trained to be a leader.

So with great enthusiasm I started to pray and think through how I could raise up a spiritual Timothy. I'd ask God to show me who to invite with me on trips and who I should invest more time in. I'd throw out invites to everyone and see who had the desire to go deeper and take on more responsibility in the work.

One of the first questions I asked myself was what does a leader do? If we weren't clear on what a leader does then how could we train people to be leaders?!

So what do you think we did?

Yes, we turned to the scriptures and asked ourselves, "what does a leader do"

Why don't do it as well with the following scriptures and make a note of what you discover,

"This is a trustworthy saying: "If someone aspires to be a church leader, he desires an honorable position." So a church leader must be a man whose life is above reproach. He must be faithful to his wife. He must exercise self-control, live wisely, and have a good reputation. He must enjoy having guests in his home, and he must be able to teach. He must not be a heavy drinker or be violent. He must be gentle, not quarrelsome, and not love money. He must manage his own family well, having children who respect and obey him. For if a man cannot manage his own household, how can he take care of God's church? A church leader must not be a new believer, because he might become proud, and the devil would cause him to fall. Also, people outside the church must speak well of him so that he will not be disgraced and fall into the devil's trap. In the same way, deacons must be well respected and have integrity. They must not be heavy drinkers or dishonest with money. They must be committed to the mystery of the faith now revealed and must live with a clear conscience. Before they are appointed as deacons, let them be closely examined. If they pass the test, then let them serve as deacons. In the same way, their wives must be respected and must not slander others. They must exercise self-control and be faithful in everything they do. A deacon must be faithful to his wife, and he must manage his children and household well. Those who do well as deacons will be rewarded with respect from others and will have increased confidence in their faith in Christ Jesus."
1 Timothy 3:1-14

"If you explain these things to the brothers and sisters, Timothy, you will be a worthy servant of Christ Jesus, one who is nourished by the message of faith and the good teaching you have followed. Do not waste time arguing over godless ideas and old

wives' tales. Instead, train yourself to be godly. "Physical training is good, but training for godliness is much better, promising benefits in this life and in the life to come." This is a trustworthy saying, and everyone should accept it. This is why we work hard and continue to struggle, for our hope is in the living God, who is the Savior of all people and particularly of all believers. Teach these things and insist that everyone learn them. Don't let anyone think less of you because you are young. Be an example to all believers in what you say, in the way you live, in your love, your faith, and your purity. Until I get there, focus on reading the Scriptures to the church, encouraging the believers, and teaching them. Do not neglect the spiritual gift you received through the prophecy spoken over you when the elders of the church laid their hands on you. Give your complete attention to these matters. Throw yourself into your tasks so that everyone will see your progress. Keep a close watch on how you live and on your teaching. Stay true to what is right for the sake of your own salvation and the salvation of those who hear you."
1 Timothy 4:6-16

"Again I say, don't get involved in foolish, ignorant arguments that only start fights. A servant of the Lord must not quarrel but must be kind to everyone, be able to teach, and be patient with difficult people. Gently instruct those who oppose the truth. Perhaps God will change those people's hearts, and they will learn the truth. Then they will come to their senses and escape from the devil's trap. For they have been held captive by him to do whatever he wants."
2 Timothy 2:23-26

An elder must live a blameless life. He must be faithful to his wife, and his children must be believers who don't have a reputation for being wild or rebellious. A church leader is a

manager of God's household, so he must live a blameless life. He must not be arrogant or quick-tempered; he must not be a heavy drinker, violent, or dishonest with money. Rather, he must enjoy having guests in his home, and he must love what is good. He must live wisely and be just. He must live a devout and disciplined life. He must have a strong belief in the trustworthy message he was taught; then he will be able to encourage others with wholesome teaching and show those who oppose it where they are wrong."
Titus 1:5-10

From these scriptures I saw the following points about leaders,

- It's good if people want to be leaders

- A leader's life must be above reproach

- A leader must be faithful to their partner (I'm not going into the gender debate in this book!)

- A leader must be self controlled, have wisdom and have a good reputation with people

- They must be able to teach others and enjoy having guests in their home

- They must not be a heavy drinker or be violent

- They must not quarrel but be gentle and not love money

- They must manage their family and children well

- Not a new believer

- Not be dishonest with money

- They must be closely examined and tested

- Committted to the faith

- They explain spiritual things to other people

- They follow good teaching in their own life

- They don't waste time arguing about unnecessary things

- They train themselves physically and spiritually

- They are hard workers

- They are an example to others by what they say and how they live

- They read the scriptures to those they are discipling and gathering

- They remember prophetic words given to them and build their lives on them

- They don't neglect their spiritual gift

- They are kind to everyone

- They are patient with difficult people

- They are gentle with people who oppose them and are able to show those people where they are wrong

- Not arrogant or quick tempered

- They must love what is good

When I did this for the first time it de-mystified the whole area of appointing leaders. It was like my father in law de-mystifying the world of carpentry for me. Like with so many things in life, knowing what you're looking for makes things a whole lot clearer. Because I identified what I was looking for in a leader I could now pray for people in a much more focused way and set about training and testing people in these areas.

I didn't do anything that clever. I just asked God for opportunities to grow and test people's faith and lives in all of these areas. When they did a good job I encouraged them and thought about how to entrust more to them. If deeper personal issues were brought up in people's lives then we worked them through together. Some people began to avoid me because they were not prepared to be disciples or consider how they could grow. But that was ok because I was looking for those who could sail through the storm and get to the other side.

Here are some ways in which I did this.

I talked a lot more with the team and churches about being a leader and how it is a good thing to aspire to. For many of our disciples they don't even know there are meant to be leaders in the church because they haven't grown up with it all like I had. With hindsight you could say that I was casting vision for leadership. I asked people if they felt God was calling them to be a leader. Some said yes.

We began to address relational issues amongst those we were discipling. I must confess that this is a bit of a minefield when you're working in the harvest as people's lives are messy to say the least. But we started to teach more intentionally about faithfulness and marriage and how God's work starts at home in our family. I started to spend a lot more time with some of the fruitful disciples to help them think about their life and building their reputation amongst people. Some of our most fruitful disciples come from a background of drugs and crime so this area is important.

I deliberately invite myself and other team members to people's homes and ask who can show hospitality to guests. If people are not willing to open their home to you then they are unlikely to open their heart to you.

I started to ask others to teach and answer questions instead of doing it myself. This meant I started to do more coaching behind the scenes and less 'work' myself.

I looked for who seemed to be able to settle arguments amongst people and intentionally asked them to speak into other situations. I also made a note of people who seemed to always be quarreling and arguing with people.

Instead of handling money and planning issues myself I entrusted more to others on the team. I entrusted things that are valuable to me into the hands of others (Money, team members, sometimes my own children) and watched to see who 'added' to the work. This was hard for me but as I let go of things it helped others to grow.

I'd ask others to answer people with difficult questions!

I spent more time helping fruitful disciples discover their purpose and calling from God and I'd remind them often of prophetic words they had received from God.

I spent more time laying hands on people and speaking prophetic words over them.

All of these things helped to develope other people as leaders, but it was also sometimes hard for me as it dented my pride and ego. Other people increasingly experienced the joy of pressing through trials and seeing God at work in amazing ways. Other people started to feel God helping them to baptize and teach others. But I kept asking God to show me how I could become less.

I remember one particular occasion where I was reading the Gospel of John and the following two verses stood out to me. Does anything stand out to you from them,

"Then Jesus and his disciples left Jerusalem and went into the Judean countryside. Jesus spent some time with them there, baptizing people."
John 3:22

"Jesus knew the Pharisees had heard that he was baptizing and making more disciples than John (though Jesus himself didn't baptize them—his disciples did) So he left Judea and returned to Galilee."
John 4:1-4

I'll let you work out what God showed me, but after seeing it I made a decision to stop (unless absolutely necessary) baptizing people and encouraged others to do it. It helped everyone in our team to see that they were disciple makers and not to rely on me. I'd said this to people over and over again but it was only when I made this practical step that I saw others baptizing more people. On reflection, it was another situation where it was good for me to go away. As I removed myself it meant others could step up.

I also looked for ways to help others swing the sword of the spirit. For me, making disciples and being a leader is all about empowering others and giving others the opportunity to grow. People will never become good at using a sword if they don't get to practice. The word of God is the sword that we use to fight the lies of satan. I've attempted to model how we must turn to the scriptures for guidance in every circumstance and how we can then teach and apply the scriptures to other people's lives,

All Scripture is inspired by God and is useful to teach us what is true and to make us realize what is wrong in our lives. It corrects us when we are wrong and teaches us to do what is right. God uses it to prepare and equip his people to do every good work."
2 Timothy 3:10-17

God uses His word (not me or you) to prepare and equip people to do every good work so we better get teaching people how to swing the sword,

"Work hard so you can present yourself to God and receive his approval. Be a good worker, one who does not need to be ashamed and who correctly explains the word of truth. Avoid worthless, foolish talk that only leads to more godless behavior."
2 Timothy 2:15

Whenever a question is raised I take the opportunity to train others how to go to the scriptures to find the answer and then how to act on it immediately. That way they can find the answer whether I am there or not! I look for those on my team and amongst the churches we're planting who bring the word of God into situations and conversations. They are the wise ones!

322   Accidental Apostle

The Lord cares for them more than we do

Before I share a few stories at the end of this chapter I wanted to
say one final thing about appointing leaders,

"With prayer and fasting, they turned the elders over to the care
of the Lord, in whom they had put their trust."
Acts 14:23

It's really not about your work, it's about the Holy Spirit. God
cares for those you're appointing as leaders far more deeply than
we do. Paul and Barnabus turned the elders over to the care of the
Lord because they belonged to Him. It's hard to let go of people.
Especially those who have become faithful co-workers. Yet the
apostolic call invites us to let go of those we love and to turn them
over to the care of the Lord.

We do this with much prayer and fasting!

Why do you think they appointed the leaders with prayer and
fasting in Acts 14:23?

If we think back to when Jesus sent out His disciples in Matthew 10
we read something very interesting which reveals why Jesus also
appointed his leaders with much prayer (and probably fasting as
well!),

"Look, I am sending you out as sheep among wolves. So be as
shrewd as snakes and harmless as doves. But beware! For you
will be handed over to the courts and will be flogged with whips in
the synagogues. You will stand trial before governors and kings

because you are my followers. But this will be your opportunity to tell the rulers and other unbelievers about me. When you are arrested, don't worry about how to respond or what to say. God will give you the right words at the right time. For it is not you who will be speaking—it will be the Spirit of your Father speaking through you."
Matthew 10:16-21

Appointing leaders is like sending out sheep among wolves! Jesus knew what would happen to His disciples and we know what will happen to leaders we appoint. They face a humanly impossible task with dangers on every side. BUT in the heat of those trials and sufferings, leaders are those who take the opportunity to preach the Gospel to others and to speak the words that God gives them. The work of being a leader is nothing like managing people in the world. It requires supernatural empowerment and complete dependence on the Spirit.

Apostolic workers know what it will take because they have gone through it themselves and still are!

When considering how to appoint leaders and encourage them to fight the good fight it's interesting to look at Paul and Timothy's relationship.

Here are just a few things that Paul wrote to Timothy,

"This is why I remind you to fan into flames the spiritual gift God gave you when I laid my hands on you. For God has not given us a spirit of fear and timidity, but of power, love, and self-discipline."
2 Timothy 1:6-8

"Hold on to the pattern of wholesome teaching you learned from me - a pattern shaped by the faith and love that you have in Christ Jesus. Through the power of the Holy Spirit who lives within us, carefully guard the precious truth that has been entrusted to you.
2 Timothy 1:13-16

Don't be afraid of suffering for the Lord. Work at telling others the Good News, and fully carry out the ministry God has given you."
2 Timothy 4:1-6

If you want to develope leaders then you must love them deeply and then be prepared to let them go! You must let go of what you're holding onto so you can lay your hands on others instead! You must be an example of how to be joyful in suffering, how to be fearless and how to carry out ministry in the face of great hardship.

Then you will be able to say with Paul,

"As for me, my life has already been poured out as an offering to God. The time of my death is near. I have fought the good fight, I have finished the race, and I have remained faithful. And now the prize awaits me—the crown of righteousness, which the Lord, the righteous Judge, will give me on the day of his return. And the prize is not just for me but for all who eagerly look forward to his appearing."
2 Timothy 4:6-9

Timothy, my son

Jesus didn't treat everyone the same, so nor do I.

I'm constantly on the look out for Timothy's who have the capacity and calling to be leaders. One guy was brought to our house during a mission week we were doing. He had a notorious reputation in our area for drugs and violence but I felt God had shown me who this man could be in Christ. From the moment I met this guy I treated him completely differently to others I've met and discipled. He wasn't coming to our house to become a christian or to sit down and learn some nice things from the Bible. He was coming to enlist in an army, but he didn't know it yet.

So we welcomed Him into our hearts and home and I trained Him like a soldier. Of course we had times where we messed around and had fun. But this guy wasn't looking for churchianity or to be part of a christian club that met on a Sunday. He wanted to be involved with a family and to be put to work in the mission.

Because I perceived He was a leader, I treated him like a leader. The day after he gave his life to Jesus we took him out and trained him how to heal people and find people of peace. Throughout our relationship I deliberately looked for opportunities to throw this new brother into the deep end, and more often than not he rose to the occasion with a simple faith and great joy. He led a number of people to Jesus that week before He got baptized. And after his baptism he went onto baptize and train others. The last time I tried to work it out I think he was part of 6 generations of baptized disciples. (And by that I mean that I baptized "S", "S" baptized this brother, this brother baptized "C", "C" baptized "A" and I believe

"A" baptized someone else.) He'd be at my side when I travelled to other parts of the UK and over time I learned to trust him to train people in my absence. Like us all, he had some things in his life that Jesus was working on, but he understood what it meant to be a disciple and learned how to teach others as well. I look back and see that this brother coming to faith was a major turning point in the work we were doing and through him many doors were opened to people

This brother is now with Jesus but his example lives on amongst those we are working with. Many looked at his life and couldn't believe how God was changing him. What they didn't see however was the many hours I'd invested in this brother driving around the country together and sharing meals at home. I learned that pouring yourself out into faithful willing Timothy's produces much fruit and that developing leaders produces 30, 60 or 100 fold fruit. Of course it's all God's work in people and all glory goes to him. But we have the privilege of working with God by making disciples and helping others to solve problems rather than treating them like babies!

It's not me doing the work

I'm a practical kind of a guy who likes to get on with it. So I have had to learn a lot about how to equip and empower others to lead. And I still have lots to learn. At the start of one year I felt like God was challenging me to become an equipper and a trainer rather than just a do-er. So I committed myself to doing this.

The first thing I had to do was to 'pray in' some people to train. So I did that. Within a couple of months I had two brothers by my side and we were going regularly to a town in our area to plant a church.

Of course I was concerned about actually planting a church in that town and making disciples in the harvest. But I also deliberately went very slow because I realized that this was an opportunity to multiply the number of travelling workers in our region so it wasn't just me running around doing everything. I'd tried to train people before with mixed success, I often found that instead of developing leaders I was just giving people instructions and tasks to do. I was operating as a leader myself rather than helping others to become leaders. So I forced myself to take a different approach with these two brothers.

Instead of giving them answers and lots of tools that would help them to plant a church I asked them lots of questions, spent hours helping them to wrestle with the scriptures and did not hold back in telling them the truth when they needed to hear it. Sometimes it felt like I was wasting a lot of time sitting around with these guys when I could have been out doing the work myself, but God gave me patience and grace to pour myself out into these brothers. We had lots of arguments and I had to find lots of ways to try and manoeuver around differences of opinions and personality clashes. I constantly tried to build humility and trust amongst us rather than trying to prove my point or argue about who was right.

After a few months I began to see such a change in them both. They were starting to solve problems themselves, take initiative for the disciples and churches in our area and would come to me when they needed help. I learned to appreciate them as brothers who I could share my burdens with rather than as projects or people I was just training. These two brothers are now important leaders in the work we are doing and are starting to respond to God's call on their lives to preach the gospel, make disciples and strengthen believers across the UK and beyond. Maybe soon they will also begin to develope and appoint leaders themselves from amongst the people they are working with. I hope that my example will be helpful to them and provide a foundation for them to build on.

Shepherd your flock (Part 1)

We had trained a team how to find people of peace and sent them out into a housing estate. After they'd been out for around 30 minutes I took a walk around to pray for the area. I headed into the housing estate and I must admit that I was quite surprised to find some of the team already sat in a front garden eating and drinking with some of the locals. The team told me that knocked on the door of this house within the first 5 minutes and offered prayer. I quickly identified who the person of peace was so I could begin to train them as a potential leader immediately. So many people fail to recognize the importance of what we say and do with people when training them. They expect people to somehow just "get it" when actually Jesus is calling them to train these new disciples how to obey Jesus. From the moment I set foot in that house I treated this person of peace like a leader. I explained to her that God had sent us to this area to find people just like her and that we would help her to gather her people and form a church. I constantly encouraged this lady to pray for her people and tried to find ways to lovingly provoke her to good works. This lady had people in her home 24/7 and was known in the area for her care and love for others. To me it was so obvious that she was a leader in the area who had a calling on her life to shepherd her flock. I told her this every time we met.

I could see others on the team struggling with my upfront approach though and whenever we visited the lady and her flock some on the team would constantly try to water down the expectation or vision I was trying to impart into her. I used to get annoyed by this but now I've learned that people don't do it deliberately and it's part of working with others in teams. Not only was I training the new believers to be disciples but I was training the team I was working with to be apostolic and not revert to the charitable, pastoral, need-meeting version of christianity that they were familiar with. That version of christianity doesn't make disciples and it certainly doesn't develope leaders.

After a while this lady began to develope as a shepherd in her area and regularly gathered her friends and family to bring and share food, care for one another and look at the scriptures. Some on the team celebrated what God had done in this lady as if through our prayers He had just waved His magic wand over her. I rejoiced that God had helped me and some others on the team to patiently correct, rebuke and encourage her as a beloved sister and co-worker.

Shepherd your flock (Part 2)

I met a man in Glastonbury a few years ago. He seemed to have a faith in God and was clearly a leader in the community there.

After our first encounter I remember feeling like he was exactly the kind of person we were searching for! He had a genuine faith and desire to be part of a disciple making movement and was clearly a born leader. I watched him with his people on the street, encouraging them, rebuking them and trying to plant spiritual seeds into them. For various reasons we lost contact after a few initial meetings and then our paths crossed again a year or so later.

I was encouraged to see that his faith was still strong and he now seemed ready to be baptized and be more focused in trying to gather his people for church. He recently got baptized in a river along with one of his flock who he has helped to rescue from a life of drugs and crime. When we meet with him I don't treat him like a baby. He's a soldier who wants to lead others so we help him understand God's vision for His life and challenge him about how he is going to faithful to this. I'm very humbled by this brother who is also an encouragement to the rest of the disciples and churches in our region.

The other week I heard that he may be baptizing another of his flock soon so we'll continue to pray for him and entrust Him and his flock into the care of the Spirit.

Who are the leaders in the work you are doing?

How are you developing leaders?

Chapter 9

Condemned to die

1 Corinthians 4:9

As I write this, two of my closest brothers and team-mates are heading to a country where it is illegal to preach the Gospel and where becoming a follower of Jesus can lead to torture and death.

They may not return.

When I look at Jesus, His first disciples and also many other people throughout history, I feel deeply ashamed about my own selfishness and unwillingness to suffer hardship for the sake of Jesus. True disciples of Jesus count suffering for the name of Jesus as a joy. We have fallen far short of this in the UK and Europe and that is why our continent has become the spiritually darkest place in the world,

"And if the light you think you have is actually darkness, how deep that darkness is"
Matthew 6:23

We are walking in deep darkness where even the light we think we have is such a dim reflection of the true gospel. My purpose for the writing this book is to help create a completely different understanding and framework for what it means to be a disciple of Jesus. I'm convinced that everything we think we know regarding

Jesus and His work needs to be overhauled and radically transformed. I am not really concerned if some people feel this book is too harsh or critical of churches and christians because I am contending for a whole new kingdom culture which births disciples, churches and leaders in the harvest. My hope is that a few good men and women will rise to the challenge and commit themselves to be faithful to Christ and His gospel.

Some things have got to die.

Our immaturity and fear needs to die. Church as we know it has to die. And we may have to die for the sake of the gospel,

"And now I am bound by the Spirit to go to Jerusalem. I don't know what awaits me, except that the Holy Spirit tells me in city after city that jail and suffering lie ahead. But my life is worth nothing to me unless I use it for finishing the work assigned me by the Lord Jesus – the work of telling others the good news about the wonderful grace of God."
Acts 20:22-25

I believe the body of Christ needs a strong wake up call. Many so called leaders are enjoying the benefits of being ministers and pastors. They've got their own pulpits, nice houses and cars and congregations that regularly support them and their families. The concept of suffering, sacrifice and apostolic work is foreign to them. Jesus was amongst us as a suffering servant and called us to follow His example.

"I am the good shepherd. The good shepherd sacrifices his life for his sheep. A hired hand will run when he sees a wolf coming. He will abandon the sheep because they don't belong to him and he isn't their shepherd. And so the wolf attacks them and scatters

the flock. The hired hand runs away because he's working only for the money and doesn't really care about the sheep."
John 10:11-14

Are you working for money and what you can get out of life or do you really care about the sheep? Deep down are you really only concerned with building up yourself and your family, or are you willing to pour yourself out to make disciples and equip others?

Being called by God is being appointed to death. Committing yourself to the gospel and equipping others to become mature disciples of Jesus is essentially saying that you are handing over your right to exist and have a life. For those who God calls, the work of the gospel and building up others is more important than building your reputation or protecting your own interests. It has nothing to do with money because you haven't been hired by man but appointed by God. People should think very carefully before they become disciples of Jesus so they understand the cost involved,

"Several days later a man named Agabus, who also had the gift of prophecy, arrived from Judea. He came over, took Paul's belt, and bound his own feet and hands with it. Then he said, 'The Holy Spirit declares, so shall the owner of this belt be bound by the Jewish leaders in Jerusalem and turned over to the Gentiles." When we heard this, we and the local believers all begged Paul not to go on to Jerusalem. But he said, "Why all this weeping? You are breaking my heart! I am ready only to be jailed at Jerusalem but even to die for the sake of the Lord Jesus.' When it was clear that we couldn't persuade him, we gave up and said, "The Lord's will be done."
Acts 21:10-15

We need a radical re-think about what the normal life of a disciple looks like. Fervent prayer is normal. Bold preaching is normal. Planting churches amongst new groups and households of people is normal. Appointing leaders from these new churches is normal. And joyfully facing suffering, persecution and death for the gospel is normal. Hudson Taylor the great missionary to China once said,

"It is not so much the greatness of our troubles, as the littleness of our spirit, which makes us complain."

In these dark times God is calling for men and women of faith who will embrace suffering and hardships as part of the territory. Is that the kind of life that people sign up for when they go to Bible college? Is that the job description given to potential pastors? Real ministry involves you dying (sometimes literally) to give life to others,

"But I will rejoice even if I lose my life, pouring it out like a liquid offering to God."
Philippians 2:17

What's our reward?

We live in a world that is infested with ego. Everyone is searching for recognition and adulation. For a long time, the uncrucified insecurities in my own life led me to seek praise and recognition from men. I wasn't interested in being on the stage or in the limelight, but somewhere deep down I wanted to get some recognition for my hard work and a cocktail of selfish ambition and determination to be successful meant I found it hard to rejoice when God lifted others up. Yes we can all put on the act that it's all about others, but secretly inside we all harbor the desire for recognition. I see this spiritual jostling everywhere, I hate it when I see it in my own life and in God's church.

Jesus never promised us recognition or success. Actually, he promised that all of his followers would be mocked, persecuted and lied about. Sharing in Jesus' suffering is part of our reward and is a privilege,

"For you have been given not only the privilege of trusting in Christ but also the privilege of suffering for Him."
Philippians 1:29

One of the people who God has greatly used in my life told me a story that I have never forgotten. He was receiving prayer at the end of a meeting one Sunday and someone gave him a prophetic word that included the phrase "You are blessed". My friend wanted to understand this word more so he went through the whole New Testament and searched for every reference to the word blessed. He soon realized that to be "blessed" according to the New Testament is very different from what most christians and churches believe. This guy demonstrated what it meant to be "blessed" in his life as he endured much suffering and persecution in his life and continued to do the will of God. I often remember his example.

Make no mistake, if God is calling you then you too will be blessed with all manner of persecution, including hostility and abuse from those nearest and dearest to you and from people you thought were on the same side as you. It is a blessing though because it will transform you more into the likeness of Jesus and grow your character.

Recently I have had a number of significant challenges in my life. Whilst I have not feared for my life as some believers do around the world, there has been many times where I have simply not known what to do or how to endure the trials that kept coming my way. It felt like wave after wave had been sent my way to try and knock me down and stop obeying Jesus. As I cried out to God for help, He kept reminding me about Jesus on the cross. He endured the pain of the cross without fighting back and literally allowed himself to be killed because of the joy that was set before him,

"Because of the joy awaiting him, he endured the cross, disregarding it's shame"
Hebrews 12:2

We all talk about being like Jesus, but I often wonder what people mean by that. Are they referring to when Jesus offended people to such a degree that they wanted to throw him off a cliff to kill him? Are they referring to when Jesus was rejected by all his friends in his hour of need? Or are they referring to when he became a public spectacle and allowed himself to be killed?

I suspect we mean that we'd like to be the miracle working, glorified Jesus who solves the problems of the world with a click of his fingers. Wake up. There is no glory without suffering and death. Do you want to be a faithful servant of Jesus and His church? Well prepare yourself to drink the same cup that Jesus did,

"Then the mother of James and John, the sons of Zebedee came to Jesus with her sons. She knelt respectfully to ask a favour. 'What is your request?' he asked. She replied, 'In your Kingdom please let my two sons sit in places of honour next to you, one on your right and the other on your left.' But Jesus answered by

saying to them, 'You don't know what you are asking! Are you
able to drink from the bitter cup of suffering I am about to
drink?'
Matthew 20:20-23

You want to be a missionary?

You want to be a pastor?

You want to be 'in ministry'?

Think again.

Are you ready for a life of unimportance where everything is about
God and not you?

"After all, who is Apollos? Who is Paul? We are only God's
servants through whom you believed the good news. Each of us
did the work the Lord gave us. I planted the seed in your hearts,
and Apollos watered it, but it was God who made it grow. It's not
important who does the planting, or who does the watering.
What's important is that God makes the seed grow."
1 Corinthians 3:5-8

Each day I am learning more about what it looks like to be a
faithful servant of Jesus and it looks less and less like what I'd
imagined and hoped it to be. I'm talking here about the real work
that Jesus calls us to. The trench warfare of making disciples,
planting churches and appointing leaders. This is very different
from the life that many so-called servants of Jesus seem to enjoy.

There are very few pats on the back but that's OK because we're
just doing the work that the Lord has given us.

I often think about how being a servant of Jesus and His church is like being a father. I have the joy of being a father to 4 biological children. I am trying with God's help to love them and train them in the way to go so that they will be prepared when the time comes for them to start growing their own families. My wife and I haven't been blessed with children to make us feel better about ourselves or so our life feels more fulfilled or successful. God has entrusted children into our family for us to serve and pour ourselves into them. It really is all about them. Our reward as parents is to see our children flourishing, making Godly choices in their lives and ultimately leaving our direct care to have families and children of their own.

How would you feel however if you met a father who kept his children all for himself? Imagine them growing up but being forced to live in the same house together with him until old age, unable to have their own families. You'd think that Father was sick right? Instead of serving his children and lovingly sending them out to grow and develope their own lives and families, they'd become imprisoned and conditioned to serve him and his needs. That scenario would probably be considered abusive and completely opposite to the biblical reason for being blessed with children.

Yet isn't this the scenario that is happening in most churches?

A good father produces more families, not lifelong dependant children. A father's reward is an empty home. He has spent his life investing in his children and empowered them to go out and build their own homes.

His children are his reward,

"After all, what gives us hope and joy, and what will be our proud reward and crown as we stand before our Lord Jesus when he returns? It is you! Yes you are our pride and joy."
1 Thessalonians 2:19-20

I have some questions about leaders and 'ministers' who want to build the biggest churches and ministries in their town. Whilst there's nothing wrong with numbers, we need to seriously question our motivation and what reward we are looking for.

For me, I'd rather have nothing left at the end of my life if it means I have poured everything out into my biological and spiritual children. I'm not bothered about my reputation or ministry, my joy and crown is other people and helping them to go further and higher than I ever could.

Accidental apostles pour out their lives to quietly equip others to do the work of ministry. They endure whatever comes their way and will do whatever it takes because it's not about their own reputation or glory. They will honour others at every opportunity instead of themselves and will constantly work to do themselves out of a job,

"But now I have finished my work in these regions."
Romans 15:23

Reading Paul's words in Romans 15 always inspires me. He describes how he has fully presented the good news of Christ from Jerusalem all the way to Illyricum (Romans 15:19) and has finished his work in those regions (Romans 15:23) I believe one of the marks of those men and women with an apostolic call is that they are working with the end in mind. They constantly work to empower others and provide a foundation for others to build on. They don't settle down and build their own empire, like Diotrephes and other men and women throughout history who seek power and reputation,

"I wrote to the church about this, but Diotrephes, who loves to be the leader, refuses to have anything to do with us."
3 John 9

While everyone is clamouring to be the top dog like Diotrephes, the apostolic call pulls people down to the bottom where they lay the foundation for movements which others build on. Whilst it's amazing to think that Paul could say he fully preached the gospel and finished his work across entire regions, I also feel the sense of loneliness that would come with this realization. While everyone continued to build the work, Paul humbly realized his work was done and bowed out, making room for others to be the stars.

Jesus described his life as being like a grain of wheat which fell to the ground and produced many more seeds. Eventually Jesus would fully lay his life down, but every day He lived as a man condemned to die.

Paul had great authority but yet was very aware that he was not indisposable. Throughout his ministry he was constantly falling to the ground so that many more seeds could grow. When he was present he was preparing others for his absence and when he taught, his teaching led people to know God more deeply for themselves. He made disciples of Jesus! Paul was a spiritual father to many and the gospel multiplied through the disciples, churches and leaders that were birthed through his ministry. The apostolic gift is necessary because it causes gospel work to grow everywhere and not just around a few gifted individuals. Everyone is empowered to do the work and disciples make disciples who make disciples.

Human leaders are not the stars, Jesus is, and He directs affairs through His Spirit.

Just as apostles pour out their lives sacrificially to build others up. so the churches they found send out their best workers sacrificially to multiply the work in other places,

"Among the prophets and teachers of the Church at Antioch of Syria were Barnabus, Simeon (called "the black man"), Lucius (from Cyrene), Manaen (the childhood companion of King Herod Antipas) and Saul. One day as these men were worshipping the Lord and fasting, the Holy Spirit said, "Appoint Barnabus and Saul for the special work to which I have called them." So after more fasting and prayer, the men laid their hands on them and sent them on their way"
Acts 13:1-4

Here in our region, my constant prayer and message to the team is that we want to be a network that sends out our best people just like the church in Antioch. Instead of keeping God's gifts for ourselves to enjoy we want to share them with the world. How else will all the nations be discipled?

As this book comes to an end I'll give Paul the final word and I pray that God will help you to get on with the work He has called you to. I'd encourage you to write down your own reflections and to put into practice the things that God has said to you through these pages.

May Jesus be glorified and may you be found faithful on the day of the Lord's return,

"Instead, I sometimes think God has put us apostles on display, like prisoners of war at the end of a victor's parade, condemned to die. We have become a spectacle to the entire world – to people and angels alike. Our dedication to Christ makes us look like fools, but you claim to be so wise in Christ! We are weak, but you are so powerful! You are honoured, but we are ridiculed. Even now we go hungry and thirsty, and we don't enough clothes to keep warm. We are often beaten and have no home. We work wearily with our own hands to earn our living. We bless those who curse us. We are patient with those who abuse us. We appeal gently when evil things are said about us. Yet we are treated like the world's garbage, like everybody's trash – right upto the present moment. I am not writing these things to shame you, but to warn you as my beloved children. For even if you had ten thousand others to teach you about Christ, you have only one spiritual father. For I became your father in Christ Jesus when I preached the good news to you. So I urge you to imitate me"
1 Corinthians 4:9-17

Lightning Source UK Ltd.
Milton Keynes UK
UKHW051934070220
358393UK00011B/190